The Boston Globe

GUIDE TO

BOSTON

Help Us Keep This Guide Up to Date

Every effort has been made by the author and editors to make this guide as accurate and useful as possible. However, many things can change after a guide is published—establishments close, phone numbers change, walking trails are rerouted, facilities come under new management, etc.

We would love to hear from you concerning your experiences with this guide and how you feel it could be made better and be kept up to date. While we may not be able to respond to all comments and suggestions, we'll take them to heart, and we'll also make certain to share them with the author. Please send your comments and suggestions to the following address:

The Globe Pequot Press
Reader Response/Editorial Department
P.O. Box 480
Guilford, CT 06437

Or you may e-mail us at:

editorial@GlobePequot.com

Thanks for your input, and happy travels!

INSIDERS' GUIDE®

The Boston Globe

GUIDE TO

BOSTON

SEVENTH EDITION

JERRY MORRIS

INSIDERS' GUIDE®

GUILFORD, CONNECTICUT

AN IMPRINT OF THE GLOBE PEQUOT PRESS

To Mary Beth

To buy books in quantity for corporate use
or incentives, call **(800) 962–0973, ext. 4551,**
or e-mail **premiums@GlobePequot.com.**

917.4
Morris

INSIDERS' GUIDE ®

Spot photography throughout courtesy of Greater Boston Convention
and Visitors Bureau, Inc.

Text design by Sue Cary

ISSN 1546-5780
ISBN 0-7627-3430-2

Manufactured in the United States of America
Seventh Edition/First Printing

CONTENTS

MAPS

The prices and rates listed in this guidebook were confirmed at press time. We recommend, however, that you call establishments before traveling to obtain the most current information.

Please note: When dialing local phone numbers, ten digits are required. Use the area code 617 with the seven-digit numbers given in this book for Belmont, Boston, Brookline, Cambridge, Chelsea, Everett, Milton, Newton, Quincy, Somerville, Watertown, and Winthrop.

Most museums and services mentioned have facilities for, or are accessible to, the disabled. It is always best, however, to call first about particular needs.

PART ONE

GETTING TO KNOW BOSTON

Boston: An Overview

oston is not your everyday American city. It has been shaped by geography, history, religion, and politics more than any other city in the country. And it's fun. There is a lively mix of history within a downtown where people still live and shop. Just about everything, from a bustling waterfront, beautiful parks, major department stores, acclaimed restaurants, a national historic park, and a sports mecca to towering buildings and architecture that span the centuries, can be experienced without effort. How many cities can boast that?

That's saying a lot, but to know the city—and enjoy it—you have to know a little about its history and geography.

Boston is, after all, the oldest American city. Perhaps we should modify that a bit and say the oldest permanently settled city. The Indians were here first, and that's how this place got its first name as the Shawmut Peninsula. Up until recently, a recognizable symbol from that period could be seen throughout the region in the Indian chief logo of the former Shawmut Bank, a Boston institution for years. The Shawmut tribe were Boston's first settlers, and the Indian who used to be the bank's symbol was Chief Obbatinewat. The chief is no longer a corporate symbol. As a result of the mergers of the 1990s, Shawmut is now part of Fleet Bank, which in 2004 merged with Bank of America. It is about the latest in a round of mergers that has seen many Boston institutions becoming subsidiaries of New York, Canadian, or other firms.

There are even stories that the Vikings were here. A Scandinavian historian has written a book to prove it, though Harvard University professors have disputed it. You'll find a statue to the most famous Viking of them all, Leif Eriksson, standing far inland, almost in Kenmore Square along Commonwealth Avenue and pointing to the interior. Why, no one seems to know.

Captain John Smith, the great English explorer (of Pocahontas fame), came along in the early 1600s and even named the Charles River, for his beloved king.

Like the legendary phoenix, Boston has risen from the ashes of revolution, wars, blockades, devastating fires, economic depressions, and indifference to become one of the great cities of not just the United States but the world. Indeed, a few years ago a survey by *Condé Nast Traveler* only confirmed that Boston is a world-class city. That survey put Boston in third place, ahead of Paris, Washington, London, Rome, Vienna, and Venice and surpassed only by San Francisco and New York. Boston possesses the charm of many other cities. In fact, the visitor to Boston often finds among its streets evocative reminders of London, Paris, Rome, and other cosmopolitan centers.

The joy of Boston today comes from many sources. It is not only the city where "the child Independence was born" but also a city of literary triumphs, educational prominence, and medical leadership; the center of the country's industrial revolution and today's high-tech corporations; the home of a great symphony, magnificent museums, architectural delights, lively politics, and myriad cultural happenings; and a sports town that proudly wears an Emerald Necklace of greenery through its center.

In 2003 the population of Boston was approximately 582,000, and the Greater Boston area is now home to more than three million people. The city itself covers 46 square miles; the Greater Boston area, 1,100 square miles. Whereas the Puritans are credited with having founded the city, at present it is the bountiful immigration of people from other parts of the country and from Canada, Europe, and Asia that is enriching the city's character and building on its past.

But the "city upon a hill" that John Winthrop, the first governor of Massachusetts Bay Colony, so proudly noted has not always been the city you see today. Indeed, had it not been for the search for a good drink of water, Boston might still be the Shawmut Peninsula, a point of land marked by three hills, known as Trimountain.

As history tells us, in 1620 the Pilgrims accidentally settled in Plymouth, some 30 miles to the south of Boston, and in their struggle to survive did not see their community grow for years. The Puritans, arriving ten years later, came better prepared, with advance parties and great numbers of settlers, and chose Salem, a shore location 20 miles to the north of Boston. But conditions in Salem forced the Puritans to seek another place to settle, and

Charlestown, just across from Boston, would have been the choice had its water supply been better.

Boston's history is marked by colorful and sometimes heroic people. The first resident and the person most responsible for the Puritans' discovery of Boston was a recluse by the name of Reverend William Blackstone (often spelled *Blaxton*), who had been living alone on a side of Beacon Hill with his collection of 200 books—perhaps an indication of Boston's future role in the literary and educational arena (eight years later, in 1638, John Harvard's gift of 400 books formed the foundation for one of the greatest libraries in the world at America's first college, which bears Harvard's name for this gift). Blackstone, having left an earlier settlement south of Boston in Wessagusset, now Weymouth, knew some of the Charlestown settlers from his college days in England and invited them to enjoy the sweet water of the spring he used.

The Puritans, like Blackstone, brought a wealth of knowledge with them, for their party included many members of the clergy and other well-educated settlers. They also brought with them the charter granting them the right of settlement and how they were to be governed. Unlike the Pilgrims, who with the Mayflower Compact had to create their own government, the Puritans, armed with the tools of government, extensive knowledge, and religious fervor, did not have to look to London for anything but trade—a factor that was to greatly influence the outcome of the later conflict between the colonists and the English.

The center of the new town of Boston was the area around the Old State House and grew from there.

Although for many people the Boston Tea Party signifies the great offense of "taxation without representation" that led to the Revolution, that event was but one—albeit a highly emotional one—act against the motherland that in its struggle to overcome financial distress continually provoked revolution through its harsh actions to put down the freethinking colonists.

Liberal as the first settlers were, they had little tolerance for religious beliefs other than their own. One of the prime reasons for leaving England was to escape the domination of the Anglican Church, with its rigid beliefs and rules. The anger of the early Puritans was against not just the Anglicans but also the differing beliefs of Baptists, many of whom fled, with the Quakers, to more liberal Rhode Island. For many, their beliefs led to death, with Boston Common becoming the site of four hangings between 1649 and 1651 (a statue to one Quaker, Mary Dyer, now sits in front of the East Wing of the State House).

The new colony's troubles began in 1675 when Indians broke the treaty signed with the Pilgrims and King Philip's War wreaked havoc, resulting in the destruction of twelve communities. It would be years before the colony recovered.

In case you wondered . . .

Boston was named for an English town from which came some of the first Puritans. The name of St. Botolph, the city's saint, comes from the English church in old Boston, whose former pastor was one of the first settlers in Boston, Massachusetts. Today you'll find the name St. Botolph gracing a private, formerly all-male club, as well as a lovely street.

Then England stepped in, nullifying the colony's charter, making Massachusetts a Crown Colony, and installing Sir Edmund Andros as a royal governor who ruled like a despot, creating new taxes and granting lands to his favorite friends. Andros also ordered the building of King's Chapel, the first Anglican church in North America, and thereby further angered the Puritan settlers.

New Englanders became caught up in the French and Indian War, begun in 1689 as a dispute between King William III and France and lasting for seventy-four years. The war had an intangible side effect for the colony, though, since in 1745 a New England militia was sent from Boston Common to capture the mighty French fortress at Louisburg, Nova Scotia, and succeeded in doing so. This experience later gave proof to the colonists that they could indeed defeat a major world power—first France and then England.

The years of royal government saw a succession of taxes imposed, each doing damage to the young Boston's economy and exacerbating the colonists' displeasure with England. To avoid the taxes, many colonists—including John Hancock—engaged in smuggling. In 1761 England imposed a new law, the Writs of Assistance, to give the British free entry into the colonists' homes and businesses to seek out the smugglers. That year, when James Otis spoke against the writs in the Old State House, as John Adams noted in his autobiography, "the child Independence was born." In 1734 the Molasses Act, which imposed taxes on rum and sugar, brought about a decline in shipbuilding. And England's Charles Townshend came up with new taxes to pay England's growing debt from its wars and expansion. First was a sugar act in 1764. Then in 1765 came the Stamp Act, which outraged the colonists—who were to place stamp taxes on everything written, from deeds to newspapers—and prompted them to form the Continental Congress, a first gathering of all the colonies affected by these new taxes and the beginning of the colonists' unification in spirit and action against England. The Stamp Act was rescinded, only to be replaced by new taxes on glass, paper, and tea. Again these taxes were dropped, except for that on tea, and it was against this situation that more than 5,000 Bostonians gathered in the Old South Meeting House one December evening in 1773 to protest English taxes. In the dark hours that followed, a group of "Indians" could be seen dumping British tea into Boston Harbor.

England responded by sending in more than 4,000 troops. They were led by General Thomas Gage, who was also named governor and closed the port of Boston. With so many troops in a town of just about 16,000, the tension that had exploded years earlier in 1770 with the Boston Massacre only continued against the Redcoats.

Once again, the colonists activated militias and formed Committees of Correspondence throughout New England to communicate over the grievances with English rule. With the city's economy suffering, some 9,000 colonists left Boston, the town now having more British troops than residents. Gage, seeking to further halt the revolutionary spirit aboil in Boston, ordered the capture of two of its leaders, Samuel Adams and John Hancock, who at the time were visiting in Lexington, 17 miles away.

On the night of April 16, 1775, the British set out from the foot of Boston Common, then waterfront, for Lexington, and the famed "one if by land, and two if by sea" lanterns were lit in the spire of the Old North Church. In the morning hours, the "shot heard round the world" was fired in Concord, and the Revolution began.

Boston, though, was not to be rid of British troops for more than a year. With the city under siege, the Second Continental Congress, meeting in Philadelphia, undertook formation of the Continental army under the leadership of George Washington. Just two days before Washington was to take command of the troops on Cambridge Common, however, one of the most decisive battles of the Revolution took place on Bunker Hill. On June 17, 1775, the Battle of Bunker Hill—still celebrated in Boston—saw patriots with few military skills and little gunpowder take on the might of the British army. Although England won, its loss of troops was horrendous, effectively making the battle a political loss for the British and a moral victory for the colonists.

Another event still celebrated in Boston, though now more for the Irish, marks the day the British peacefully left Boston: March 17, 1776. On March 5 the British had awakened to find huge cannon power looking down on their vessels from Dorchester Heights. The cannons, captured from the British, had been brought from Fort Ticonderoga, hundreds of miles away. At first the British were going to attack, but fate was on the side of the colonists, as a violent storm on March 6 halted those plans. The British took the sensible approach, packing 8,900 troops on seventy-eight vessels and leaving town.

In the know . . .

Islands—Boston Harbor has many, with easy access from the down-town waterfront. And if you don't mind stretching a point, Boston itself is an island, thanks to colonists who in 1639 built the first canal in North America, stretching 3 miles from the Charles River in Dedham (next to the Dedham Mall) to the Neponset River. And Dedham, which is only 12 miles from the h eart of Boston, at one time had the distinction of showing just how provincial the city was, for every place beyond that town was referred to as "west of Dedham."

With independence, Boston once again saw vessels from its harbor engage in world commerce; from Salem, ships began trade with China in 1786. But the years of conflict and two major fires, one in 1761 and another in 1787, saw Boston's population at only 18,000—just 2,000 more than its level fifty years previously. New York and Philadelphia were now the largest American cities. And two more shipping embargoes virtually ended Boston and Salem's ship-ping commerce: In 1801 President Jefferson placed an embargo on shipping with England, and the War of 1812 served to seal the fate of the shipping industry.

In 1822 Boston became a city, and its second mayor, Josiah Quincy, initi-ated the first major renewal of the city with the filling in of a huge section of the waterfront and the building of Quincy Market (which, 154 years later, once again became a symbol of the "new Boston," its structure turned into a lively collection of shops and restaurants, once more drawing people into the city). In the years that followed, the face of Boston changed dramatically as its hills were leveled—only Beacon Hill remains, at 60 feet lower than its for-mer height—and fill was brought in by rail from nearby Needham to create Back Bay. More fill produced new land along the Boston waterfront and across the Charles River in Cambridge. These were the years that the indus-trial revolution took place in nearby Lowell and other towns and cities, turn-ing their waterways into powerful forces for generating the textile mills that helped transform not only New England but the country from an agricul-tural to an industrial nation. These were also the years when the literary giants—Thoreau, Longfellow, Emerson, Alcott—wrote the words that so inspired the new nation and the world and when Boston became a leader in the abolitionist movement. It was a period in which a great famine occurred in Ireland, sending the first major wave of immigrants to America and chang-ing forever the ethnic and political character of Boston.

In 1865 Massachusetts Institute of Technology began on Boylston Street, soon moving across the river to Cambridge and adding to what is now the greatest concentration of colleges and universities in the United States. At present, some fifty schools of higher education serve more than 300,000 students—many from around the world—who contribute greatly to the city's youthful and vibrant spirit.

In 1872 another fire devastated Boston, burning sixty-five acres of land in the heart of the city and destroying 770 buildings. Miraculously, the fire halted just feet from the Old South Meeting House. But it did destroy the old Trinity Church, thereby inspiring its members to build anew, creating one of the masterpieces of American church architecture in Copley Square.

At the turn of the century, Boston again began a slide back, a period marked by depression and indifference. The public spirit, evinced by people like Henry Lee Higginson, who in 1881 founded the Boston Symphony Orchestra and financially supported it for the next thirty-seven years, seemed at an end. Yet following World War II, veterans began flocking to area universities, and as the graduates set up shop in the old warehouses and factories of Cambridge and elsewhere, the new technology began to flourish. Soon this new industrial revolution was marked by a highway that rings the city—Route 128, lined with so many high-tech firms that it is known as America's Technology Highway.

Boston's renaissance did not take hold until 1960, when Mayor John Collins began the great redevelopment that eventually transformed Boston into the city it is today. Between 1936 and 1956, there was little construction in the city; Boston could look only to its past.

Since 1960, however, more than fifty major projects have metamorphosed Boston. And today even more projects are in the works to change the face of the city, depress the Central Artery, and make the waterfront more accessible. The waterfront, formerly a dilapidated wharf area, has become a lively district with hotels (the Boston Harbor Hotel at Rowes Wharf has become the picture-perfect symbol of the new Boston, and the Marriott Long Wharf is one of that chain's busiest), the nationally acclaimed New England Aquarium, and renovated granite and brick warehouses that now house condominiums, wonderful restaurants and museums, shops, and offices; a huge rail yard in the heart of the city is now the Prudential Center; an extensive part of the city, including the famed Scollay Square known to soldiers worldwide, has given way to create a new city hall and other structures of Government Center; the John Hancock Tower now rises sixty floors above Copley Square, mirroring the architectural beauty of that square; and Copley Place has sprung up to reflect the new Boston, with luxury stores from Texas and New York. The city now has four convention centers, the largest of which is in the Seaport District, and some of the finest hotels in the country to serve visitors. With its new convention facilities and new hotels with national and international status, Boston's provincial status has been relegated to the past.

The Prudential Center, which was modern Boston's first renewal, is now linked to Copley Place by a glass-enclosed walkway and pleasantly designed open areas, including a grand courtyard with sidewalk cafes and unique boutiques as well as fine stores such as Saks Fifth Avenue. The renewed Pru offers an all-weather way for enjoyable diversions on the way to the Prudential Tower, the Hynes convention center, or the Sheraton Boston Hotel.

The city has also learned from all this renewal. Outrage followed the destruction of the West End—home to Lithuanian, Irish, Italian, Russian, Albanian, Polish, and Jewish settlers—and the tearing down of old landmarks. New construction is now marked with a lengthy review period, keeping height and looks in mind. The New England Building, at 500 Boylston Street, for example, was to be duplicated next door until neighborhood opposition to its size and "un-Boston look" forced a complete redesign of the project's second phase. And some say that the redesigned 222 Berkeley Street is a triumph of architecture, a more humanly scaled building that is more characteristic of Boston.

Boston is also a city of contradictions or seemingly misnamed places. Fort Hill, the area around South Station, is certainly no hill, but in colonial days it was. Now leveled, Fort Hill contains only one reminder of its former height: a street named High, which no longer is. Those who decide to reside here can expect to pay dearly for it—housing costs in Boston are among the highest in the nation. A $100,000 home purchased in 1991 is today valued at $176,531 (the national average is $151,445), but try to find one even at that price (homes on Beacon Hill or condos overlooking the harbor can top $10 million).

Boston is a city of treasures and experiences. It is a city of newcomers—45 percent of heads of households have moved into the city since 1978, and the majority of newcomers are between eighteen and forty years old. Boston is no longer the city that banned books and plays, but though its nightlife has swelled, it still closes down by 1:00 or 2:00 A.M.

It is a city that has rediscovered its past without forgetting about the future, one that is opening more of its land to recreational use. And in 2004 the Big Dig project to depress the Central Artery was basically completed, creating some thirty acres of open space in the heart of the city. If you have been to Boston before, do visit this area by the North End and waterfront. You will not believe the sight or the peacefulness of this new oasis in Boston.

Discover Boston's history, which like a fabric is woven throughout the

Boston Neighborhoods

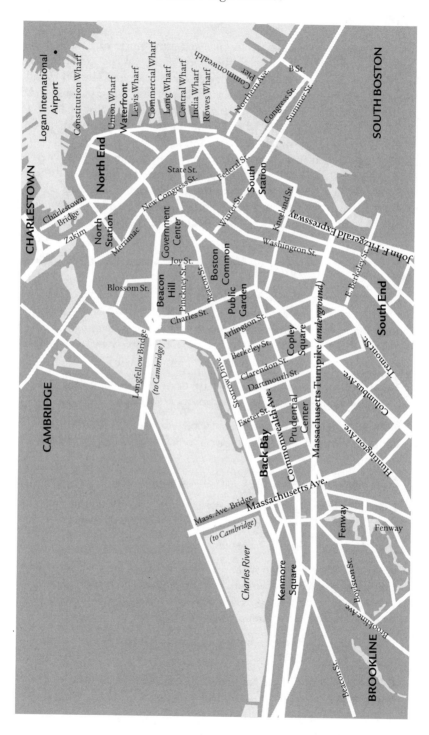

CHARLESTOWN

CAMBRIDGE

Logan International Airport

Constitution Wharf

Union Wharf

Lewis Wharf

Commercial Wharf

Long Wharf

Central Wharf

India Wharf

Rowes Wharf

Waterfront

North End

Commonwealth Pier

Northern Ave.

B St.

Congress St.

Summer St.

SOUTH BOSTON

Charlestown Bridge

Zakim

North Station

Merrimac

New Congress St.

State St.

Federal St.

South Station

Government Center

Joy St.

Pinckney St.

Blossom St.

Beacon Hill

Beacon St.

Charles St.

Boston Common

Public Garden

Winter St.

Washington St.

Kneeland St.

John F. Fitzgerald Expressway

E. Berkeley St.

South End

Longfellow Bridge

(to Cambridge)

Arlington St.

Berkeley St.

Clarendon St.

Dartmouth St.

Exeter St.

Storrow Drive

Copley Square

Commonwealth Ave.

Prudential Center

Massachusetts Turnpike (underground)

Columbus Ave.

Tremont St.

Back Bay

Huntington Ave.

Mass. Ave. Bridge

Massachusetts Ave.

(to Cambridge)

Charles River

Kenmore Square

Fenway

Fenway

Boylston St.

Brookline Ave.

Beacon St.

BROOKLINE

city. Get to know its people, the aromas and atmosphere of the North End, the Victorian splendor of Back Bay, the charm of Beacon Hill. Go up high and look down on the city's redbrick and green landscape, over which the golden and sparkling dome of Charles Bulfinch's classic State House gleams. And do go off to discover the riches of Plymouth, Concord, Salem, New Bedford, and Lowell. For the Boston area is more than a place in history; it has also provided the roots for much of the country. Some of the very first wagon trains to go west left from Ipswich to found towns in Ohio and elsewhere.

Boston is on a roll. It is no longer just the home of the bean and the cod or the place where "the Lowells talk to the Cabots / and the Cabots talk only to God." It may not be the "paradise" that English explorer John Smith described on his 1614 journey, but it is a wonderful place to explore and enjoy.

Major Happenings in Boston's History

1614 Captain John Smith sails into the Boston area, naming the Charles River, noting the islands lush with corn grown by Indians, and declaring the area a "paradise."

1624 William Blackstone, Boston's first resident, settles on the Shawmut Peninsula with his collection of 200 books.

1630 Boston is founded under the leadership of John Winthrop, who declares, "We shall build a city upon a hill; the eyes of all people are upon us."

1634 Boston Common is purchased as a public park.

1635 The Public Latin School opens; in later years, Benjamin Franklin, John Hancock, Samuel Adams, and others study here.

1636 Harvard College is founded.

1761 "The child Independence was born," notes John Adams, lawyer and future second president of the United States, on hearing James Otis denounce the Writs of Assistance, enacted to give the British free access to the colonists' homes and businesses.

1764 Taxation without representation is denounced at town meetings and in citywide protests.

1770 March 5 marks the day of the Boston Massacre, in which five colonists are killed by British bullets outside the Old State House.

1773 The Boston Tea Party takes place the evening of December 16, when colonists dressed as Indians leave the Old South Meeting House to board British ships and toss 342 chests of tea into Boston Harbor.

1775 The evening of April 18, two lanterns gleam from Old North Church, signaling to Paul Revere and William Dawes that the British will be leaving by sea for Concord and Lexington. On June 17 occurs the Battle of Bunker Hill—a hollow and disastrous victory for the British, their army almost destroyed—marking the beginning of the end of British might in the colonies.

1776 On March 17 the British troops, overwhelmed by colonial artillery, secretly move to Dorchester Heights and evacuate Boston by ship for the final time, taking with them many Tories—those loyal to the crown. The Declaration of Independence is read to Bostonians from the balcony of the Old State House.

1821 Horace Mann opens the first free public high school in America.

1826 Mayor Josiah Quincy begins Boston's first renewal—filling in the waterfront for the construction of Quincy Market.

1841 The Irish, fleeing the potato famine at home, begin arriving in Boston.

1852 The first public library in the country opens in Boston.

1852 The filling in of Back Bay begins.

1872 The Great Fire sweeps Boston, burning 65 acres and 770 buildings in the heart of the downtown area, stopping just short of the Old South Meeting House.

1877 The Swan Boats of the Public Garden make their debut.

1897 The first subway in the United States opens at Park Street under Boston Common.

1910 John F. "Honey Fitz" Fitzgerald, grandfather of John F. Kennedy, is elected mayor of Boston.

1946 Boston politics, always lively and sometimes unpredictable, sees James Michael Curley elected mayor for the fourth time, this time while serving a five-month jail sentence.

1960 John Fitzgerald Kennedy casts his ballot in the Old West Church hours before being elected president of the United States.

1962 Boston's famed Scollay Square is demolished to make way for Government Center.

1976 Quincy Market, once again the scene of restoration, reopens on August 26.

1980 Boston celebrates its 350th birthday.

1992 The Big Dig, a more than ten-year project that will return Boston's waterfront to the city once again, begins.

1995 The FleetCenter replaces the Boston Garden as the new home of the Celtics and Bruins. Also opening is the Ted Williams Tunnel, the city's third harbor tunnel, which provides a direct connection to Logan International Airport and is named for the famed Red Sox slugger.

2000 The 200-mile Bay Circuit Trail, first proposed in 1929 as an outer "emerald necklace," becomes a reality. This mix of colonial farm, river, and ocean landscape runs from Plum Island on Boston's North Shore to Kingston Bay on the South Shore.

2001 Rail service to and from Boston grows. Boston to Portland, Maine, is back with the start of the "Downeaster." Also high-speed Amtrak Acela service between Boston and New York City is increased.

2004 The Big Dig, the most expensive highway project in the nation, is all but completed. The Central Artery, which once loomed overhead, is gone. The city opens a new huge, state-of-the-art convention center in the Seaport District. The city adds another landmark: the soaring Leonard P. Zakim Bridge. After 86 years, the curse of the Babe is lifted. The Red Sox defeat the New York Yankees and St. Louis Cardinals in a stunning eight-game winning streak to win the World Series.

The People of Boston

While Boston is known as the land of Brahmins, Pilgrims, and Puritans, it is today a very much diversified city. The Chinatown section alone has greatly expanded in recent years. And, in most cases, it is the "newcomers" from around the world who have helped to change the face of Boston and helped to make it one of the most livable cities in the nation.

Just as these people are changing the face of Boston, so, too, did the earlier settlers. In your journey about Boston, you will run into Puritans, Pilgrims, Brahmins, and the Irish. While the Pilgrims are famed for the founding of America, they did little in Boston. It was the Puritans who created this "City on a Hill," the Brahmins who later ruled it, and the Irish who changed everything.

Puritans: These were the original settlers of Boston. The Puritans earned their name as they originally sought to "purify" the Church of England, leading to civil war there. They came to the New World, where they would be free to worship as they believed. Their belief that they were "chosen by God" soon led to conflicts here with those who did not believe or behave as they did. Some people were banished from Boston—including Roger Williams, who not only helped found Rhode Island but also the Baptist Church in America. Another focus of conflict was during the Revolution with the Anglican Church (Church of England), which represented the British rulers of the colonies. The Puritans first arrived in Salem on the North Shore.

Pilgrims: These were the settlers of Plymouth, about 40 miles south of Boston, often referred to as "America's Home Town," as it did become the first permanent settlement in America. The Pilgrims were considered a radical faction of Puritanism, as they were more liberal in their religious beliefs. About one-third of the 102 colonists who sailed on the *Mayflower* were Pilgrims.

Brahmins: In the nineteenth century the Brahmins, of Puritan stock, mostly aristocratic, highly educated, and set in their ways, ruled Boston (see the South End on page 92 for how shocked a Brahmin could be). An early saying of two of the more prominent Boston families goes: The Lowells only speak to the Cabots, and the Cabots only to God.

The Irish: While the Irish have been represented in Boston since its beginnings, it was not until the great potato famine of the 1840s and 1850s that they arrived, pennyless and often sick, in startling numbers. The Irish, who found many an unwelcome sign (IRISH NEED NOT APPLY), soon became politically adept, and by the twentieth century would take control of the city from the Brahmins. The Irish led the way to changing Boston and were soon followed by massive waves of Italians, Jews, and others. One of the early fears was of their Roman Catholic faith. It wasn't until John F. Kennedy was elected president in 1961 that America elected a Catholic to the highest office.

When visitors tour Boston, they see certain names appearing constantly. People of history, the arts, politics, architecture—their names are immortalized on Boston's plaques, statues, and buildings. Here are just some of the persons whose names figure prominently during a tour of Boston.

ARCHITECTS

Charles Bulfinch, Boston's master architect of the State House and other capitols—including the nation's—and of Beacon Hill mansions and St. Stephen's Church in the North End. His Federal style is still imitated.

Charles F. McKim, architect of Boston Public Library.

Frederick Law Olmsted, designer of Boston's Emerald Necklace, a 5-mile stretch of greenery through the city; famous as well for his design of Central Park in New York City.

Alexander Parris, whose granite designs are reflected in Quincy Market, the Somerset Club on Beacon Hill, and St. Paul's Cathedral.

I. M. Pei, the twentieth-century architect who has helped change the face of Boston by overseeing the design of Government Center, the Christian Science Center, John Hancock Tower, and the Kennedy Library.

Henry H. Richardson, best known for designing Trinity Church in Copley Square. The influence of his Romanesque style is found in churches and public buildings throughout the country.

COLONIAL FIGURES

Reverend William Blackstone (who spelled his name *Blaxton*), Boston's first settler, who invited the Puritans to enjoy the good waters of the future city.

John Harvard, who on his death donated 400 books and a sum of cash and now has the country's oldest university named for him.

Mary Dyer and *Anne Hutchinson,* colonial women who were persecuted for their liberal religious beliefs. Dyer was hanged on Boston Common, and Hutchinson was killed by Indians while exiled in New York; both are remembered with statues in front of the State House.

LITERARY FIGURES

Louisa May Alcott, Oliver Wendell Holmes, Henry Wadsworth Longfellow, and *Henry David Thoreau,* all part of the Golden Age of Literature in the mid-1800s, their writings still known around the world. They regularly gathered at the Old Corner Bookstore on Washington Street; one may visit the homes and sites associated with them in Concord, as well as Longfellow's home in Cambridge.

Spenser, who for many people is more than just the central character in the Robert B. Parker mystery stories, most of which are set in the city. (Parker, however, is a resident of Cambridge.)

POLITICAL LEADERS

Michael Dukakis, governor of Massachusetts from 1975 to 1979 and from 1983 to 1990, streetcar rider, Brookline resident, and 1988 Democratic candidate for president.

John Forbes Kerry was elected senator from Massachusetts in 1984 and twenty years later was named the Democratic presidential candidate. While not a native of Massachusetts (he was born in Denver), he lives at a most proper Boston address on Louisburg Square on Beacon Hill. He once served as lieutenant governor to another presidential candidate, Michael Dukakis.

The *Kennedy* name spells magic in Boston: *John F. Kennedy,* elected president of the United States in 1960; his brother Senator *Edward (Ted) Kennedy;* and *Joseph (Joe) Kennedy,* congressman from the Cambridge area and son of the late *Robert Kennedy,* who served as attorney general under his brother JFK. The family story can be found at the Kennedy Library, or visit the home in Brookline where JFK was born.

Boston mayors: *James Michael Curley,* three times in office, once elected while in jail, and known as the mayor who took from the rich to give to the poor; *John F. "Honey Fitz" Fitzgerald,* the Irish mayor who perhaps founded the Kennedy legacy and whose daughter Rose became the mother of President John F. Kennedy; *Josiah Quincy,* Boston's second mayor, who in the nineteenth century sparked the city's first renewal project with the construction of Quincy Market; and *Kevin White,* controversial mayor who left office in 1983, following a sixteen-year term during Boston's major renewal period. *Thomas Menino,* the present mayor, is the city's first of Italian heritage. For a city of politics, Menino has accomplished a first by running unopposed since 1997.

REVOLUTIONARY WAR FIGURES

Adams, of which there are many: *Samuel Adams* (whose name now graces a beer), considered the leading figure in the fight for independence and honored by a statue in front of Faneuil Hall; *John Adams,* the second president of the United States; and *John Quincy Adams,* the son of John Adams and the sixth president of the United States. Both presidents lived just 8 miles from Boston, and you can tour their homes. They are the first of four presidents to have been born in Norfolk County, the area just outside Boston (the other two are John Fitzgerald Kennedy in Brookline and the first George Bush in Milton).

Benjamin Franklin, who may have made his name in Philadelphia but was born and bred in Boston.

John Hancock, whose grand signature appears on the Declaration of Independence. Hancock did not found an insurance company, but his money financed the early part of Boston's revolutionary spirit.

Marquis de Lafayette, the famed Frenchman who came to the aid of the American Revolution, serving beside George Washington. Remembrances of him can be found throughout the city.

Paul Revere, who did much more than ride to Lexington shouting, "The British are coming!" Revere was a silversmith, made bells, developed the copper industry, and was a leading patriot; his home is in the North End, and his grave is at the Granary Burying Ground.

George Washington, Father of His Country, who was a frequent visitor to Boston, taking command of his troops in Cambridge and residing in the home later bought by Longfellow.

A True Bostonian
A soul from earth to heaven
    went, to whom the saints, as he drew near,
Said, "Sir, what claims do you present to be admitted
    here?"
"In Boston I was born and bred,
and in her schools was educated,
I afterward, at Harvard, read and was with honors
    graduated.
In Trinity, a pew I own, where Brooks is held in
    such respect.
And the society is known to be the cream of the select.
In fair Nahant, a charming spot, I own a villa, lawns,
    arcades.
And last, a handsome burial plot in dear Mt.
    Auburn's hallowed shades."
St. Peter mused and shook his head. Then as a gentle
    sigh he drew,
"Go back to Boston, friend," he said. "Heaven isn't
    good enough for you."
                    —ANONYMOUS, circa 1900

Key Information for Visitors

For the visitor to the Boston area, each season brings its pleasures. Though summer can be hot and humid, it's a time for taking a harbor boat ride, spending a day at the ocean, relaxing at a sidewalk cafe, or attending a Boston Pops concert on the Esplanade. Fall brings back the thousands of students who attend the fifty colleges and universities in the area; it's a time for visiting country fairs, picking your own apples, and enjoying the glorious foliage. Winter offers skiing within two hours of the city, cross-country skiing on nearby golf courses, and a lively theater season. And spring heralds the flower shows, the return of the Red Sox, the great marathon, observances of Paul Revere's ride to Concord and Lexington, and even maple sugaring.

Tourist Information and Visitor Services

IN BOSTON

Boston is in the 617 area code, which is required even when making local calls. In addition to Boston proper, use area code 617 with the seven-digit numbers given in this book for Belmont, Brookline, Cambridge, Chelsea, Everett, Milton, Newton, Quincy, Somerville, Watertown, and Winthrop.

The Greater Boston Convention and Visitors Bureau has two walk-in offices that provide information, maps, and brochures:

Prudential Center, Center Court, open Monday through Friday 9:30 A.M. to 6:00 P.M. Saturday and Sunday 10:00 A.M. to 6:00 P.M.

Boston Common, 147 Tremont Street, open Monday through Saturday 8:30 A.M. to 5:00 P.M., Sunday 9:00 A.M. to 6:00 P.M. Located just 50 feet from Park Street subway station (where the Red and Green Lines meet). Site also marks the start of the Freedom Trail, along which are some of the most historic sites in the United States. The trail is about 3 miles long, but you'll see most sites in just over a half mile of easy walking. This is "America's Walking City."

The toll-free number for information on Boston is (888) SEE–BOSTON (888-733-2678) throughout the United States and Canada. The visitors bureau can also be reached in Boston by calling 536-4100. The Internet address is www.bostonusa.com.

Discounts and Services

Boston-by-Phone, a free reservation service that allows a direct connection to whichever hotel or service the visitor needs. The service is available twenty-four hours a day. Callers will be able to speak directly with a tourist planner Monday through Friday between 8:30 A.M. and 5:00 P.M. Telephone (888) SEE–BOSTON (888-733-2678). This service and all others can be found on the Web site www.bostonusa.com.

Boston Family Friendly ValuePass provides discounts to attractions and tours. Free by calling (888) 733-2678.

Boston CityPass provides a 50 percent discount on six attractions: The Skywalk Observatory at Prudential Center, the New England Aquarium, the John F. Kennedy Library and Museum, the Harvard Museum of Natural History, the Museum of Fine Arts, and the Museum of Science. The pass is $36.75 for adults, $25.50 for youths three through seventeen. CityPass can be purchased at any of the attractions and in other locations.

The Go Boston Card provides all-inclusive admission to more than fifty attractions, discounts at shops and restaurants, free gifts, and a pocket guidebook to the city. Passes also include trolley and duck tours, whale watching, and harbor cruises. The Go Boston Card is available at visitor information centers and the Gray Line tour office. For information, call 742-5950.

The Visitor Passport is a public-transit pass offering unlimited travel on all subway lines, local buses, inner-harbor ferries, and travel on commuter rail lines within 5 miles from downtown Boston. A one-day pass is $7.50, a three-day pass is $18.00, and a seven-day pass is $35.00. Visitor Passports are available at the information center on Boston Common and at the Prudential Center. For information on routes and schedules, call the MBTA at 222-3200.

Campus Visit Travel Desk, (888) 998-4748. With more than fifty colleges and universities in the region—sixteen with Boston area campuses—the service provides families with trip planning assistance and travel discounts. Also available are fax-on-demand directions to Boston area schools.

Massachusetts Office of Travel and Tourism, 10 Park Plaza, is a good source of information for planning a Massachusetts vacation and especially day trips from Boston. Call 973-8500. The office also offers a toll-free number, (800) 227-MASS (6227), for a free guide to travel in the state as well as seasonal information such as foliage and ski reports. On the Web, visit www.mass-vacation.com or e-mail VacationInfo@state.ma.us. The office is open Monday through Friday 8:45 A.M. to 5:00 P.M.

Boston National Historical Park and Boston African American National Historic Site, 15 State Street. Call 242-5642. Open daily 9:00 A.M. to 5:00 P.M. Located on the Freedom Trail opposite the Old State House and the State Street subway entrance. Offers free walking tours of the Freedom Trail and the Black Heritage Trail, has maps and brochures as well as books and other items for sale. It is wheelchair-accessible, has restrooms, and offers, on the second floor, an art exhibit and slide show on area sights. The park includes Charlestown Navy Yard, Bunker Hill Monument, and African Meeting House.

Travelers Aid Society of Boston, 17 East Street (across from South Station). Call 542-7286. Open Monday through Friday, 8:30 A.M. to 5:00 P.M.; closed Saturday and Sunday. A national service that helps with travel-related problems and works with robbery victims, lost persons, and wayward children.

Massport Information Booths are located at Logan International Airport in the baggage claim areas of Terminal E (international arrivals), A, and C.

For visitors driving into Boston from the Massachusetts Turnpike, there are information centers on the Pike in Lee, near the New York state line; in Charlton, the first service area after entering the toll road from Interstate 84; and at the last service area on the turnpike in Natick, just before entering Greater Boston. For persons traveling on Interstate 95 from points south, there is a center in Mansfield, a few miles from the Rhode Island state line.

Foreign visitors needing assistance will find some consulates and honorary consulates in Boston. Most consulates are open Monday through Friday from 9:00 A.M. to 5:00 P.M. A complete listing of consulates can be found in the White Pages of the Boston telephone directory under "Government Listings" (pages with a blue border). For information on multilingual city tours, see page 25.

In Charlestown

The visitor center in Charlestown Navy Yard is located near the USS *Constitution* and is operated by the National Park Service. The center offers exhibits, guided tours, brochures, and restrooms. Call 242–5642.

A Walking City

Boston is not known as "America's Walking City" for nothing. Just about every Boston attraction is within easy walking distance from just about anywhere in the city. Most attractions are within the first mile from Boston Common, where a fine information center is located with details and maps of all these tours. A look at the city's walks:

The **Black Heritage Trail** is a 1.6-mile walking tour on the history and contributions of Boston's nineteenth-century African-American community. What surprises many is that so much takes place on the north slope of Beacon Hill.

The **Boston Immigrant Trail** begins at the Dreams of Freedom Museum across from the Old South Meeting House. The trail includes a memorial to the Irish famine, the Holocaust, the Museum of African American History, Ping On Alley in Boston's Chinatown, and the statue of the "father of public education in South America," Argentina's president Domingo Sarmiento.

Check out your ancestors at the Web site www.BostonFamilyHistory.com, which not only offers information on the twenty-seven-site Boston

Immigrant Walking Trail but also includes historical background on ancestor groups and identifies genealogical resources in Boston. The site also has an electronic message board for people searching for ancestors in New England.

Boston Women's Heritage Trail takes you to the homes, churches, and social and political institutions where twenty women lived or made contributions to society. The women range from Julia Ward Howe and colonial religious leader Anne Hutchinson to Phillis Wheatley, a slave who became the first published African-American poet.

Emerald Necklace Trail is a 5-mile green space designed by Frederick Law Olmsted in 1887 that stretches from Franklin Park to the Boston Common. Along the way are a Victorian garden, an internationally known arboretum, a golf course, riding trails, and a zoo.

Freedom Trail, the most famous walk in Boston and one of the most historic walks in the nation, is 2.5-miles long. Most sites are within the first mile. The Freedom Trail brings the story of the American Revolution to life. A great way to see it is with the Freedom Trail Foundation's Audio Guide (357–8300) available at the Boston Common Visitor Center for $15. Designed to see the trail at your own pace, simply click on the site number and listen to the stories and music of the times.

The **Irish Heritage Trail** commemorates the Bay State's Irish heritage. Some 26 percent of Massachusetts residents trace their ancestry back to Ireland, giving the state the highest concentration of Irish Americans in the country. The 3-mile trail often follows the Freedom Trail, as Irish Americans were very involved in helping to found both Boston and the nation.

The **Literary Trail** explores the heritage of some of the country's greatest authors and poets as it winds it way through Boston, Cambridge, and Concord. Stops include the Boston athenaeum, Omni Parker House, Longfellow National Historic Site, Thoreau's serene Walden Pond, Louisa May Alcott's Orchard House, and the Old Manse, home to both Emerson and Hawthorne.

Getting around the City

From a Bostonian's view, driving in the city is not recommended. Boston is known for its confusing array of tiny, twisting, some say, cow paths and one-way streets. And while the Big Dig (replacing the former overhead Central Artery with a tunnel for traffic underground) is over, work continues on related above-ground projects such as parks and road resurfacing—causing additional traffic headaches. The Big Dig, the most expensive road project in the nation, took more than fourteen years to complete.

There also appears to be a lack of street signs. Plus there are rotaries, places where four or more roads converge on a circle. The law says to yield to the vehicle in the rotary. And there is perhaps no square Boston Square.

Most of present-day Boston was at one time under water, which might help explain some of the confusion over streets. The Faneuil Hall area was mostly part of Boston Harbor in colonial days; the Back Bay was a bay until the mid- to late 1800s.

The best advice is to park your car and then walk, take the T (which is very convenient), join a tour, or let a taxi maneuver you through the streets.

TOURS BY TROLLEY OR DUCK

The best introduction one can have to any city is to take a tour. Boston has two excellent ways to discover its attractions and get one's bearings: by trolley or duck. Yes, I did say duck.

While the duck tours—on former World War II craft that were designed to travel on both water and land—are the most fun, as the vehicles take a ride up the Charles River, and on land passengers are encouraged to "quack" at those on the street, my first choice would be to go by trolley.

Why? The trolley tours have two advantages. One, most will pick up visitors at hotels as well as locations throughout the city; and two, while the tour in its entirety lasts about an hour, visitors can get off at sights they wish to explore and return later on another trolley.

The Trolley and Duck Operators

Beantown Trolley, 236-2148, offers tours in reproduction turn-of-the-twentieth-century trolley cars. Covers all historic sights.

Boston Duck Tours, 723-3825, leave from the Prudential Center opposite the Boston Marriott Hotel and Museum of Science for an eighty-minute tour of the city and a dip into the Charles River. Seasonal. Call for reservations (very popular).

Cityview Trolley Tours, 383-7899. Offers unlimited on-and-off all-day pass, also admission to New England Aquarium or free harbor cruise.

Discover Boston Trolley Tours, 742-1440. Fully narrated tour of Boston and Cambridge available in six languages. Includes all-day pass, guided walking tours, and free harbor cruise. Twilight tours available.

Old Town Trolley, 269-7150. This is the largest trolley company and has frequent departures from many locations. Tours are fun, are fully narrated, and last around ninety minutes. Old Town Trolley also offers a variety of special tours in season: a chocolate tour, a haunted Boston tour, holiday lights, JFK's Boston, a beer tour, and even a seafood tour to three of the area's best restaurants.

MULTILINGUAL CITY TOURS

Discover Boston, 742–1440, about ninety minutes. Tours are offered in six languages.

PRIVATE TOURS

Exciting Tours of Boston by Ralph Spinelli, 699–6140. Spinelli, a "historian and raconteur," offers a variety of part-day tours (in minivans that accommodate from one to fourteen passengers) of the Boston and Cambridge area, Lexington and Concord, Salem, and Marblehead, and all-day tours to Newport, Cape Cod, and Plymouth.

SIGHTSEEING TOURS BY FOOT

Walking tours are the best way to see the city. You'll see the sites at a civilized pace, on their own level, and with interesting and informative guides. Do wear comfortable shoes, as you will travel on cobblestone and brick walkways, and on Beacon Hill some walks are at a steep incline. Except for National Park Service tours, all walks charge a fee. Most tours are seasonal, so it is best to call for times. The tours include:

Boston Art Tours, 732–3920, offers "cultural fun with style" in and around Boston.

Boston by Foot, 367–2345, has been conducting tours throughout the city for years. Volunteers experienced in the city's architectural, historic, and cultural areas lead the tours. Tours include Boston underground, the waterfront, and North End.

Boston by Little Feet, 367–2345, offers hour-long tours for children ages six through twelve.

Boston History Collaborative, 350–0358, offers guided and self-guided tours of Boston.

City of Boston, 635–7383, offers park ranger tours.

Colonial Boston Walks, (781) 648–0628. Let "Benjamin Franklin" lead you on a walk of the Boston of his childhood. Another walk is with "Abigail Adams," the first woman to marry one president and mother another. She conveys life during the city's occupation by British troops.

Freedom Trail Foundation, 227-8800, offers a variety of walking and behind-the-scene tours such as a visit to the Old North Church crypt and bell tower.

Hip & Historic: Celebrating the South End, 426-5000. Take a walking tour of the South End along with the opportunity to view open artist studios.

Innovation Odyssey, 350-0358, visits sites associated with the area's inventors and innovators that include the invention of the Internet, medical firsts, and the birth of the telephone. The tour covers Boston and Cambridge, bringing to light both the triumphs and tribulations of those involved with the innovations.

Literary Trail of Greater Boston, 574-5950, covers 20 miles from Boston to Cambridge and to Concord, exploring the history and writings of some of America's greatest writers. Tour stops include homes of the authors, museums, and the Boston Athenaeum.

Maritime Trail, Boston History Collaborative, 350-0358. Offers guided and self-guided tours of Boston. The Maritime Trail connects a variety of sites and activities on the city's rich seafaring past. Pick up a map at the Boston Common information center or call for a tour.

MyTown, 536-5763, is a multicultural youth tour of the South End that explores the history of one of Boston's most diverse neighborhoods. The tours are led by high-school students.

National Park Service, 242-5642, has tours of the Freedom Trail and the Black Heritage Trail.

North End Market Tour, 523-6032. Led by chef Michele Topor, this three-hour tour covers the city's historic Italian neighborhood. Those on the tour learn the secrets of Italian cooking ingredients and sample authentic flavors.

North End Walking Tour, 268-6882. A one-hour tour celebrating colonial Boston and its mostly proud, sometimes scandalous people.

Society for the Preservation of New England Antiquities, 227-3956, offers historical and architectural tours of houses and neighborhoods, including the weekly Magnificent and Modest: Beacon Hill Walking Tour. Tours also include the elegant Federal-style Otis House Museum.

WalkBoston, 451-1570, includes tours of Brookline's Secret Pathways and East Cambridge.

Do it yourself. Visit one of the information centers for free maps and tips on touring; follow the walks in this book; buy a copy of *Shawmut Peninsula Walk,* which traces Boston's original shoreline, or a copy of walks in Boston from *WalkBoston* (available in bookstores or by calling 367-9255). Follow the Black Heritage Trail or the Women's Heritage Trail, both easy walks. Maps and information are found at the city information centers.

TOURS BY BUS

Boston Tours, (781) 899-1454. Tours of Boston from suburban hotels.

Brush Hill/Beantown Trolley/Gray Line, (781) 986-6100, offers bus tours of Boston, Cambridge, Salem and Marblehead, Cape Cod, Plymouth, Newport, Foxwoods Casino, and, in season, foliage. Tours range from two hours to a full day.

Peter Pan Tours, (800) 343-9999, provides tours to Foxwoods Casino, Newport, Salem and the North Shore, Cape Cod, and Martha's Vineyard.

SPECIAL TOURS NOT TO BE MISSED

Boston Public Library Tour, 536-5400. A library that is magnificent in its architecture, art, and collections.

Boston Symphony Hall Tour, 266-1492, home of the Boston Pops and Boston Symphony, one of the most acoustically perfect buildings.

Fenway Park Tour, 482-4SOX, home of the Boston Red Sox baseball team and one of the most famous ballparks in the country.

Make Way for Ducklings, 635-7483, introduces children to the famed Mallard family of ducks as a Boston park ranger reads the classic children's story by Robert McCloskey. Takes place at the ducklings' statues in the Public Garden.

Museum of Fine Arts, 267-9300, one of the finest museums in the country; a one-hour introductory tour.

TOURS BY BICYCLE

Boston Bike Tours, 308-5902, offers low-impact bike tours from Boston Common visiting the city's neighborhoods, the Esplanade, Fenway Park, and Victory Garden. Tours include bike, water, and helmet.

TOURS BY BOAT

One, if not the best, way to appreciate Boston's mix of the old, the new, and magnificent scenery is to see it from the water.

Since 1989, when this book was first published, Boston's water-viewing opportunities have blossomed. From its wharves, one can catch Boston's changing skyline on a variety of harbor tours, explore its many islands, climb to the top of the country's oldest lighthouse, take a whale-watch tour, enjoy a midday or dinner feast or just a sandwich at lunch, head off to Provincetown on the tip of Cape Cod or Cape Ann on the elegant North Shore, or take an ocean cruise to Bermuda and other exotic destinations. How many urban destinations offer all of that?

From the Cambridge side of the river, you can cruise up the Charles. And there is now ferry service from downtown Boston to the John F. Kennedy Library, "Old Ironsides" (the USS *Constitution*), other areas of the city, and a wonderful water trip to and from Logan International Airport.

In addition, one can take a sail, or even sailing lessons, join a pirates' sail, and, as earlier mentioned, ride a duck into the Charles River. For more information on whale watching, see page 139.

The Wharves

Commonwealth Pier, at 164 Northern Avenue, serves Bay State Cruises to Provincetown. There are music cruises on weekends in summer. The *Spirit of Boston* also sails from here. The pier is a half-mile walk from Atlantic Avenue. A shuttle boat runs from Long Wharf to connect with ferry service.

Fan Pier, located along Northern Avenue beside the Joseph Moakley Federal Courthouse. Located almost opposite Rowes Wharf. The harbor islands Discovery Center is here, and boats to Boston Light leave from here.

Long Wharf, on Atlantic Avenue (by MBTA, take the Blue Line to Aquarium Station), serves Bay State Cruises and Boston Harbor Cruises.

Rowes Wharf, at 350 Atlantic Avenue (just behind the Boston Harbor Hotel), is 2 blocks from Aquarium Station. It serves the Water Shuttle, Boston Harbor Commuter, *Odyssey,* and Massachusetts Bay Lines.

Harbor and Island Cruises

Bay State Cruises, 748-1428, offers both a high-speed and leisure cruise to Provincetown as well as harbor sightseeing cruises. Entertainment cruises in the harbor on weekends. Leaves from Commonwealth Pier at the World Trade Center on Northern Avenue.

Boston Harbor Cruises, 227–4321, leaves from Long Wharf by the aquarium. The city's oldest and largest cruise company offers harbor sightseeing, whale-watch cruises, and sunset and music cruises. Also, ninety-minute cruises to Provincetown on a high-speed boat are an option. Cruise to George's Island and inner harbor cruise with a stop at the USS *Constitution.*

Boston Light Tours, 223–8666, offers seasonal visits to America's oldest lighthouse, dating from 1716 (the present lighthouse dates from 1783). Cruises leave from Fan Pier by the Federal Courthouse in South Boston and from the John F. Kennedy Library in Dorchester.

Boston Steamship Company, 542–8000, offers tours aboard replica steamships. Options include hourly tours as well as sunset and moonlight cruises.

Charles River Boat Co., 621–3001, offers cruises on the Charles River lower basin. The river divides Boston and Cambridge, and there is a dam where it enters Boston Harbor, with entry through a series of locks. Cruises leave from CambridgeSide Galleria.

The Liberty Fleet of Tall Ships, 742–0333, offers sails from Long Wharf on the 125-foot schooner *Liberty Clipper,* a replica of eighteenth-century New England fishing schooners and Revolutionary warships. Noon, afternoon, sunset, brunch, and dinner sails.

Massachusetts Bay Lines, 542–8000, leaves from Rowes Wharf behind the Boston Harbor Hotel. Offers whale-watch, harbor, sunset, and rock music cruises.

Brunch, Lunch, Dinner Cruises
Odyssey Cruises, (800) 946–7245, offers jazz brunch and weekly lunch cruises and three-hour dinner cruises. Leaves from Rowes Wharf. Live music, entertainment.

Spirit of Boston, (866) 211–3807, offers two-hour narrated lunch cruises and three-hour dinner cruises with live entertainment. Leaves from Commonwealth Pier. Ample parking nearby.

Cruise to Cape Cod (Provincetown)
Bay State Cruise Company, 748–1428, offers both high-speed and leisure service. From Commonwealth Pier.

Boston Harbor Cruises, 227–4321, offers high-speed ferry service. Leaves from Long Wharf by the aquarium.

Cruise to Bermuda

The *Norwegian Majesty* sails from April through October to Bermuda; weekly departures from the Black Falcon Cruise Terminal. Also cruises to Montreal including fall foliage cruises. Travel agents have details.

OTHER NEARBY SUMMER WATER ADVENTURES

Black Falcon Cruise Terminal

For visitors thinking of taking a cruise, or planning on arriving in Boston as a port of call on a cruise, the city now has a modern cruise center, located in what was once referred to as the old Boston Army Base. With the exception of the *Norwegian Majesty,* which sails May through October on seven-day cruises to Bermuda, most cruise lines come to Boston only as a port of call. However, the port is showing new popularity with short cruises to Canada and elsewhere. There is ample parking in the area for persons leaving their cars for the duration of the cruise. It is not an area where taxis are readily found, but telephones are found in the building. (The center was named for a disaster. The *Black Falcon* was a freighter that burned and sank here, killing many longshoremen.) Three of Boston's longtime and favorite seafood restaurants are within a mile of the pier—Jimmy's, No Name, and Anthony's Pier 4—as well as Jimbo's and the Daily Catch, offering more reasonably priced fare. There is also a Harpoon Ale brewery tour nearby.

Just across from the entrance to the cruise terminal is the Boston Design Center, which takes up one-third of the old Boston Army Base. The eight-story building, as long as the Prudential Tower is high, contains showrooms for fabrics, furniture, and carpets. The building is not open to the public, except for those persons with a referral from an architect or interior designer.

To get to Black Falcon Cruise Terminal from Atlantic Avenue, take a right onto Northern Avenue and follow it to its end, passing by an information booth at the Marine Industrial Park entrance. Take a right onto Tide Street and an immediate left onto Drydock Avenue. The terminal may also be reached by taking Summer Street from South Station to the entrance of Marine Industrial Park, turning left into the park.

Private Transportation

BY CAR

Parking is at a premium—in both cost and space—in Boston. The average rate for parking anywhere from two to twelve hours is now $10 to $15, with some rates as high as $30.

The largest parking areas in the city are the garages at the Prudential Center, at Government Center, at Boston Common, at New England Aquarium, at Winthrop Square, at Lafayette Place, at Copley Place, and at Faneuil Hall Marketplace.

One of the handier parking areas, especially on weekends, is the Garage at Post Office Square, hidden beneath a beautiful park and within a very short walk to Faneuil Hall, Downtown Crossing, and the waterfront. The garage and park replace an ugly parking area with a small oasis of beauty. The garage has weekend rates and entrances on Pearl and Congress Streets.

The Massachusetts Turnpike runs 135 miles from Boston to the New York border. It is a toll road. For highway conditions, call 237-5210. For the State Police, which patrols the highway, call 727-6781 or (800) 525-5555 statewide. Tourist information centers are located at service areas in Lee (eastbound), Natick (eastbound), and Charlton (eastbound and westbound).

RENTAL CARS

All major rental-car firms have offices at Logan International Airport and throughout the area. Be aware that in addition to the usual taxes imposed on a rental, Boston now has a $10 flat fee on each rental to help pay for its new convention center. You can avoid the fee by renting in Cambridge or other places outside the city of Boston.

BY TAXI

Some people might argue that Boston has an inadequate number of taxis; most complaints today come between 3:00 and 7:00 P.M.

The fare for a taxi in Boston is $1.75 for the first ¼ mile plus 30 cents for each additional ⅛ mile. You can also expect to pay an extra charge for trunk service and bridge, turnpike, and tunnel tolls. Boston now has a third harbor tunnel, the Ted Williams Tunnel—named for the legendary Boston Red Sox home-run slugger. Although a tip is not required, most people leave the driver an additional 15 to 20 percent.

Call 536-8294 for complaints or information.

Boston Taxi Companies
  Boston Cab, 536-5010
  Checker, 536-7000
  City Cab, 536-5100
  ITOA, 825-4000
  Metro Cab, 782-5500
  Town Taxi, 536-5000

Public Transportation

THE T

The Massachusetts Bay Transportation System (MBTA, or just plain T) has five rapid transit lines—Red, Green, Orange, Blue, and Silver—serving the greater portions of Boston, Cambridge, Brookline, Newton, Somerville, Milton, Quincy, and other areas; a color-coded map of these rail lines can be found at most T stations. In addition, the T includes an extensive bus line system and commuter rail trains. Most tourist-related areas are easily reached by the rapid transit lines. All four lines intersect in Boston, allowing transfers at no charge between lines. Both the Red and the Green Lines have branches off them, which, depending on where you are going, requires checking the front of the train for its destination. The Red Line, for example, runs between Cambridge and Quincy or Ashmont in the Dorchester section of Boston. All Red Line trains stop at the JFK/UMass Station, from which shuttle buses go to the John F. Kennedy Library, the Massachusetts Archives and Commonwealth Museum, and the University of Massachusetts at Boston. Stations are identified by the area they are in, such as *Copley* for Copley Square, or by an attraction, such as *Symphony* for Symphony Hall.

The newest line, the Silver, presently offers bus service between Dudley Square in the Roxbury section to Downtown Crossing. The second phase will go underground and connect with South Station, and the third will go via a tunnel into South Boston to the waterfront, new convention center, and World Trade Center. The final phase will go to Logan International Airport via the Ted Williams Tunnel.

T service is offered Monday through Saturday between 5:00 A.M. and 1:00 A.M., with Sunday and holiday service from about 5:30 A.M. to 12:45 A.M. from Boston.

Most subway rides are $1.25, with some exceptions on the Red Line's Braintree branch and the Green Line's D branch. Children five to eleven and junior-high- and high-school students pay 60 cents, senior citizens and those with disabilities pay 35 cents. For those boarding the Red Line at Braintree, Quincy Adams, or Quincy Center, the fare is $2.50, children $1.25, and seniors 35 cents. There is an exit fee of $1.25 at Braintree and Quincy Adams for adults, 60 cents for children, and no charge for seniors. The Green Line has added fees of $1.50 (75 cents children five to eleven, 35 cents seniors) boarding inbound between Reservoir and Fenway; inbound between Riverside and Chestnut Hill is $3.00 ($1.50 children, 35 cents seniors).

Most bus fares, including the Silver Line, are 90 cents adults, 45 cents children five to eleven and students, and 25 cents seniors. Some zoned routes can cost up to $1.55, Night Owl service is $1.50 to $4.00, and express buses range from $2.20 to $3.45.

Commuter rail fares range from $1.25 to $6.00 depending on distrance traveled.

Inner-harbor ferries are $1.50 and commuter boats are $6.00.

The Visitor Passport is a bargain-filled way to get around Boston. It's a pass on the T that allows unlimited travel on subways, buses, and trolleys and limited travel on commuter rail lines. Seven-day T passes are available at Logan Airport, hotels, visitor bureau offices, and other locations. Pass holders get a wallet-size card with use dates stamped on it. For prices and details, see page 21. For MBTA information, call 222-3200.

Finally, don't forget that Boston had the first subway in the nation, opening the line from Park Street in 1897.

By Bus

Boston has a major bus station located in South Station, the major terminal for Amtrak service. The terminal is located at 700 Atlantic Avenue. MBTA Red Line service, with connections throughout the city, is also located there.

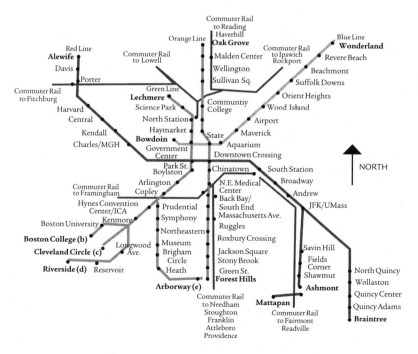

T Subway Lines and Commuter Rail Routes

Among bus lines offering service are **Greyhound,** with service throughout the United States, (800) 231-2222; **Peter Pan,** with service in New England and along the East Coast, (800) 343-9999; **Plymouth** and **Brockton,** with service to the South Shore and Cape Cod, 773-9401; **Vermont Transit,** 526-1800; **Bonanza Bus Lines,** with service to Providence, Cape Cod, Fall River, and Newport, 720-4110; and **Concord Trailways,** with service to New Hampshire, (800) 639-3317.

By Rail

South Station, at Atlantic Avenue and Summer Street, serves Amtrak and the MBTA. The building has been grandly restored; it's worth a visit even if you're not traveling. Access to the MBTA, buses, and trains is available from one central location. For Amtrak information, call (800) 872-7245. High-speed Amtrak Acela rail service (3 hours, 23 minutes) is offered nine times daily between Boston and New York from South Station.

North Station, at 150 Causeway Street, serves the MBTA commuter rail to points north and west of the city, as well as the Green and Orange MBTA lines. Call 222-3200.

Train service between Boston and Portland, Maine, is now available from North Station. The 114-mile trip takes 2 hours and 20 minutes and includes stops in Haverhill, as well as in Dover and Exeter, New Hampshire, and Saco and Wells, Maine. Stops in Durham, New Hampshire, are added on Saturday and Sunday.

By Air

Logan Airport is the closest major airport to a city of any in the country—just under 3 miles. If you are driving, however, at times it feels as though it might be 100 miles, with traffic snarls that cause long delays going through the tunnels to and from Boston. Yet being close to the city does have its advantages for getting both to and from the airport. And should you be delayed by a flight, rather than sitting at the airport, you can easily visit the city.

Traveling between Boston and Logan by MBTA is easy on the Blue Line between the city and Airport Station. From the station, a free airport shuttle bus (number 22 to Terminals A and B; number 33 to Terminals C, D, and E) operates every twelve minutes.

For information on transportation to and from Logan, call (800) 23-LOGAN (800-235-6426).

Manchester, N.H., Airport is just about an hour's drive from Boston. The airport is served by many low-cost airlines, which makes it a popular alternative to Boston's Logan Airport. Its location adjacent to Interstates 93 and 293 also makes it convenient to reach the seacoast and lakes of New Hampshire and Maine, and in winter, the ski areas. For information, call (603) 624-6539.

T.F. Green Airport (Providence) is just over an hour's drive from Boston. It is conveniently located just 1 mile off Interstate 95 at the end of exit 13. The airport is just ten minutes from downtown Providence, handy to Newport, and convenient to both Cape Cod and Mystic, Connecticut. For information, call (888) 268-7222.

Pease International Tradeport is located about 2 miles from Portsmouth, New Hampshire. Pan American Airways, (800) 359-7262, offers service to Florida and other destinations. About one hour from Boston just off I-95.

By Ferry

Harbor Express, 222-6999, from Long Wharf to Quincy, Hull, Logan Airport, and harbor islands.

MBTA Harbor Express, Boston Harbor Cruises, 227-4321, from Long Wharf, service to Charlestown Navy Yard, North Station, World Trade Center, and Hingham.

Water Taxis

City Water Taxi, 422-0392, service to entire waterfront including Logan Airport, USS *Constitution,* Faneuil Hall, Museum Wharf, Anthony's Pier 4, and FleetBoston Pavilion.

Rowes Wharf Water Taxi, 406-8584, offers on-call service to Logan Airport, World Trade Center, and Moakley Federal Courthouse.

For information on water transportation between Logan Airport and downtown, call (800) 23-LOGAN.

For more information on the wharves, see page 28.

Public Toilets

When in a walkable city, it is always good to know where to go should you have to go. Unfortunately there are few signs indicating where public restrooms are located. Most businesses do not allow access to their facilities unless you happen to be dining there or a customer of some stores. The best advice is to use the restrooms of the attraction or dining place before leaving it. Boston does have three public, self-cleaning toilets, found in Copley Square, outside the New England Aquarium, and on Congress Street near City Hall.

Weather

New Englanders love to say, "If you don't like the weather, just wait a minute"—which can be very true, for the weather here is fickle: It can be almost completely sunny overhead and still raining right on you.

Boston average mean temperature is 49° F (9° C) in spring, 71° F (22° C) in summer, 55° F (13° C) in fall, and 31° F (-1° C) in winter.

Local weather, 936–1212
Marine weather (spring and fall), 976–1212
Time and temperature, 637–1234

In the know . . .

For weather, you can also look to the tower of the old John Hancock Building (next to the new glass-walled tower), where, since the building opened in 1949, Bostonians have looked for a clue to the weather. Its beacon proclaims the forecast in a red-and-blue code that goes like this:

Steady blue, clear view;
Flashing blue, clouds are due;
Steady red, rain ahead;
Flashing red, snow instead.

And, in baseball season, flashing red means the Red Sox game is canceled.

Holidays and Closings

Unless otherwise noted, most museums, attractions, and information centers are closed on major holidays, such as Thanksgiving, Christmas, and New Year's Day.

Blue Laws are the Massachusetts laws that once kept just about everything closed on Sunday and holidays and still prevent the drinking of alcoholic beverages in restaurants and taverns before noon on Sunday. Since 1983, however, the Blue Laws have been greatly liberalized; now retail stores may open on Sunday and most holidays. Sale of beer, wine, and liquor is now allowed on Sunday beginning at noon. The Blue Laws are strictly applied on Easter, Thanksgiving, and Christmas, however.

Legal holidays in Massachusetts or Boston are as follows:

New Year's Day, January 1.

Birthday of Martin Luther King Jr., third Monday in January.

Presidents' Day, third Monday in February.

Evacuation Day in Boston (also *St. Patrick's Day*), March 17, the day the British left town in 1776. Schools, libraries, and government offices in Suffolk County—Boston, Chelsea, Revere, and Winthrop—are closed. (The St. Patrick's Day parade is usually held on the weekend closest to March 17.)

Patriots' Day, Monday nearest April 19, a holiday in Massachusetts, mainly in the Greater Boston area, to mark the beginning of the American Revolution in 1775 when the first shots were fired on the Lexington Green (reenacted at the crack of dawn on the 19th every year). Schools and state and county offices are closed; some banks may be closed.

Memorial Day, last Monday in May.

Bunker Hill Day, June 17, marks the famed battle ("Don't shoot till you see the whites of their eyes") between colonists and the British. Although a victory for the Redcoats, the British troops were so badly mauled that they quickly left town for good. Schools, libraries, and government offices are closed in Suffolk County (Boston) only.

Independence Day, July 4.

Labor Day, first Monday in September.

Columbus Day, second Monday in October.

Thanksgiving, fourth Thursday in November.

Christmas, December 25.

Publications

NEWSPAPERS

The *Boston Globe,* published daily, offers an excellent "Calendar" section on Thursday, containing a complete listing of the latest attractions, concerts, and so on, as well as information on lectures, walks, nightlife, workshops, special-interest groups, and programs for children. On Sunday, the "Sunday Best" listing in the paper's "Arts Etc." section gives ideas for that day. The *Boston Globe* is also available online at www.boston.com.

The Sunday issue of the *Boston Herald* also offers information on events.

The *Boston Phoenix* is an excellent source of information on entertainment and nightlife. Published each Friday, it is aimed primarily at Boston's burgeoning university crowd, with most listings reflecting that age-group's interests.

The *Improper Bostonian* is free and available in news boxes throughout the city. It offers a sophisticated look at the city and a huge listing section.

MAGAZINES

Boston magazine offers trendy stories monthly on the city and its people, as well as guides to dining and an annual "Best and Worst" listing.

Where is a free magazine found in most hotels, as well as at information centers. Updated monthly, it contains listings of attractions, restaurants, and shops, particularly at Faneuil Hall Marketplace.

Currency Exchange

At Logan Airport there is a currency exchange in the Volpe International Terminal (Terminal E), and banks are also located in Terminal B and C.

Bank of America. Call (800) 225-5353 for locations offering immediate currency exchange.

For the most favorable rates, use your bank or credit card in one of the ATMs found throughout the city.

Exposition and Convention Centers

Boston Convention & Exhibition Center, 415 Summer Street; 954-2000. This is a state-of-the-art facility with 516,000 square feet of contiguous exhibit space as well as plenty of meeting rooms and other facilities. It is located in the waterfront area and just ten minutes from Logan Airport. A Westin hotel (under construction in 2004) is adjacent. Other hotels nearby.

The **John B. Hynes Veterans Memorial Convention Center,** at 900 Boylston Street (954-2000). Parking is available in the Prudential Center garage beneath the center and at nearby garages. By T, take the Green Line to Auditorium/ICA Station. Major conventions are held here.

In case you wondered . . .

The drinking age in Massachusetts is twenty-one, and the state maintains a rigid traffic code that calls for the loss of one's driver's license for a year if convicted of driving under the influence.

Most bars and restaurants serve drinks until 1:00 A.M., some until 2:00 A.M. On Saturday night, service stops at midnight and does not resume until 11:00 A.M. or 1:00 P.M. on Sunday.

Some Massachusetts residents like to refer to the state as Taxachusetts. Visitors will feel the pinch with the state sales tax, a 5 percent addition to all purchases except food and clothing. Food, however, is taxed if you purchase it at a restaurant; the tax is 5 percent. Hotel tax varies, but allow 9.7 percent; check to see if your room rate or package includes this tax or if it is an additional charge.

Massachusetts has a lottery. Call 848-7755. The results are published on page 2 of the "Metro" section of the *Boston Globe* daily and on page 2 of the *Sunday Globe.*

The **World Trade Center Boston,** at Commonwealth Pier (385-5000). Parking is available. Among events held here are computer shows, the New England Home Show, and various conventions. By bus, take T-Bus 7; by the Red Line, go to South Station, then take a three-quarter-mile walk south on Summer Street, then left onto Viaduct Street. (Shuttle buses from South Station operate to some events.) Northern Avenue is off Atlantic Avenue near the Boston Harbor Hotel. The center is a half-mile walk from Atlantic Avenue.

Bayside Exposition Center, in Dorchester (825-5151). Parking ($10) is on the premises. By T, take the Red Line to JFK/UMass Station; the center is a short walk from the station. Among shows held here are the New England International Auto Show, the World of Wheels, and the New England Flower Show.

Religious Services

Note: This listing is designed to point out historical churches. The Yellow Pages of the telephone book has complete listings for all faiths under "Churches and Synagogues."

Boston's historic churches—see the listings in chapter 14—become more meaningful during Sunday services. Most offer refreshments after the service—a good time to meet the people of the city. Emmanuel Church on Newbury Street features Bach during its services, and one of the largest organs in the world—with 13,595 pipes—can be enjoyed only during Sunday or Wednesday services (and on First Night) at the Mother Church, First Church of Christ, Scientist. Trinity, in Copley Square, offers tours by members after the service. Visitors interested in history might enjoy attending services at St. Stephen's in the North End—the only Bulfinch-designed church standing in Boston and one that began life as a Protestant church and is now serving the Catholic faith—or at the Old North Church of Paul Revere's ride fame. King's Chapel, the first Anglican church, and one detested by early Puritans, is now Unitarian but has an Episcopal service and a Congregational church government. The Old South Church in Copley Square is the "new" home of the Old South Meeting House congregation—where Ben Franklin was baptized and the Tea Party began. Park Street Church was the point of departure for the first missionaries to Hawaii and the setting where "America" was first sung. Tremont Temple is America's first integrated church.

For tourists and others seeking meditation, chapels that are open weekdays and other times include:

The Paulist Center and Chapel, 5 Park Street, 742–4460
St. Anthony Shrine, 100 Arch Street, 542–6440
St. Francis Prudential Chapel, Prudential Center, 437–7117

At the airport:

Our Lady of the Airway Chapel, 567–2800

Medical Facilities

Boston is home to some of the finest medical centers in the world, attracting people from all over the globe for the treatment offered. Here is a partial listing.

In the downtown area, along the Charles River, is **Massachusetts General Hospital** (726-2000, medical walk-in 720-2707); **Massachusetts Eye and Ear Infirmary** (523-7900) is adjacent to Massachusetts General. Clustered together in the Fenway area are the **Beth Israel Deaconess Medical Center,** a merger of Beth Israel and Deaconess Hospitals (667-7000, emergencies 754-2300); **Children's Hospital** (355-6000, emergencies 355-6611); and **Brigham and Women's Hospital** (732-5500, emergencies 732-5636).

In the South End of Boston is the **Boston Medical Center** (638-8000, emergencies 414-4075). In the Theater District of Boston is the **New England Medical Center** (635-5000, emergencies 636-5566).

Among other hospitals in the area are **St. Elizabeth's** in Brighton area (789-3000, emergencies 789-2666), **Mt. Auburn Hospital** in Cambridge (492-3500, emergencies 499-5025), and **New England Baptist Hospital** (754-5800).

Inn-House Doctor (859-1776) provides twenty-four-hour medical hotel visits and dental service.

All-Night Drugstores

CVS has pharmacies in Cambridge in Porter Square, 876-4037, and East Boston, 567-3236; open until midnight is the store at 155 Charles Street, 227-0437. For other locations, call (800) 746-7287.

Walgreen's, 757 Gallivan Boulevard, Dorchester, 282-5246. For other locations, call (800) 925-4733.

Discounts

Discounts are offered to senior citizens over the age of sixty-five at museums, at attractions, and on the MBTA. College-age students are given discounts at many area museums and attractions; a valid student ID is required. If you are a member of the American Automobile Association, your card may qualify you for a discount at some attractions. Also:

· Stop at information centers and ask for any discounts.

· Pick up free tourist guides, many of which contain discount coupons.

· Look in newspaper calendar and entertainment sections for discount coupons.

- Thinking about the circus or ice shows? Many area TV and radio stations and stores offer discounts on certain performances, and Bostix in Faneuil Hall Marketplace has discounted tickets to that day's performances.

- Pick up a copy (around $30) of *Entertainment,* a coupon book with free and discounted coupons good for meals, attractions, and accommodations throughout the Greater Boston area. For information on the Boston edition or guides for other cities in the country, call (888) 231-7283.

- Call the Boston Convention Bureau for a discount-coupon book and weekend-hotel-package guide: 536-4100 or (888) 733-2678.

Handy Telephone Numbers

Boston is in the 617 area code. Massachusetts has four additional codes: 413 for the western part of the state; 781 for areas just outside Boston; 978 for north and west of Boston; and 508 for Cape Cod, south and southwest of the city. All numbers given in this book, unless otherwise noted, are in the 617 area code, which must be dialed even for local calls.

Emergencies

Boston Police, 911
Boston Fire Department, 911
Massachusetts State Police, 737-8980 or (800) 525-5555
Poison Information, 232-2120
Dental Emergency, (508) 651-3521
Children's Hospital Emergency Room, 355-6611

Consumer Protection Agencies

Attorney General's Office, 727-8400
Better Business Bureau, 426-9000
Consumer Affairs, 727-7755

Other Resources

Angell Memorial Animal Hospital, 522-7282

Ask a Nurse (free medical information and referrals), (800) 544-2424

Automatic Teller Information, (800) 424-7787 (Cirrus Network), (800) 843-7587 (Plus System)

Boston City Hall (information on city services and official events), 635-4000

Boston Public Library Telephone Reference Information (if you have a ready-reference question, here's your source for an answer—open Monday to Thursday 9:00 A.M. to 9:00 P.M. and Friday and Saturday 9:00 A.M. to 5:00 P.M.), 536-5400

Bostonian Society (answers questions about local history), 720-3285

Center for International Visitors, 542-8995

Citizen Information Center, 727-7030

Disabled Information Center, 727-7440

Jazzline (recorded information on events), 787-9700

Lost or Stolen Credit Cards: American Express, (800) 528-2121; Diners Club/Carte Blanche, (800) 525-7376; MasterCard, (800) 826-2181; Visa, (800) 227-6811

Massachusetts Audubon Society, (781) 259-9500

Massachusetts Horticultural Society, 536-9280

Massachusetts State Parks and Forests, 727-3180

Metropolitan District Commission Recreation, 727-9547

State Highway Conditions, 973-7500

PART TWO

THE TOURS

The Grand Tour by Car

Anyone from outside Boston will tell you not to drive in the city. Its streets are narrow, winding, and confusing. It's a city of cow paths from the seventeenth century coexisting with twenty-first-century traffic.

But for those with visiting family or friends, or even tourists wishing to catch the city's flavor, history, sights, and sounds, here is a grand tour that takes under three hours and covers some 24 miles of Boston and Cambridge. The route can be adapted to start anywhere, allow for detours for special stops, and eliminate some segments. The route makes provisions for one-way streets, which account for some of the meandering, and covers some three centuries of Boston history. It is planned for little backtracking, and there are plenty of parking areas along the route. The route can also be expanded easily, and it offers many opportunities for easy stops to get out and wander.

With the Big Dig—the massive $14 billion project to bury the former Central Artery through the city—now essentially completed, Boston has once again reconnected its waterfront and North End to the heart of the city. The tour may not be as much fun as a duck or trolley tour, but this can be done just about anytime you wish.

A few tips first: Bring lots of quarters for parking meters. Don't attempt this tour anywhere close to rush hour (3:00 to 7:00 P.M. or before 9:30 A.M.). And be prepared for a slow crawl through the North End and in the Beacon Hill area.

Whether you are coming from the north, south, or west, the tour can begin in one of many places. The mileage numbers in parentheses indicate a progression from start to finish, not the distance between sights.

We begin the tour at the **Christian Science Center** on Massachusetts Avenue near the intersection of Huntington Avenue, with your vehicle heading north or toward Cambridge. From here you can see **Symphony Hall** just behind you.

Religion has long played a major role in Boston history. It was the Puritans from England—not the Pilgrims who founded Plymouth—who settled the city. And it was in the churches that events surrounding the Revolution, including the Boston Tea Party, took place. And in the twentieth century the influence of the Roman Catholic Church was dominant.

The Christian Science Church, while small in membership, has a commanding presence along Massachusetts and Huntington Avenues with its open plaza and reflecting pool. The church believes in healing through the Bible.

No matter what your beliefs are, this is an interesting stop on your journey through Boston and Cambridge. Within the Mary Baker Eddy Library is one of Boston's top attractions: the Mapparium, a unique reproduction in glass of the world as it was in 1932–35, when the replica was built. A fascinating look at the world from inside can also be noisy due to the reflection of sound off the glass panels. From this center the internationally known *Christian Science Monitor* is published

Across the street is **Symphony Hall,** home to the Boston Symphony Orchestra and Boston Pops, and offering a hall that is almost acoustically perfect.

The area is also a music lover's heaven. Not only is it home to the renowned symphony and pops orchestras, diagonally across from Symphony Hall is the **New England Conservatory** and just up Massachusetts Avenue on the right is **Berklee College,** two outstanding music institutions.

Continue your drive along Massachusetts Avenue, crossing grand Commonwealth Avenue, which has the feel of Paris with its monument-lined mall and Victorian mansions. On the right-hand corner of Commonwealth and Massachusetts Avenues is the ornate former **Ames Mansion,** at 355 Commonwealth Avenue. Built in 1882 for Oliver Ames, who made a fortune in manufacturing and railroads and later was a governor of the state, the mansion is in the style of a French château of the Loire Valley (like many of the buildings here, it has been converted into office space and condominiums). Before crossing Harvard Bridge, note on the right what appears to be a church but has apartments sprouting out of it. The former **Mount Vernon Congregational Church** burned in a fire, and architect Graham Gund retained the facade for his apartment complex (he also designed the pyramid-shaped **Cambridge Hyatt Regency Hotel,** which can be seen to the left across the Charles River). Crossing the bridge, you'll be entering Cambridge and the **Massachusetts Institute of Technology** comes into view; if you stop near the traffic lights ahead (about 1 mile), you can do a little exploring of the campus on foot. Continue, passing on your left 250 Massachusetts Avenue, the former home of the **New England Confectionery Company,** maker of those distinct Necco wafer candies (the plant now is a center of biomedical research), and proceed through **Central Square,** where a diversity of ethnic restaurants can be found, past the distinguished **Cambridge City Hall** on the right (2 miles) and on to **Harvard Square.** Harvard Yard, enclosed by brick walls, is on the right, as are the university's main museums (if you wish to visit, take a left for a parking garage; the visitor information center is next to the Cambridgeport Trust). Because of traffic, you will have to continue out of the square, but taking the first left-hand turn you can return into it, passing **Cambridge Common** (3.1 miles), where George Washington took command of the Continental army, and then turn right onto **Brattle Street,** and pass Brattle Hall, the American Repertory Theatre, and the classic homes of **Tory Row,** where those loyal to the Crown once lived. On the right you'll pass more Harvard buildings and the Episcopal Divinity School. And do stop at the home of **Henry Wadsworth Longfellow** (3.7 miles), the poet who made Paul Revere a household name. This National Historic Site is furnished just the way Longfellow left it. Even George Washington once lived here.

Continue on up to Mount Auburn Street (stay in the left lane) and enter the Egyptian gate of **Mount Auburn Cemetery** (4.8 miles). America's first parklike cemetery, it became in the 1800s one of the most popular tour sites for visitors to Boston. Since then, this garden setting, with many a famous Bostonian resting within it, has become the model for other cemeteries around the country. At the office you can pick up a map for a guide to the graves of Longfellow, Mary Baker Eddy, and others; you can even see an Americanized version of the Sphinx and view the city from an easy-to-climb tower.

Leaving the cemetery, turn right onto Mount Auburn Street, then follow signs for Memorial Drive, taking in the beauty of the **Charles River** (on Sunday in summer the first section of Memorial Drive is closed, necessitating a slight detour) and the college rowers on the river, while enjoying splendid views of Boston across the river. You'll pass buildings of many high-tech companies and those of the emerging biomedical field, many spawned in the universities on both sides of the river.

On the left as you pass **Boston University Bridge** is a large building

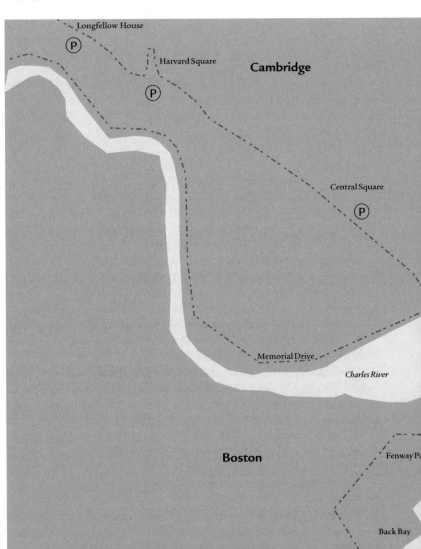

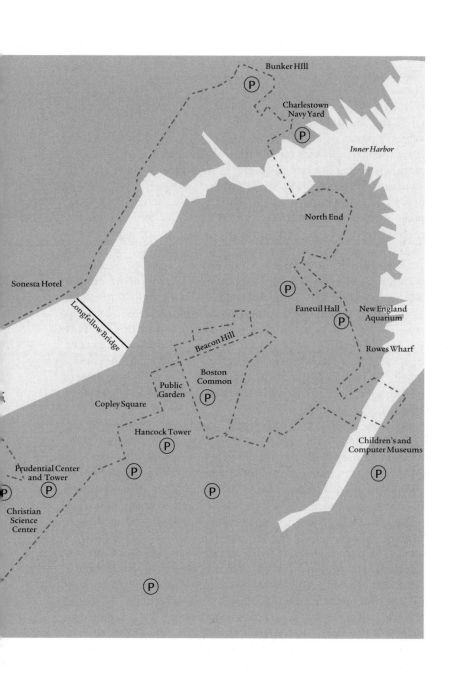

Bunker Hill

Charlestown
Navy Yard

Inner Harbor

North End

Sonesta Hotel

Longfellow Bridge

Faneuil Hall

New England
Aquarium

Beacon Hill

Rowes Wharf

Public
Garden

Boston
Common

Copley Square

Hancock Tower

Children's and
Computer Museums

Prudential Center
and Tower

Christian
Science
Center

rounded on one end that at one time was an early Ford Motor Company factory for the assembly of cars. Now it has been converted to offices and research development, and in 1995 it was among the few structures cited by the Urban Land Institute for excellence in rehabilitation.

Continue along Memorial Drive (take the underpass and you will now be in front of M.I.T.) passing another university boat house, then bear right onto **Edwin Land Boulevard** (named for the inventor of instant film process, Polaroid) passing CambridgeSide Galleria and the Hotel Marlowe on the left and the Royal Sonesta Hotel on the right.

Just beyond the Royal Sonesta (10.1 miles), if you take a right, you can visit the **Museum of Science.** Or just continue straight ahead, over Gilmore Bridge (Bunker Hill College is at its end), where once stood the foreboding Massachusetts State Prison. Continue straight ahead for Sullivan Square. The 99 restaurant to your left offers great meals at reasonable prices. (Be aware this was the scene in 1995 of an apparent mob-related murder of four men during the lunch hour—no reason not to stop by, however! Unfortunately for the suspects, off-duty policemen in a nearby booth quickly apprehended them.) Head up Green Street (if you turn right onto Main Street, you can make a stop at the **Warren Tavern** for lunch or dinner or sip a beer, as Paul Revere did here), turning right at the top to **Bunker Hill Monument.** This is a good place to get out and stretch, explore the base of the monument, and, if you have the strength, climb it. Bunker Hill, of course, is the site of the first major battle of the Revolution, one that the colonists lost but one that left the British in such a shambles that they never recovered and soon left Boston.

Continue down Winthrop Street, while noting the **Freedom Trail** marker (a 3.2 mile red line in the sidewalk that traces colonial history from Boston Common to Bunker Hill). Cross Warren Street and turn left onto Main Street into Charlestown's City Square. On the left is **Olives,** where celebrity chef Todd English, whose signature restaurants are now found throughout the country and aboard the *Queen Mary 2,* first began. Bear right with the park to your left, then turn right onto the highway and at the first traffic light make a U-turn back to the first left. Then follow signs to the **USS Constitution** (11.6 miles) and drive into the Charlestown Navy Yard where it is always easy to park to explore the nation's oldest commissioned battleship. Across from the *Constitution* is an interesting museum on naval history. Also to be seen is the USS *Cassin Young,* a World War II destroyer, and dry-docks dating to the nineteenth century. If you have forty-five minutes or more, take in the **Bunker Hill Pavilion** for a vivid multimedia show about the Battle of Bunker Hill and the events leading up to it. There are also a dining area and snack shops here, if you wish to take a break.

In case you wondered . . .

Only in Boston will you find the Smoot. The Harvard Bridge—that link between Boston and Cambridge—is exactly 364.4 Smoots and one ear long, for a Smoot is a measurement using the body of Oliver Reed Smoot, M.I.T. '62 (5 feet, 7 inches). The Smoot marks, originally a prank, are now so legendary that officials, in rebuilding the bridge, kept the marks. Oh yes, there was some thought as the bridge was being rebuilt of re-marking the bridge using Smoot's son, Stephen, also an M.I.T. lad. But it was decided that "there's no Smoot like an old Smoot," and so the Smoot, which joined the angstrom, the meter, and the light-year as a standard of length in 1958, remains. An original Smoot mark can be found in the M.I.T. Museum. Other student pranks, such as putting a police car on the school's great dome, are recounted at the M.I.T. Museum.

Now return to Boston, taking a left out of the naval yard to the second light and turn left again. Ahead of you is a good view of the **Zakim Bridge,** Boston's newest landmark. Turning left onto the Charlestown Bridge you will see Paul Revere Park and the Richard Gridley locks (named for the former British colonel who designed the Bunker Hill fortifications for the colonists). The locks at the mouth of the Charles River control seawater entering into the river. At the traffic light, turn left, noting the sign informing you of entering the **North End.** We now drive along Commercial Street, passing Copp's Hill Burying Ground on the right and above on a hill (one of Boston's oldest cemeteries). Pass the Coast Guard center on the left where the USS *Constitution* was built in colonial days. Then turn right onto **Hanover Street** for a look at the North End, Boston's oldest neighborhood and home to **Paul Revere** and the **Old North Church** (both places are handy, but parking is at best difficult; try the Faneuil Hall area coming up, then walk over). You will pass Paul Revere Mall and, across from the mall, **St. Stephen's Church,** the only Bullfinch-designed (architect of the State House) church left in Boston. Today the North End is an Italian neighborhood, famed for its restaurants and festivals.

Continue on Hanover Street into the **Faneuil Hall** area. Turn left and you will be in **Haymarket.** On Thursday, Friday, and Saturday, this vicinity is crowded with market stalls selling fresh fruits and vegetable. At the end of the market area, turn right, passing on the left Faneuil Hall, where the call of freedom has echoed since colonial days, and **Quincy Market,** where former warehouses have been turned into a lively shopping-and-dining experience. On the right is the **Millennium Bostonian Hotel,** built around a historic alleyway. Continue bearing right and you will see on the right the **Blackstone Block,** Boston's oldest commercial block, which has with it the **Union Oyster House,** the country's oldest restaurant (a king of France once lived here!) and one you will want to return to. Across from it are six glass monuments that bear witness to the **Holocaust.** Just in front of New City Hall on the left you might catch a glimpse of the two statues of **James Michael Curley,** who was one of the most colorful mayors in Boston's history and who was once reelected to office while serving a jail term.

Just after the Union Oyster House, turn left onto Hanover Street then right and right again onto Blackstone Street. On your left is the **Rose Fitzgerald Kennedy Park,** named for President Kennedy's mother. It's hard to imagine now, but an elevated Central Artery was here and now runs silently underneath the park. This time bear left following the Kennedy park. You are not only driving on land once occupied by the water of the harbor but also above the tunnel that now whisks traffic through the city. On the left is Boston's waterfront, no longer hidden by the **Central Artery** that was torn down for the Big Dig. If you take a left here, you can visit the **New England Aquarium,** Boston's foremost attraction in terms of number of visitors. Many harbor cruises also leave from here (parking is available).

Continue on Purchase Street to Congress Street and then turn left, and again left onto Atlantic Avenue. This is the area where the Boston Tea Party took place. Then turn right at the **James Hook Lobster Company** onto Seaport Boulevard. If you continue straight, you will be entering the **Seaport District,** with its Fish Pier and some fine seafood restaurants and the new **Boston Convention Center.** To the left is the Moakley Federal Courthouse. Boats leave from here for trips to **Boston Light,** the oldest lighthouse in the country. We will be taking a right onto Sleeper Avenue, passing behind the **Children's Museum.** Turn right again, and note the giant milk bottle, which serves as a dining spot, in front of the Children's Museum. As you cross Fort Point Channel, you will pass the **Tea Party Ship and Museum.** Then take the next left, then a right onto Summer Street, passing venerable **South Station** on the left, which has once again become a center of Boston transportation for both trains and buses. Notice the white building with the hole in the middle on the right: That's the **Federal Reserve Bank.** Turning left at the second set of lights onto Lincoln Street, you will soon see the Chinese arch that marks the entrance to **Chinatown,** the nation's third-largest such community. The entrance, however, is just for walkers. Then turn right onto Kneeland Street, heading quickly past **Boston's Theater District** and the **New England Medical Center,** which is hidden within the many buildings on the left. Turn right at the end of the large, redbrick Transportation Building onto Charles Street (16.3 miles), going between the **Public Garden** on the left and **Boston Common** on the right. In colonial days this was the shorefront. Under Boston Common is a large garage, its entrance on the right of the road, should you want to explore this area. Otherwise, take a right onto Beacon Street. This is the intersection where the famed ducks from *Make Way for Ducklings* crossed with the help of a friendly police officer. Heading up Beacon Street on the left is number 45, the third and grandest of homes Charles Bullfinch designed for Harrison Gray Otis, and next door is the white granite **Somerset Club,** one of Boston's most exclusive clubs (firemen responding to a fire there were once asked to use the rear entrance), originally designed by Alexander Parris, who was also the architect of Quincy Market. Pass the **State House** (17.1 miles) with its gold-leaf dome. On the right is the monument to black soldiers who served in the Civil War. Take the next left, then the first left onto Derne Street, and take another left onto Hancock Street and a right onto **Mount Vernon Street**—a classic **Beacon Hill** street, with Bullfinch-designed homes, brick sidewalks, and gas lamps. If you have a photographer onboard, you'll want a picture of Louisburg Square, where Senator John F. Kerry has a home. Then take a left at the square, stopping almost immediately for a shot of **Acorn Street,** perhaps the most photogenic street in the city. Take a right onto **Chestnut Street,** another Beacon Hill classic, and a left onto Charles Street. A left turn back onto Beacon Street will take you past the State House again, only this time continue straight ahead. A short distance ahead you will face **King's Chapel;** then take a right onto Tremont Street. There you will pass the **Old Granary,** where patriots of the past are buried, and **Park Street Church,** where "America" was first sung and from which missionaries left for Hawaii. On the right, just beyond the church, is Boston Common, America's oldest park. If you were to follow the street on the left (on foot, as it is one-way), you would soon be in **Downtown Crossing,** Boston's lively shopping district and home to the famed Filene's Basement, where they still automatically mark down clothing on a daily basis.

At the end of Boston Common, turn right onto Boylston Street. **Emerson College** occupies a large portion of the buildings and a theater here. Then take the next right back onto Charles Street, only this time bear left and take the next left onto Beacon Street at the end of the Public Garden (everything to your right was once under water, giving the upcoming area the name Back Bay); on the right you will see the **Bull & Finch Pub,** home to the *Cheers* TV series. Then take a left onto Arlington Street. At the third intersection, just past the Ritz-Carlton, turn right onto **Newbury Street,** which is famous for its art galleries, boutiques, and sidewalk cafes. Turn left at

Clarendon Street, passing on the right **Trinity Church,** one of America's most beautiful churches (there is parking either to the left, at Skipjacks Restaurant, or straight ahead). Turning right onto St. James Avenue at the church, you enter **Copley Square,** with the sixty-story glass John Hancock Tower on your left. Continue straight ahead for Huntington Avenue, noting to the right **Boston Public Library.** On the left you'll pass Copley Place with its lavish shops and a large garage, should you wish to explore this area further. Huntington Avenue returns to where you began—or you might want to detour to the right on Belvedere Street. Park under the **Prudential Center,** and head to the Pru's top floor for a magnificent 360-degree view of the city.

At the intersection of Massachusetts Avenue (20.8 miles), you may want to continue on Huntington Avenue, going past **Northeastern University,** one of the largest private universities in the country. Continue on to the **Museum of Fine Arts** just ahead—one of the finest museums in the country, with extensive collections of American and European art, Egyptian treasures, and more. There are parking (turn right onto Museum Road) and restaurants here, if you wish to visit. Otherwise, continue to the next right, Louis Prang Street. Just ahead in the Fenway area on the left is the **Isabella Stewart Gardner Museum**—"the house that Mrs. Jack built" and a lovely place to linger, with its indoor garden and eclectic collection, all in a palatial setting, a tribute to a woman who truly left her mark on the city (21.7 miles). **Simmons, Emmanuel, and Wheelock colleges,** all for women, are located in this area.

From here you can continue along through the Fenway, part of the **Emerald Necklace** that winds through the city; turn right onto Brookline Avenue (with the CITGO sign facing you) to pay homage to **Fenway Park** (on the right), where baseball pennant dreams are renewed each spring. Continue through Kenmore Square. At the third traffic light to the left is a statue to **Leif Eriksson** (the Vikings are said to have explored the area, but why he is looking inland is unknown). At Massachusetts Avenue turn right and return to where you began.

There's more to see, but this excursion should whet your appetite and provide a view of the area's most appealing sights. You've covered old Boston, new Boston, eminent universities, historic sites, and architectural delights. You've also observed how Boston, with its narrow, twisting streets and compact size, can easily be seen—on foot.

Walking Tours:
Where to Begin

Now it is time to see the city as it should be seen: by foot.

The question for any visitor (or even native Bostonian) is, Where does one begin to see the city? Often the answer is simply determined by where one is now.

Each of the tours in this section of the book will take, if you are just out for a walk, less than two hours; some could even be done in an hour. Boston is that kind of city—one that is compact and made for walking. Most of the Boston tours are presented so that one leads into the next; however, the sequence is readily adaptable to visitors' individual needs and interests. And tours of Charlestown and the Boston Harbor Islands have been included as well, to highlight those aspects of the area's attractions. (For a walking tour of Cambridge, see chapter 20.)

As Boston may not appear to be laid out very logically (some say its streets resemble cow paths, but actually the city is laid out in a fine example of seventeenth-century planning), it is best seen on foot. With its narrow, twisting streets, multitude of one-way streets, construction that hampers traffic, and limited parking spaces, Boston toured by car can be frustrating. Instead, enjoy the city on a walking tour. From Copley Square to Faneuil Hall is about 2 miles, a thirty-minute walk. From Faneuil Hall to Beacon Hill is only 1 mile, and you'll cover 350 years of history on the way.

There are three logical places to begin a walking tour of Boston. First is Copley Square, one of the most notable intersections in the country and the place to begin your tour if you are staying in one of the many hotels within a few hundred feet of it: the Fairmont Copley Plaza, the Westin, the Boston Marriott Copley Place, the Sheraton Boston, the Colonnade, the Back Bay Hilton, the Lenox, the Copley Square, or the Midtown. Copley Square is also an area rich in Victorian architecture, cultural attractions, and fine shopping.

Second is Faneuil Hall, chosen because it is without a doubt the most visited section of Boston. From here radiate four of the most favored tours of the city—the North End, the Waterfront, the Freedom Trail, and, of course, Faneuil Hall. The area is also convenient for visitors staying at the Millennium Bostonian, which has an old alleyway cutting through it, or at the Boston Marriott Long Wharf, the Boston Harbor Hotel, the Wyndham Boston Hotel, or the Langham.

Some hotels, incidentally, are right on the walks. The Omni Parker House is part of the Freedom Trail. The Ritz-Carlton and the Four Seasons overlook the Public Garden. The Ritz-Carlton Boston Common obviously overlooks the Common. The Boston Marriott Long Wharf has the Waterfront walk going right through it, the tour continuing beside the Boston Harbor Hotel.

Third is Boston Common, site of the Park Street subway station—a major transportation center—and of a city information center that offers multilingual service. Just a few feet from Boston Common is the Swissotel. In this book, Park Street marks the beginning of the Beacon Hill walk, the start of the Freedom Trail walk, and the start of the Boston Common and Public Garden walk.

If you are staying outside Boston, using public transportation to visit the city is a sensible approach. Major MBTA stations located outside the city will bring you to Park Street or Copley Station to begin most of these tours; for the Freedom Trail and Faneuil Hall tours, exit at either Government Center or State Street Station.

WALKING TOURS AND THE T

Beacon Hill
Take the Red Line or Green Line to Park Street.

Boston Common and the Public Garden
Take the Red Line to Park Street or take the Green Line to Park Street or Boylston Street.

Boston Harbor Islands
Take the Blue Line to Aquarium.

Charlestown
Take the number 92 or 93 bus from Haymarket, reached via the Green and Orange Lines or from in front of Woolworth's in Downtown Crossing. Get off at Charlestown Navy Yard.

> *By boat:* In summer take the cruise from Long Wharf to the Charlestown Navy Yard. Commuter boat service also goes from Long Wharf to Charlestown, with a connecting bus to the USS *Constitution*.

> *By car:* The route should be well marked from downtown Boston over the Charlestown Bridge to the Charlestown Navy Yard.

Copley Square, Back Bay, and the Prudential Center
Take the Green Line to Copley or Convention Center/ICA or take the Orange Line to Back Bay station.

Faneuil Hall
Take the Orange Line or Blue Line to State or take the Green Line to Government Center.

The Freedom Trail
Take the Orange Line or Blue Line to State to begin the tour at the Old State House or take the Red Line or Green Line to Park Street to begin from that end of the tour.

The North End
Take the Orange Line or Blue Line to State and walk or take the Green Line to Government Center and walk.

Waterfront
Take the Blue Line to Aquarium, the Red Line to South Station.

One Final Note

Wear comfortable shoes, as many of these walks are over cobblestone streets and uneven brick sidewalks, not to mention subway ventilation grates set in sidewalks.

GO TO THE TOP FIRST

The best way to discover the compactness—and beauty—of Boston is to go to the top of the Prudential Tower. Until September 11, 2001, the John Hancock Tower, which is a bit closer to downtown, was my first choice. Unfortunately, after 9/11 the observatory, with its great historical items, has been closed indefinitely, maybe forever. The Prudential Skywalk, though, has advantages over the Hancock Tower—a 360-degree view of the city, for one. From the fiftieth floor, on a good day, you can see to the mountains of New Hampshire and out to Cape Cod. One great sight is to look down into Fenway Park when the Red Sox are playing, especially at night. There are also many interactive displays on Boston's history, famous residents, and important buildings. On the floor above is an excellent restaurant, along with a superb jazz lounge where you can relax and drink in the view as well as your favorite beverage.

Boston Common and
the Public Garden

Boston Common

There is very little that is common about Boston Common. It's here that the first Bostonian lived (Reverend William Blackstone, alone but with 200 books to keep him company); cows roamed; Quakers, pirates, and others were hanged; a duel was fought; love flourished; the British camped and set sail for Lexington from the city's former shoreline; and large celebrations, even a mass by Pope John Paul II, were held. It's here that children splash in the Frog Pond; panhandlers wander; speakers hold forth; and the country's first subway runs below. And it's here that one end of the Emerald Necklace, the 5-mile stretch of greenery that flows through the city, is situated.

Boston Common is the oldest public space in the country, having been set aside in 1640, following its purchase from Blackstone. In those days the Charles River washed the Common where Charles Street is now, and along that shore the British left on the night of April 16, 1775, for Lexington. The shore was also the scene of hangings, the bodies being buried in the shallow sand. Other hangings were held from a great elm that formerly stood in the center of the Common; the ashes of Mary Dyer, a Quaker whose statue can be seen in front of the State House, were scattered about the site of the tree.

The Common's forty-five acres served as a campground during the Revolution for as many as 6,400 troops. On the first Monday in June, the Ancient and Honorable Artillery Company, the Western Hemisphere's oldest military organization, still gathers its force here.

Boston Common is rich with monuments, statues, and memorials. Rising above **Flagstaff Hill** in its center is the 70-foot Soldiers' Monument to Civil War veterans. It was from this hill in 1824 that Lafayette, during a visit, fired cannons to mark the occasion. Near the Park Street subway entrance and information center is **Brewer's Fountain,** a gift of Gardner Brewer that is a bronze replica of the Parisian Fountain that was the sensation of the Paris Exposition of 1855. One of the most impressive sights is the bas-relief **memorial to Robert Gould Shaw** and his black Civil War company (of the film *Glory* fame). Along the Beacon Street side of the Common is **Founders' Monument,** a fanciful depiction of Blackstone's meeting with John Winthrop and others.

At the corner of Tremont and Boylston Streets is the city's fourth-oldest cemetery, the **Central Burying Ground,** where you may be walking over the remains of Gilbert Stuart, the painter of George Washington. Also buried here are the Bradlees, the largest family to partake in the Boston Tea Party.

Frog Pond is the site of the first water piped into the city from Lake Cochituate in Natick, solving the city's early needs for water. Children are likely to be seen wading in its waters today. Although cows no longer roam in the Common, having been banned in 1830, you can still play ball or, on an early morning's stroll, see an exercise class in t'ai chi ch'uan, a Chinese way to refresh and relax used since the thirteenth century. Despite the panhandlers, the Common is a delightful place to spend time.

The Common is also a place for love. In 1728 two young men fought over a young love; one died and is buried not far from the grave of Peter Faneuil—the man who helped the other escape to Europe—at Granary Burying Ground. Oliver Wendell Holmes, the Autocrat of the Breakfast Table, standing at the grave site with his wife, said how women love to love, as she dropped rose petals on the grave. How well he should have known, for though Holmes was so wise with words on paper, he was said to have been too timid to ask his beautiful schoolmistress to marry him. It was along the Long Walk, now the Holmes Walk, that Holmes, ready to leave on a ship to London that day if she said no, finally asked if she would take the Long Walk, meaning marriage. She replied that she would. If you look over to Beacon Street, it was on the second floor of number 39 that Fanny Appleton married Henry Wadsworth Longfellow. The couple then moved to Brattle Street in Cambridge to a home, now known as the Longfellow Mansion, that was the gift of Fanny's parents. And what ever happened to Blackstone? He retreated to Rhode Island (southwest of the city is a town indirectly named for him, Blackstone; it is located in the Blackstone Valley, a region in both Massachusetts and Rhode Island) for the peace he lost when the town became settled, only to return to Boston in 1659 upon a white ox to marry Governor Endicott's widow. The two returned to Rhode Island, where Blackstone died in 1675.

The Common also marks the beginning of the **Emerald Necklace,** a creation by Frederick Law Olmsted that was begun in 1887 and continues for 5 miles along Commonwealth Avenue, the Riverway, the Fenway area, and Arnold Arboretum and ends at Franklin Park. For Olmsted, a romanticist and the creator of New York's Central Park, the necklace was a way to commune with God through natural wonders.

The Public Garden

Cross Charles Street and enter the **Public Garden** and you will immediately be struck by its difference from the Common. The garden sits on some of the first filled-in land in Back Bay and looks very Victorian, with its lagoons, flower beds, and wandering paths.

No matter what the season, the Public Garden is a pleasant place to walk. Two of the best times are spring, when tulips brighten the paths, and summer, when the garden's prized Japanese pagoda trees are in full blossom.

Although its paths meander almost aimlessly, you can cut through the garden directly from Boston Common to Commonwealth Avenue, passing over a small suspension bridge constructed in 1869.

No visit to Boston is complete without a ride on the famed **Swan Boats,** which have paddled around the garden since 1877 and are still run by the Paget family. The idea for the ride came to Robert Paget from the opera *Lohengrin,* in which the hero comes to the rescue of his love on a boat pulled by a swan. Paget, who had been operating boat rides elsewhere, took the then-new bicycle propulsion technology and concealed it within a swan. The ride captured the fancy of the Victorians and remains popular to this day. In and around the garden's pond are plenty of ducks to be seen and fed, but the most famous are in bronze and near the Beacon and Charles Streets entrance: the eight ducklings made famous by the 1941 classic *Make Way for Ducklings* by Robert McCloskey, the tale of Mr. and Mrs. Mallard's journey through Boston in search of a new home for Jack, Kack, Lack, Mack, Nack, Ouack, Quack, and Pack.

Like the Common, the garden is a place of monuments and statues. Among the more famous are those portraying **Edward Everett Hale,** a

Unitarian minister and the author of *Man Without a Country,* and **Charles Sumner,** an advocate of emancipation and free speech who, during a fight against the expansion of slavery into the country's new territories, was struck and so severely injured by a Southern senator that it took three years for Sumner to recover. During this time Sumner was reelected to the U.S. Senate, his seat left vacant to speak for him. The garden's most prominent statue is of **George Washington** astride his horse; Washington's sword has been broken so many times that it is now made of fiberglass. Another statue commemorates the Polish captain **Tadeusz Kosciuszko,** who rallied to the American cause during the Revolution, and still another honors an Irishman, **Colonel Thomas Cass,** who led an all-Irish regiment in the Civil War and was killed in action in Virginia. **George Robert White,** who in 1908 gave the princely sum of $5 million to the city for clinics and art, is also honored here.

Overlooking the garden are two outstanding hotels—the **Ritz-Carlton** on Arlington Street and the **Four Seasons** (both offer afternoon tea in stylish settings)—and the third-most popular spot in the city to visit, the **Bull & Finch Pub**—more popularly known as *Cheers*—is at 84 Beacon Street.

Detours

Downtown Crossing, the heart of Boston shopping, is only a few hundred feet from here; or you could continue your walk by following the Freedom Trail or Beacon Hill tours, which begin and end at the Common. After going through the Public Garden, follow Newbury Street for gallery viewing or a snack at one of the many outdoor cafes.

Faneuil Hall

Perhaps the liveliest corner of Boston, Faneuil Hall is said to attract more people a year than Disney World—the world's most popular tourist destination. There's good reason for this, as Faneuil Hall is one of the most historic, most fun, and most colorful areas in the city, one filled with shops, restaurants, and bars. If people-watching and window-shopping are among your hobbies, Faneuil Hall is a feast for the eyes. And **Quincy Market** is a symbol of renewal, having twice played that role in the city's history.

Before touring the historic area, explore the **New England Holocaust Memorial** on Union Street. Its six luminous glass towers that recall the death-camp chimneys are etched with six million numbers, a reminder of the Jews who died in the Holocaust.

Being practical, we offer a circular tour that begins between Faneuil Hall and the entrance to Quincy Market, enters **Government Center,** passes through one of the oldest blocks in the city, and finally goes into Quincy Market for shopping or refreshments. You can't miss the starting point, which is marked by a large flower shop, usually a circle of people watching a street performer, and, of course, the red brick of Faneuil Hall contrasting nicely with the granite face of Quincy Market.

Faneuil Hall, the Cradle of Liberty, began life as a marketplace, being located next to Dock Square, the main landing place in Boston for years (a marker to the front of the hall gives a good perspective on the area), and was

Faneuil Hall Walk

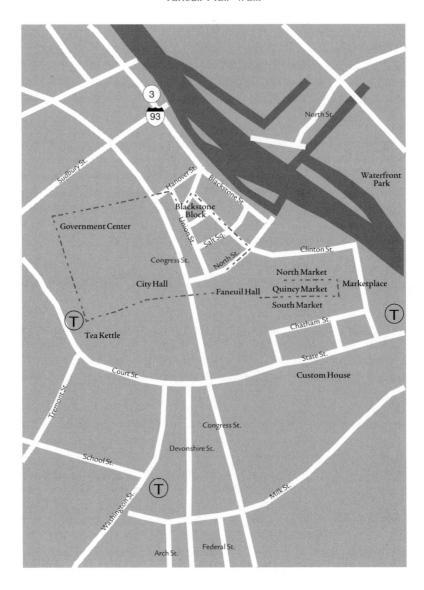

given to the city in 1742 by a wealthy merchant, Peter Faneuil. Its lower floors still contain markets and shops. The building was enlarged, doubling its space and adding a third floor, by Charles Bulfinch. The hall is famed for the fiery orations by patriots, abolitionists, and others that have taken place here during its history. The large painting over the stage shows Daniel Webster, one of the most vocal members of the U.S. Senate, defending the Union in 1830 against a South Carolina senator's view that states could veto federal laws. *Webster's Reply to Hayne,* as the canvas is called, was "Liberty and Union, now and forever, one and inseparable" and helped unify the country. The painting was commissioned by King Louis Philippe of France, but he was overthrown before it could be hung at Versailles. Philippe wanted a painting depicting all the famous politicians of the day, with an audience that included the elite of Washington society.

At the end of a steep stairway to the third floor are the museum and headquarters of the **Ancient and Honorable Artillery Company,** the nation's oldest military organization. Among the items here is a cannon used by the British at Yorktown in 1783 and again by Confederate troops before its capture at Williamsburg in 1862. High above all is the gilded grasshopper weather vane that has perched here since Peter Faneuil had Shem Drowne construct it in 1742; the grasshopper is a copy of one that sits atop London's Royal Exchange.

Leave the building and walk toward New City Hall, the mammoth concrete structure, noting the statue of **Samuel Adams,** perhaps the leading figure of the American Revolution. **New City Hall,** built in the 1960s, is the focal point of the city's Government Center, a vast and open setting, lined on one side by federal and state offices and on the other by the **1816 Sears Crescent,** with the landmark 227-gallon steaming kettle retained from when the building housed the Oriental Tea Company in 1873. Today it is the site of a Starbucks coffee shop. Before Government Center was built in the early 1960s, this was the site of Scollay Square, known to World War II servicemen around the world; today visitors may happen upon a free outdoor concert being given here.

Walk around New City Hall, descending the stairway to a small park containing two bronze statues of **James Michael Curley,** who, it was said, could charm anyone. One of the most colorful politicians in the city's history, Curley served as mayor four times, congressman twice, and governor once—at one time being elected to office while serving a prison term. Although it was said, "Vote often and early for Curley," he is credited with many improvements in the city, including the establishment of Boston City Hospital, now Boston Medical Center.

In the know . . .

Quincy—you'll run into that name a lot on a Boston visit. It's a city, a former mayor, an MBTA station, and a market. But while we're at it, first learn how to pronounce Quincy so that you can talk like a Bostonian. It's *Quin*-zee, not *Quin*-see. And Worcester is *Woos*-ter, and Faneuil is *Fan*-yoo-ell. And you can't park your car in the *Haa*-vaad Yard, so don't ask. But if someone asks what the neighboring country is and the answer is Canadeer, not Canada, you'll know that's a New Englander—ah yup, as they might say in Maine, which is Down East—the finest kind of people, who, like true Bostonians, still drink tonic, not soda pop.

Across from City Hall Plaza is the **Blackstone Block,** a collection of buildings—some among the oldest in the city—built around small alleys with names like Marsh Lane: a reminder that this was a part of Boston's colonial waterfront. The oldest building here is the **Union Oyster House,** which just happens to be the oldest restaurant in continuous service in the United States. On its upper floors was printed the *Massachusetts Spy,* whose publisher was forced to flee to Worcester in 1775 because of the paper's stand for independence. Another occupant of the building, the Duc de Chartres (later King Louis Philippe of France), gave French lessons here to support himself. Daniel Webster was a frequent visitor to the Union Oyster House, and a plaque notes John F. Kennedy's favorite booth when he dined here. Do step inside and try some fresh oysters on the shell at the bar.

Outside, just down Marshall Alley and embedded in a wall, is the **Boston Stone,** a paint mill and grinder from colonial days that in later years was the marker from which distances from Boston were measured. **Benjamin Franklin** played near here as a youngster while working in his brother's print shop.

The **Bell in Hand Tavern,** which sits on the site of Ben Franklin's boyhood home, claims to be the oldest pub in the country, although not at this site.

When the charming **Millennium Bostonian Hotel** that faces Faneuil Hall was built, its design had to retain the seventeenth-century alleyways that pass through and under it. You can still walk through Scott Alley, or you might enter the hotel lobby to view a collection of artifacts from the past. Thursday, Friday, and Saturday are colorful days to wander in these streets, when the market vendors take over Blackstone Street, their carts loaded with fresh fruits and vegetables.

The walk ends as it began, in front of Quincy Market, the centerpiece of **Faneuil Hall Marketplace.** Named for the second mayor of Boston, Josiah Quincy, the market originally represented a major renewal of the area, calling for the filling in of the waterfront and the construction of a 535-foot-long market. Quincy Market, the middle point of the three structures, was designed by Alexander Parris in a Greek Revival style, with massive Doric columns. When Quincy Market was first completed, in 1824, Boston Harbor was at its doorstep. The flanking North and South Markets were built as warehouses in the same period.

It served its purpose well for 150 years and gave a sense of revitalization to the city when it reopened in 1976 as Faneuil Hall Marketplace. Most of the elements of the original structures have been retained. Within the Quincy Market building are more than thirty-nine food stalls offering everything including exotic teas, oysters on the shell, chowder, ice cream, and Greek and Italian specialties. A great place to get the fixings for a picnic lunch. Throughout the area are interesting shops and carts offering a variety of goods. (You might want to create a movable feast from Quincy Market and enjoy it at the waterfront park.) As the most successful of its kind, the marketplace has given rise to similar projects throughout the world.

Boston's consuming interest in its sports teams can be seen between buildings on a bench with a bronze **Red Auerbach** about to light a cigar, a symbol that this longtime coach and manager of the Boston Celtics knew he had another victory on the basketball courts in hand. Nearby is Bostix, offering discount tickets to same-day theatrical, dance, and other performances.

Detours

It's easy to explore the North End or Waterfront or to begin the Freedom Trail from here. Have a meal at Durgin Park, a restaurant that is uniquely Boston.

The Freedom Trail

Not only is the Freedom Trail the heart of Old Boston, but within this less than 1-mile-long section of the 2.5-mile trail that stretches from Charlestown to Beacon Hill transpired some of the most dramatic moments in American history, captured in the buildings in which they occurred.

The walk begins at the **Old State House,** located at State and Washington Streets, just steps from **Faneuil Hall.** State Street, once known as King Street, took its present name after the American Revolution. Washington Street, at one time the only road across a small isthmus connecting Boston with the mainland, begins here and is, of course, named for George Washington, who used this roadway to enter the city both on March 18, 1776, after the British had evacuated the city, and again thirteen years later, as president. We will follow this road only a short distance, as it continues for 38 miles to Pawtucket, Rhode Island, passing through **Downtown Crossing,** the heart of Boston's shopping district, about half a mile away, and through what was known as the **Combat Zone,** where at the intersection of Essex Street stood the Liberty Tree, around which patriots gathered to protest against the British (on the third floor of the building at Essex and Washington Streets is a bas-relief marking where the tree, cut down by Redcoats in 1775, stood). Boston's Chinatown begins here. The area is also known as the Ladder District in reference to the ladderlike grid of the streets.

The Freedom Trail

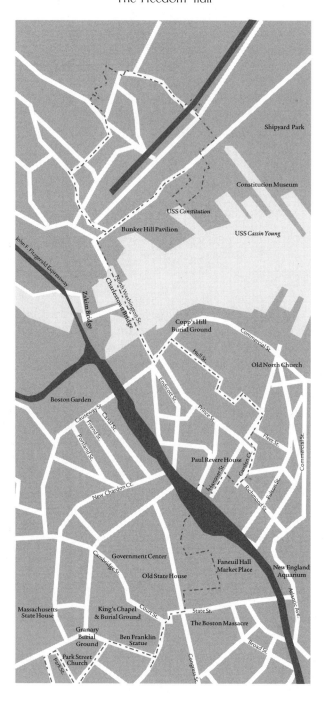

Shipyard Park

Constitution Museum

USS *Constitution*

Bunker Hill Pavilion

USS *Cassin Young*

John F. Fitzgerald Expressway

North Washington St.
Charlestown Bridge

Zakim Bridge

Copp's Hill
Burial Ground

Commercial St.

Hull St.

Old North Church

Boston Garden

Causeway St.

Canal St.

Friend St.

Portland St.

Endicott St.

Prince St.

Fleet St.

Commercial St.

Paul Revere House

Garden Ct.

Hanover St.

Richmond St.

Fulton St.

New Chardon Ct.

Cambridge St.

Government Center

Old State House

Faneuil Hall
Market Place

New England
Aquarium

Atlantic Ave.

Massachusetts
State House

King's Chapel
& Burial Ground

Court St.

State St.

The Boston Massacre

Granary
Burial
Ground

Ben Franklin
Statue

Congress St.

Broad St.

Park Street
Church

Park St.

A good place to commence your tour of the **Freedom Trail** might be the **National Historical Park Visitor Center,** at 15 State Street, where a slide show will familiarize you with this area and just maybe a free guided walk by a park ranger will be about to begin.

Outside, wander around the Old State House, noting the cobblestone circle in the center of the street that marks the site of the Boston Massacre, an event that helped fuel revolutionary emotions. On a cold night on March 5, 1770, a British sentry standing guard near here became involved in a scuffle with several young colonists and called for help. The dispute soon led to gunfire by British troops, with Crispus Attucks being the first of five colonists to die from British bullets. Above is the balcony from which the first public reading of the Declaration of Independence was delivered in Boston.

It was in the second-floor council chamber that in 1761 the words of James Otis, speaking against the Writs of Assistance, which would have given the British access to the colonists' homes and businesses, prompted John Adams to note later, in his autobiography, "the child Independence was born." This jewel of a building was almost lost to Bostonians when, in 1882, the city of Chicago offered to take the structure, then in disuse and covered with billboards, brick by brick to be rebuilt along Lake Michigan. City officials declined the offer. The replicas of the lion and unicorn, symbols of British rule, were placed on the building in 1818 to replace the originals, which were torn down by the colonists on July 18, 1776.

Before beginning your walk up Washington Street, notice the large building at Court Street and the corner of Washington. While long overshadowed by larger structures, the **Ames Building** was, when constructed in 1889, the largest building in Boston and the second-tallest building in the world to use a masonry bearing-wall construction. Also on Court Street (then called Queen Street) the notorious pirate Captain Kidd was jailed before being sent to London and his death in 1701. Since before the days of Kidd, this area was the center of government, with the Old State House, the court, and the jail nearby; it still contains many legal and financial offices.

Now continue along Washington Street, for here is what became known as **Newspaper Row,** the cradle of American journalism. From colonial days until 1958, when the *Boston Globe* moved to its present site in Dorchester, this part of Washington Street was the home of numerous publications. **Pi Alley,** which connects Washington Street with Court Square, gets its name from the jumble of metal type pieces that printers would toss into the alley from the pressrooms located along it. It was in this area that Benjamin Franklin got his start in printing.

The **Old Corner Bookstore building** is one of the most prominent colonial sites in America. In the mid-1800s it became the center of literary life, with the writers of the Golden Age of Literature—Emerson, Holmes, Hawthorne, Lowell, Longfellow, Thoreau, and others—gathering here in the office of a young publisher, "Jamie" Fields, a "literary counsellor and friend," as Holmes described him. Fields not only published these authors but also did something almost unheard of in those days: He paid them for their works. (Fields later became editor of the *Atlantic Monthly*, still published in Boston.) Almost 200 years earlier the bookstore's site was the home of Anne Hutchinson, mother of fourteen children, who, contrary to Puritan doctrine, believed that faith alone was enough for salvation; for her beliefs Hutchinson was tried and excommunicated. She has since been redeemed, in the 1990s, by an act of the Massachusetts Legislature, and a statue on the State House lawn commemorates her.

Just across from the bookstore, notice the tiny alleyway named **Spring Lane,** one of the original alleyways in Boston and, as the name implies, the spot where a spring was once located just downhill. On the south corner, at 294 Washington Street, is where Governor John Winthrop lived from 1643 to 1649.

Diagonally across the street from the Old Corner Bookstore is the **Old South Meeting House,** where Benjamin Franklin, who was born just across the way on present Milk Street, was baptized and where the "Indians" of the Boston Tea Party gathered before tossing the tea into the harbor. Do visit the Dreams of Freedom, a museum with interactive exhibits on the site of Franklin's birth, which highlights the city's immigration history. (If you continue on Washington Street, you'll find fast-food restaurants and Downtown Crossing, where Boston's largest department stores are located, including the famed Filene's Basement, in which thrifty New Englanders have been stalking bargains since long before the phrase "discount store" came into being.) Also on Milk Street is where the Great Fire of 1872 ended, just opposite the Old South Meeting House, after destroying sixty-five acres of the heart of the city. The fire was the last of six that in their days—1711, 1747, 1761, 1787, 1794, and 1872—each brought its own form of urban renewal to the city. One of the earliest lessons learned from the fires was not to build chimneys of wood, as colonists once did.

The route continues up School Street, where Boston's ornate, French Second Empire–style **Old City Hall** stands. To the right is a statue of Josiah Quincy, second mayor of the city and the person for whom Quincy Market is named, and to the left is one of Benjamin Franklin, who some say appears amused and some say serious, depending on how you view him. Franklin's statue marks the site of Boston's first school (later moved across the street), where many prominent colonists studied, including John Hancock, who learned penmanship here. Boston Latin School in the Fenway is the direct descendant of that first school.

Next is **King's Chapel.** Built as the colony's first Anglican church in 1749, it is also the first church designed—by mail-order plans, no less, from Peter Harrison in Newport, Rhode Island—in America. The church is built of granite, its columns of wood (though the wood here resembles granite). It is a church of simple beauty and interesting religious history. The Puritans, angered by having an Anglican church in their community, threw garbage at its cornerstone laying. But by 1785 the church had adopted Unitarian beliefs. It still, however, uses the Anglican Book of Common Prayer, as well as a Congregational form of government.

The burial ground next to King's Chapel is the oldest in the city, though unrelated to the church. In the graveyard lie the remains of **John Winthrop,** the first governor; **William Dawes,** who, along with Paul Revere, spread the news that the British were coming; **Mary Chilton,** one of the original Pilgrims; and **Hester Prynne,** who became the heroine of Nathaniel Hawthorne's *The Scarlet Letter.* But the strangest-looking marker is really just a ventilator shaft to the country's first subway—perhaps, as one writer suggests, a monument to Charlie, who rode the MBTA never to return but whose escapades are recalled in song ("Charlie on the MTA").

Proceeding along Tremont Street toward Boston Common, you will pass the **Omni Parker House,** the nation's oldest hotel in continuous operation. The present building dates from only 1927, but among earlier guests were Charles Dickens and John Wilkes Booth, who was seen practice shooting nearby just ten days before assassinating Abraham Lincoln.

Tremont Temple, next, dates from 1894. Now a Baptist church, it has one of the earliest records against slavery and was the first integrated church in the country.

The **Granary Burying Ground,** the most famous in the city, is named for a former grain warehouse located where Park Street Church stands. Within its two acres are the final resting places of Paul Revere; Samuel Adams; three signers of the Declaration of Independence; Peter Faneuil (whose name is spelled P. Funal on the stone), giver of Faneuil Hall; the victims of the Boston Massacre; nine Massachusetts governors; Benjamin Franklin's parents; and even Elizabeth Vergoose, who many believe is the legendary Mother Goose "who had so many children she didn't know what to do" so she wrote nursery rhymes. Elizabeth, whose gravestone has disappeared, was the second wife of Isaac Goose (also known as Vergoose). Mary Goose, whose stone is still there, was Isaac's first wife.

This walk comes to an end at **Park Street Church,** built in 1809 and described by Henry James as "the most interesting mass of bricks and mortar" in America. The church is on Brimstone Corner, named for the storage of gunpowder in the church during the War of 1812 but also, some say, for the oratory spoken from its pulpit. It was on the steps of this church that "America" ("My Country 'Tis of Thee") was first sung on July 4, 1831, and from here that the first missionaries to Hawaii were sent. Here, too, William Lloyd Garrison gave his first antislavery speech, in 1829, and the first Sunday school was organized, in 1817.

Before leaving the area, notice **St. Paul's Cathedral,** almost diagonally across from Park Street. The architects of the church, which dates to 1819, were Alexander Parris, who designed Quincy Market, and Solomon Willard, who designed the Bunker Hill Monument. With its Greek-temple look, St. Paul's Cathedral stands in contrast to the style of the period.

DETOURS

From here the walk can continue through Boston Common and the Public Garden or on to Beacon Hill. It's also just a short walk to Downtown Crossing for shopping at the large department stores and, of course, Filene's Basement. Here fast-food outlets offer inexpensive meals; for a treat, though, seek out Locke-Ober, hidden on Winter Place—a Boston dining institution.

Just opposite the Old South Meeting House is a memorial to the Irish Famine of the mid-1800s that caused a major migration to Boston and other cities. Dreams of Freedom, an interactive museum also across from Old South, highlights the city's entire immigration history.

Beacon Hill

Depending on whom you are talking to and what you are talking about, "Beacon Hill" can mean a place, the government, or a graceful tribute to colonial architecture, for here on the highest hill—named for a beacon that was at one time placed at its top—in Boston proper are the state capitol and some of the finest other examples of the architectural genius of Charles Bulfinch.

A walking tour of Beacon Hill along some of its loveliest streets begins in front of the **State House,** designed in 1795 by Bulfinch, whose work on the building earned him jobs designing the nation's Capitol as well as Connecticut's. Looking at the building, you will see some touches common to Bulfinch designs: windows set in from the brick facade, smaller windows at the top, everything in balance.

The dome of the State House is covered with copper from Paul Revere's copper-rolling mill in Canton, the first in the country. Its gilded appearance was added in 1861, and with the exception of the dark days of World War II, when it was painted gray, the dome has glowed brilliantly ever since. Topping it is a pinecone, symbolic of the lumber industry and Maine, formerly a part of the Massachusetts colony.

Before continuing, notice the bas-relief memorial on the Common facing the State House. The **Robert Gould Shaw Memorial,** by Augustus Saint-Gaudens, is considered one of the finest works of art from any American war and is the first dedicated to blacks by a white artist. The memorial is now part of the **Black Heritage Trail,** which illustrates blacks' contributions, long overlooked, to early Boston history. The Fifty-fourth Massachusetts Regiment, led by Shaw, was virtually wiped out in an assault on Fort Wagner in Charleston, South Carolina, during the Civil War. Shaw and thirty-two men with him, whose names now appear on the back of the monument, are buried at the fort. The regiment was memorialized in the film *Glory*. Before leaving, you might touch the sword—it moves.

In front of the State House is an interesting collection of statues that mark both high and low periods in the state's history. Tributes to the former are statues of **Daniel Webster,** one of the great orators of his time, a senator who spoke eloquently for the Union, and of **Horace Mann,** who as state senate president pushed for education, helping to make the state's school system a model for others; Mann later became president of Antioch College in Ohio, where he was a leader in nonsexist and nonsectarian education. The statues of **Anne Hutchinson,** to the right, and **Mary Dyer,** by the East Wing, both commemorate women who were tried for their religious beliefs. Hutchinson was banished from the state, only to meet her death at the hands of Indians in New York, and Dyer was hanged on the Common. The statue of **Joseph Hooker** on his horse stands somewhere in between. Hooker, the Civil War commander, is best known for his untimely caution that led to his defeat at Chancellorsville and for his camp followers, who gave rise to the word *hooker;* it is also said that Hooker's eyes are focused on the apartment of a lady friend across the way.

While retaining the Bulfinch front and some chambers inside, the State House has been greatly enlarged during its years of existence. A tour of the interior will reveal marble halls and an interesting display of the state seal, from royal government days to the present. In the house chamber you can view the **Sacred Cod,** symbol of the importance of the fishing industry, which has traveled with the house from the Old State House to its present location. The cod faces north, symbolizing Democratic control; to face south would give the edge to the Republicans. Massachusetts residents have the right of petition to have their representative place before the house any bill they wish. (Schoolchildren taking advantage of this have managed to get the ladybug voted the state's official insect, the tabby cat is the official state cat, Boston cream pie is the official dessert, the chocolate chip cookie is the official cookie, and corn muffins the official state muffin.) A statue by Daniel Chester French of the seated governor **Roger Wolcott** has a shiny foot from visitors rubbing it for good luck. Wolcott is credited with saving the Bulfinch State House from being torn down when the building became too small for the expanding government. (Allow about forty-five minutes for this interesting tour.)

The State House has undergone much restoration, but one sight you will not see is the private office of the senate president, restored a few years ago at a cost exceeding $160,000, perhaps to fulfill the statement made by Sam Adams at the dedication of the State House that the building should be "a suitable temple for the goddess Democracy." Although one Republican proposed making the office, then held by William Bulger of South Boston, part of the Freedom Trail, the bill has never been heard from since. The original State House cost $133,333, but even that was five times the sum appropriated.

Leaving the State House by the rear door, just ahead you will see a column marking the original height of the hill, now 60 feet lower than in colonial days. Turn left to head down **Mount Vernon Street,** said to be "the only respectable street in America" by **Henry James,** who lived at number 131. (Beacon Hill was not always so proper; at one point in colonial days the area earned the name Mount Whoredom.) As noted, the Hill is a tribute to the architecture of Charles Bulfinch, offering many examples of his work. Bulfinch, along with Harrison Gray Otis—who had three Bulfinch-designed homes here—and others, formed the Mount Vernon Proprietors for the development of the area, which began with completion of the State House.

The **Nichols House Museum,** at 55 Mount Vernon, is open to the public and offers an eclectic collection of furnishings left by its resident of eighty years, Rose Standish Nichols. Mount Vernon Street, with its brick sidewalks and gaslit streetlamps, was home to many a proper Bostonian. At number 32 lived **Julia Ward Howe,** composer of the "Battle Hymn of the Republic," along with her husband, founder of Perkins Institute for the Blind. One of the most magnificent mansions and the only freestanding one on the hill is Otis's second home, number 85. Just beyond it, at number 87, is the home Bulfinch designed for himself but never lived in, for despite his architectural riches, Bulfinch became financially bankrupt and could not afford the finished house. Although the view of these homes is best from the left side of the street, Mount Vernon, particularly in bad weather, is best negotiated down on the right, where an iron rail was installed in the nineteenth century. Another piece of iron you will notice near doorways is the boot straps, used to clean one's feet before entering the houses. Although it is not open to the public, you might notice **77 Mount Vernon,** home of the Club of Odd Volumes, one of the oldest book collectors' clubs in America. The name refers to incomplete sets of books. The house was originally built for Hepzibah Swan, who saw to it by deed that the coach houses from numbers 50 to 60 Mount Vernon Street would always remain 13 feet high. Number 56, with the wide door, is also deeded as a horse passage from Mount Vernon to the stalls below.

Louisburg Square is the most famous and prestigious location on the Hill. This elegant rectangle also happens to be a very private place: Both

Beacon Hill Walk

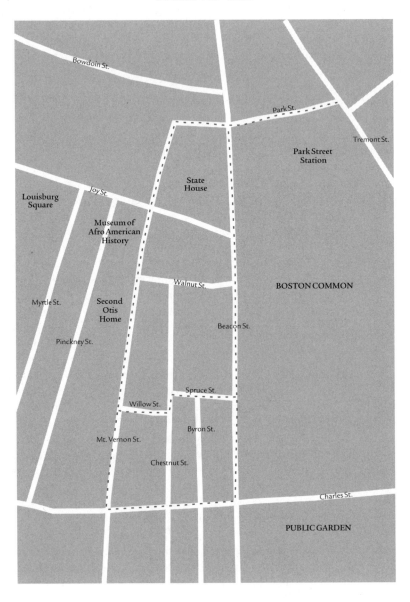

Bowdoin St.

Park St.

Tremont St.

Park Street
Station

Joy St.

Louisburg
Square

State
House

Museum of
Afro American
History

BOSTON COMMON

Myrtle St.

Second
Otis
Home

Walnut St.

Beacon St.

Pinckney St.

Spruce St.

Willow St.

Byron St.

Mt. Vernon St.

Chestnut St.

Charles St.

PUBLIC GARDEN

the street and the park in front of the homes are owned by the residents, not the city. Louisa May Alcott, Jenny Lind, and novelist William Dean Howells all lived here. Senator John F. Kerry and his wife live at 19 Louisbourg Square, at the Pinckney Street corner. Author Robin Cook lives across the street.

At this point, you could continue down Mount Vernon to Charles Street for an exploration of the antiques shops that line it, have lunch at one of the many small restaurants, or even browse along the real estate office windows to see just what it would cost to live on the Hill (some homes are selling in the multimillions; most have been split up into condos). One of the landmarks of Charles Street is the **Charles Street Meeting House,** now a collection of offices but in colonial days a Baptist church. The Charles River lapped at the building's back, making it easy to conduct baptisms in the river. The structure later became the African Methodist Episcopal Church, to serve the then-large black population on the Hill, and ended its religious days as a Unitarian meetinghouse.

To continue exploring Beacon Hill, take Willow Street, almost opposite Louisburg Square, passing Acorn Street, a tiny and perhaps the most photogenic street on the Hill. Then walk up Chestnut Street, with its lovely homes distinguished by bow windows, fancy grillwork, and lavender windows. At 29A Chestnut you can see one of the famous purple panes of the Hill; the glass, imported from England between 1818 and 1824, contained impurities that turned it lavender (you can also see some of these panes at 63 Beacon Street). The Bulfinch-designed homes at numbers 13, 15, and 17—among the most elegant on the street—were built in 1806 by Mrs. Swan for her three daughters. These houses' furnishings, sent from France by Mrs. Swan's husband, Colonel **James Swan** (for whom Swans Island in Maine is named), can be seen in the Museum of Fine Arts.

The walk continues along Spruce Street and back to Beacon Street, toward the State House. Among the architectural delights on this part of Beacon Street is the third **Harrison Gray Otis House,** one he lived in for more than forty years. Unfortunately, the house, at 45 Beacon, with its attractive entryway, is not open to the public; it is owned by the American Meteorological Society. When it was built there was a garden to the right, but Otis, seeing money to be made, developed the lot. His own home, with a bow window that looked over the garden, now extends inside the neighboring mansion. The **William Hickling Prescott House,** at number 55, owned by the Massachusetts chapter of the Society of Colonial Dames, is, however, open on occasion for viewing.

The white granite building at 42 Beacon Street now houses the exclusive **Somerset Club** but was originally built for David Sears, who owned the Sears Crescent in Government Center. The Beacon Street home was designed by Alexander Parris, using granite rather than brick for its facade. The Somerset Club, as one story goes, once had a kitchen fire for which the fire department was asked to use the servants', not the members', entrance. A male domain since 1851, the club began accepting women for membership in 1988.

The **Parkman House,** at 33 Beacon Street, is now used by the mayor for official functions. In 1849—in one of the most sensational cases of the times—Dr. George Parkman, who lived here, was murdered by John White Webster, a professor at Harvard Medical School, over a loan owed Parkman. Webster hid Parkman's body in the basement of Massachusetts General Hospital, where it was not found for days. The murder so upset Parkman's son that he became almost a recluse in the house for more than fifty years, donating it, on his death in 1908, to the city, along with a $5 million trust fund for the upkeep of Boston Common.

As you arrive back at the State House, note that in this corner John Hancock had what was described as one of the finest homes on the Hill. His heirs tried to get the state to use it as a governor's mansion and, failing that, had it torn down. The governor still has no official home.

DETOURS

If you have time, take a detour down Joy Street, where at its foot across the way is the first Harrison Gray Otis house, now the home of the **Society for the Preservation of New England Antiquities,** the largest regional preservation organization in the country. The first of three homes designed by Charles Bulfinch for Otis, the house is the only one open to the public. It has been restored to reflect the high-society taste of Boston circa 1796–1820. Next to it is the **Old West Methodist Church,** designed by Asher Benjamin. In 1776 the British, taking no chances of another Old North Church experience, had its steeple taken down. From 1894 to 1958 the church was a public library, and since 1964 it has again been a church. **John F. Kennedy** voted here when he was running for president, as he maintained an apartment at 122 Bowdoin Street. Also to be seen is Boston's first black school, at 46 Joy Street, now the home of the **Museum of Afro American History.** Next to it, on Smith Court, is the **African Meeting House,** built in 1806, the oldest black church standing in the United States. The wooden houses on Smith Court are some of the oldest buildings on the Hill.

You might also detour onto Charles Street and pick up the makings for a picnic lunch at Deluca's Market; it's only a short walk from here to the Common, the Public Garden, or the Esplanade. Or stop for a drink at the Bull & Finch, better known as Cheers, at 84 Beacon Street, opposite the Public Garden.

You may want to continue along Beacon Street to view the **Boston Athenaeum,** a very proper Boston institution that has a limited membership. This private library does welcome visitors to view its treasures, which include books from George Washington's library and a huge collection of Confederate imprints. Also within steps of each other are the **Congregational House,** at 14 Beacon Street—with facade scenes of the Mayflower Compact and John Eliot preaching to the Indians and, inside, town records from when the meetinghouse and town hall were one—and the home with the slender fluted columns, at number 16, where **Chester Harding,** an American painter, lived. The home is now the headquarters of the Boston Bar Association and is not open to the public. From here you can continue on past King's Chapel to Faneuil Hall, following the red Freedom Trail, or detour to Downtown Crossing.

Copley Square, Back Bay, and the Prudential Center

Here is a two-part walk that offers a look at the "new" Boston, beginning in Copley Square, framed by two architectural masterpieces: Trinity Church and the Boston Public Library.

The first part of the walk winds through Back Bay, the most lavish display of Victorian architecture in the country, a district with an old-world look that seems to have almost always been there but in reality is one of the city's newest areas, for until the mid-1800s Back Bay was indeed a bay. Then began an ambitious plan that by the turn of the twentieth century had added more than 400 acres to the original Boston peninsula and created what Boston did not have before: broad, well-planned streets, bearing an understandable alphabetical relationship, stretching from Arlington to Hereford Streets. From 1857 to 1900, gravel from Needham, 9 miles away, was carried twenty-four hours a day by a special railroad built for the purpose, until all the land was filled in. This "new" Boston attracted thirteen of the city's churches and nineteen schools in the thirty years between 1860 and 1890.

Then in 1959, with the construction of the **Prudential Center** over what was then a mass of dreary railroad tracks, Back Bay again became a symbol of the new and changing Boston. The center—focal point of the second part of the walk—marked Boston's first major change in years, and its fifty-two-story tower over the thirty-two-acre, city-within-a-city site made the building the tallest in New England until the hometown insurance company, **John Hancock,** built its I. M. Pei–designed, glass-enclosed (10,344 sections of half-inch tempered glass) tower in 1974. At 790 feet, the Hancock Tower tops the Prudential Center by 40 feet. In 1968 the **Christian Science Church** with the help of I. M. Pei opened up the area around its Mother Church to create a new center for its church headquarters and publishing operations with open plazas and new structures. Also changing the face of the Back Bay is the **Copley Place** center, finished in 1985 and built over the Massachusetts Turnpike. Copley Place and the Prudential Center are now linked by glass-covered walkways creating an indoor marketplace of shops, restaurants, and tourist attractions, a convention center, theaters, and hotels.

The entire area, of course, is built over a waterway. The Prudential Tower required builders to reach 172 feet below ground level for solid bedrock. Since Back Bay is on filled land, most of its buildings and homes have wood pilings for support; Trinity Church has 2,000 wooden pilings under its tower alone. The pilings must be kept moist to avoid rot, for otherwise the buildings would sink into the soft soil. A new concern is the dropping of the water table in this area and what effect it may have on many of the buildings.

There may be no better place in Boston to begin a tour of the city than Copley Square. This is not only the squarest of any Boston square (most are irregular in shape) but it is also ringed by such architectural masterpieces as Trinity Church, Old South Church, Boston Public Library, John Hancock Tower, and the Fairmont Copley Plaza hotel. From the square, you could also enter Copley Place at the Westin Hotel entrance and wander under cover to the Prudential Tower for a bird's-eye view of the city.

FROM COPLEY SQUARE THROUGH BACK BAY

Trinity Church, considered one of the finest examples of church architecture in the United States, was designed by H. H. Richardson and is in the Romanesque style, with influences from a tower of the Old Cathedral in Salamanca, Spain. The interior is richly done by John La Farge. Outside the church stands a statue of **Phillips Brooks,** the first rector of the Copley Square Church and the author of the lyrics of the hymn "O Little Town of Bethlehem."

Across from Trinity Church is **Boston Public Library,** designed by Charles Follen McKim with influences from the Bibliothèque Ste. Geneviève in Paris. The bronze doors are by Daniel Chester French, and after entering them you will find a grand marble stairway. If you go to the third floor you will see paintings by John Singer Sargent. Do visit the reading room—Bates Hall, on the second floor—as well as the wonderful courtyard, modeled after an arcade in the Palazzo della Cacciarella in Rome. Across from the library, another delight is found in the "new" **Old South Church,** at 645 Boylston Street, which uses a northern Italian Gothic design and has a splendid sanctuary.

From Copley Square follow Dartmouth Street, where you will see Old South Church on the corner, and continue to Commonwealth Avenue. **Commonwealth Mall**—the long, peaceful promenade that cuts down Commonwealth Avenue from the Public Garden to Kenmore Square and is shaded by elms—has benches for relaxing and contains statues of some of Boston's most heroic figures. It gives no hint of having been referred to, in the early 1800s, as "nothing less than a cesspool" because of a dam built across the bay to harness the tides for power in the city. To clean that mess, the plan to fill in the bay was developed, and Arthur Gilman was awarded the design for the area. Gilman's design was straight from Paris: brownstones with mansard rooftops along a French Second Empire–style grid pattern that included the 100-foot-wide promenade down Commonwealth Avenue.

As you enter from Dartmouth Street, you may want to backtrack up the mall, past the seated statue of fiery abolitionist **William Lloyd Garrison,** to view the statue of **Samuel Eliot Morison**—the Pulitzer Prize–winning author of forty-eight books and the Boston native who lived nearby at 44 Brimmer Street—sitting naturally on a twenty-ton piece of granite from Rhode Island. He seems relaxed and ready for adventure, except for his dress shoes, which seem out of place. Just beyond the statue, at 191 Commonwealth, is the former home of **Henry Lee Higginson,** a philanthropist with whom Boston seems to have been blessed, because he alone founded the Boston Symphony Orchestra in 1881. Higginson's motto—and that of the Duke of Devonshire—was "What I gave, I have; what I spend, I had; what I kept, I lost."

Another hero you will meet on your way toward the Public Garden is **Patrick Andrew Collins,** a popular Boston mayor whose statue was funded by a people's collection of money raised in six days following his death. And revolutionary days are recalled by the bronze statue of **John Glover,** a Marblehead fisherman whose marine regiment manned the boats that carried George Washington across the Delaware.

At the end of your stroll on the promenade, facing the statue of **George Washington,** who sits on his horse just inside the Public Garden, is one of **Alexander Hamilton,** the mall's first statue and the first granite statue in the country. Hamilton, who became the first secretary of the treasury, is widely known today as the face on the ten-dollar bill.

The main reason for walking down Commonwealth Avenue is to partake of the feast of Victorian architecture that can be found on either side, as well as on the side streets that branch off in such an orderly manner. Whereas the land you are walking on was filled and construction began almost immediately upon filling, your walk occurs midway in the Victorian section, as the first buildings in place were by the Public Garden and then extended down Commonwealth Avenue to beyond Dartmouth Street. At the intersection of Dartmouth and Commonwealth is the **Vendome Building,** at one time a hotel. One of the finest examples of the French Second Empire style, the Vendome was the first public building in Boston to have electricity—in 1882, from a plant designed by Thomas Edison—and was the home away from home of celebrities and presidents. A vastly different style of architecture is on the opposite corner at 152 Commonwealth, home of the **Chilton Club,** an exclusive women's club founded in 1910. The elaborate baroque-style, Beaux Arts facade of 128 Commonwealth was the home of **Chamberlayne Junior College.** Since the Great Depression, many a distinguished Back Bay residence, too expensive for one family to maintain, has become a school or has been turned into condominiums, in some cases having the interior of its Victorian splendor gutted.

At 199 Commonwealth is the **St. Botolph Club,** with its symmetrical facade, two bows, and central Ionic portico entrance in the Federal Revival style. Back in 1889 the club, for artists, writers, and professional men (nowadays all private Boston clubs, most under pressure of losing their liquor licenses, are accepting women into membership), acted in a very proper Bostonian manner when it removed a painting by John Singer Sargent that showed Isabella Stewart Gardner in a tight-fitting black dress. That scandalous painting can now be seen by all in the Gardner Museum, in the Fenway.

At the intersection of Commonwealth and Clarendon Street, look up at the bell tower of the **First Baptist Church.** This building, originally the Brattle Square Unitarian Church, is an earlier Romanesque design of H. H. Richardson. Made of Roxbury pudding stone and having a tower designed like an Italian campanile, the building displays a remarkably decorative frieze, notable because it was modeled in Paris by Frédéric-Auguste Bartholdi, sculptor of the Statue of Liberty. The faces on the frieze, depicting the sacraments, are said to be those of noted Bostonians Longfellow, Hawthorne, and Emerson, whereas the trumpeting angels on the corners give the church its nickname, "Church of the Holy Bean Blowers."

Boston Center for Adult Education, located at 5 Commonwealth Avenue, was built as a home in 1912, replacing an earlier version constructed in 1861 and similar to number 3. The center offers dozens of quick courses, from languages to crash courses in getting to know Boston, and on request will let you see its grand ballroom, said to be reminiscent of one at Versailles.

(The ballroom, like a lot of historic Boston sites, can be rented out for parties and weddings. The Boston Convention and Visitors Bureau has a complete list.)

At Arlington Street—remember, this area is the only one in Boston to have an alphabetical, logical street pattern—turn right, going past the elegant **Ritz-Carlton** (stop in for afternoon tea or a drink at its famed bar), and then turn right again, onto Newbury Street, with its collection of boutiques, art galleries (said to be the most numerous in a single location of anywhere in the country), and sidewalk cafes like no other. It's an international, lively, chic scene, with shops ranging from Burberry's of England and Brooks Brothers to Knoll International and finally to Virgin Records. At the intersection of Newbury and Berkeley Streets is Louis, a clothing store located in the former Museum of Natural History, built in the French Academic style. The Newbury, the former New England Life Building, next door was the site of the first home of M.I.T.

At **Emmanuel Church** are held regular Sunday concerts of Bach's music. The chapel next door, which is quite beautiful inside, is named for Leslie Lindsey, who, on her honeymoon, died when the *Lusitania* was sunk during World War I. When Lindsey's body washed ashore in Ireland, she was wearing the rubies and diamonds her father had given her; her family then sold them and used the funds to build the chapel in 1924. Nearby is the **New England Historical Genealogical Society,** at 101 Newbury, where it is possible to do some family research.

From here, you can return to Copley Square or continue on up Newbury Street for more shops and cafes. As you pass the **Boston Architectural Center,** at 320 Newbury, look up to see Richard Hass's trompe l'oeil cutaway drawing of a classic dome and buttress sculpture—it's a sight hard to miss from the Massachusetts Turnpike that passes almost below it.

FROM COPLEY SQUARE TO THE PRUDENTIAL CENTER

Taking the opposite route from Copley Square to explore the Prudential Center and the Christian Science Center area, you could begin indoors, walking between the Copley Plaza and Boston Public Library into the Westin Hotel and then continuing inside the luxuriant Copley Place shopping center and out across a glass-enclosed walkway into the Prudential Center.

When it was built, the **Prudential Center** contained the tallest building in New England. The fiftieth-floor skywalk of the Prudential Tower offers good views of all of Boston, and on a clear day you can see to New Hampshire; just above this floor are a restaurant and lounge. Next to the Prudential Tower is the **John B. Hynes Veterans Memorial Convention Center,** named for a Boston mayor. And just across from the Hynes on Boylston Street is the

Copley Walk

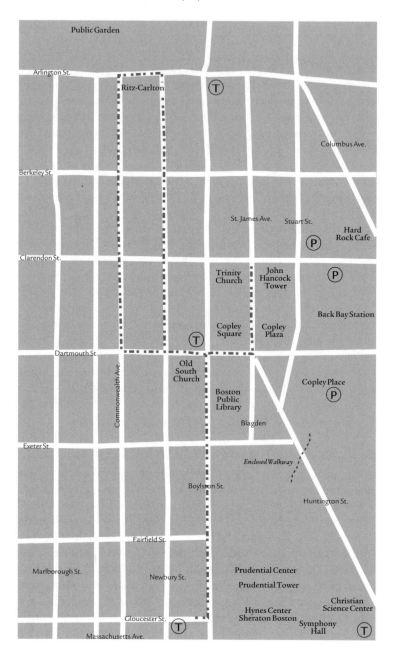

Public Garden

Arlington St.

Ritz-Carlton

(T)

Columbus Ave.

Berkeley St.

St. James Ave.   Stuart St.

Hard
Rock Cafe

(P)

Clarendon St.

Trinity
Church

John
Hancock
Tower

(P)

Back Bay Station

Copley
Square

Copley
Plaza

Dartmouth St.

(T)

Old
South
Church

Copley Place

(P)

Boston
Public
Library

Blagden

Commonwealth Ave.

Exeter St.

Enclosed Walkway

Huntington St.

Boylston St.

Fairfield St.

Marlborough St.

Newbury St.

Prudential Center

Prudential Tower

Christian
Science Center

Gloucester St.

(T)

Hynes Center
Sheraton Boston

Symphony
Hall

(T)

Massachusetts Ave.

Institute of Contemporary Art, which offers a variety of changing exhibits.

If you continue through the **Sheraton Boston Hotel,** just outside its main entrance is the **Christian Science Center**—the world headquarters of this religious group. The fifteen-acre site—with its open plaza, reflecting pool, and I. M. Pei–designed buildings to blend with the Mother Church and publishing house of this international church—is both inviting and interesting to visit. The new **Mary Baker Eddy Library,** with an entrance on Massachusetts Avenue, is filled with ideas and concepts that have shaped the world, as well as a library that offers insight into Mrs. Eddy, a remarkable nineteenth-century woman. Not to be missed is the Mapparium, a glass globe of the world made in 1935 but recently updated to show how the world has changed since then and the ideas that helped shape those changes.

Across from the Christian Science Center is **Symphony Hall,** which, for acoustics, is one of the best-built halls anywhere. Taking in a concert by the Boston Symphony Orchestra or the Boston Pops is one of the most pleasurable things to do in the city. Along Massachusetts Avenue you will find many inexpensive restaurants, as this area is also home to Northeastern University, the New England Conservatory of Music, and Berklee College of Music.

Detours

It's not far from here to the Museum of Fine Arts, the Gardner Museum, or Fenway Park.

The **Massachusetts Historical Society,** at 1154 Boylston Street and not far from the Hynes, is open from 9:00 A.M. to 4:45 P.M. and is the oldest historical society in America. Its collection includes papers of John Adams, John Quincy Adams, and other presidents; a copy by Thomas Jefferson of his original draft of the Declaration of Independence; paintings by Gilbert Stuart and John Singleton Copley; and even the pen with which President Lincoln signed the Emancipation Proclamation. You can apply at the front desk to see the society's artworks or to use the library.

If you are walking along Commonwealth Avenue, detour over to Beacon Street for a tour of the **Gibson House,** a museum of Victoriana. If you are hungry, head for the **Bull & Finch Pub,** better known as the original **Cheers** bar, on Beacon Street, but instead of following all the tourists down to the pub, head upstairs to the Hampshire House and dine in a former Victorian mansion.

Boston cannot claim to be first in the nation as to settlement. Nevertheless, a fish weir discovered during construction of the **New England Building,** now the **Newbury,** between Boylston and Newbury Streets, dates back 3,000 years; the Peabody Museum at Harvard has an exhibit showing the use of fish weirs. (If you wander up Commonwealth

Avenue, you will find a statue of **Leif Eriksson** that for some reason ended up in the middle of the roadway but originally was erected by a Bostonian who believed the Vikings did land along the Charles some 1,000 years ago. The Pilgrims do hold the title as the first white settlers to establish a permanent colony, but there were many prior explorations along the New England coast by Europeans. John Smith, the English explorer, is credited with having sailed up and naming the Charles River in 1614, and he, not the Pilgrims, gave Plymouth its name. And before the Pilgrims were thousands of Indians, most of whom died off, the victims of European diseases brought into the country by these early explorers.)

THE SOUTH END

Well before the Back Bay was laid out, the **South End** was the place to live. After years of decay, it has once again become a vibrant, diversified area in which to live. Being but a short walk from the downtown area, it's become a popular residential and dining area.

The South End's nineteenth-century streets, parks, and buildings echo those of London. It's one of the largest areas of Victorian architecture in the United States. It is an easy detour from Copley Square. Follow Dartmouth Street past Back Bay Station and Columbus Avenue and you will be entering the South End. Continue onto Tremont Street, cross it, and head up the left side, where you will see one of the more beautiful residential streets with Victorian homes gracefully winding around Union Park, filled with flowers and fountains.

How Bostonians reflected on their neighborhoods in the 1800s is best reflected in John P. Marquand's Pulitzer Prize–winning novel *The Late George Apley* (1937). Apley, who lived in splendid comfort on Beach Street (in the Back Bay), sat down in his library to write about his family for his children. He told, in a letter, of remembering how at the age of seven he lived in the South End, a neighborhood considered up-and-coming. One morning his father, home from work with a cold, was seeing him off for school, when he suddenly looked across the street and exclaimed, "Thunderation, there is a man in his shirtsleeves on those steps!" That sight—a man in shirtsleeves—had told Apley's father that the high-society days of the South End were numbered, and his father sold the house the next day and moved to the more refined neighborhood of Beacon Street. (If you visit Newburyport, take in the library to learn more about its native son John P. Marquand.)

Along Tremont Street you will see the **Boston Center for the Arts** (539 Tremont Street) and the dome-shaped Cyclorama, which once housed a sweeping painting of the Battle of Gettysburg. The area is filled with interesting shops and dining spots. The Butcher Shop (552 Tremont) offers not only fine meats but also a trendy wine bar with light meals. The Garden of Eden (571 Tremont) has a nice cafe and bakery. B&G Oysters Ltd. (550 Tremont Street) offers great seafood and kitchen showmanship. And Hamersley's Bistro (553 Tremont) is famed for elegant cuisine.

CHAPTER TEN

The North End

For both history and a "genuine neighborhood" feel, the North End can't be beat. The North End is not only Boston's oldest residential area but also its only true neighborhood, one that generations of Italians continue to call home, just as Paul Revere and some of the detested representatives of the British Crown did more than two centuries ago. It's also one of the most convivial sections of the city to visit during the many summer festivals to the saints (see chapter 23) that overflow the narrow, twisting streets with colorful, aroma-filled celebrations. There is no need to fear going hungry in the North End.

Before beginning a walk through the North End, take time to visit **Haymarket,** an area behind the City Hall and just beyond Faneuil Hall. For more than 200 years this has been Boston's market center. Although now largely confined to Blackstone Street behind the Bostonian Hotel, it still remains colorful, congested, and lively, especially Thursday through Saturday, when sellers cover the area with pushcarts purveying free fruits, vegetables, and other foods.

The easiest way to reach the North End is to follow the Freedom Trail's red line past Faneuil Hall. It's a mere five-minute walk, at your slowest, from Quincy Market into the heart of the North End. And the walk is far more pleasant and quieter these days with the completion of the Big Dig, the massive highway project that took down the Central Artery and buried it deep underfoot in new tunnels that speed traffic between the north and south of the city.

Unlike some areas of Boston undergoing gentrification, the North End appears to be clinging to its past. Although a few souvenir shops can be found and Italian restaurants appear by their prices to be catering to a tourist trade, most of the shops and restaurants serve local residents.

Taking this route along **Hanover Street** is similar to the one early colonists did. For in colonial days the North End was a peninsula cut off from Boston except for this pathway. Just beyond the Union Oyster House, America's oldest restaurant, is the Boston Stone, placed in 1737 when this was believed to be the center of the city. It marks distances to other parts of the then town. Soon you approach a remarkable oasis in the city: the **Rose Fitzgerald Kennedy Greenway,** the first step in the development of a twenty-seven-acre greenway that will be covered by trees, grass, plantings, and museums along a path once overshadowed by the Central Artery that for years cut the North End and the waterfront off from the city.

Following Hanover Street you will pass many small shops. (Jordan Marsh, at one time the city's largest department store, got its start here in a small dry-goods store opened by Eben Jordan; even Rowland H. Macy, who got his start on Nantucket, had a store here. In 1996 the Jordan Marsh name disappeared and was replaced with the Macy's name. Both stores were part of Federated Department Stores.)

Following the red line, at the intersection of Richmond and North Streets, notice the sign on the third floor—a w with a *ts* below and the date 1694—on the modern building. The sign bears the initials of former inn owner Nicholas Upsall's granddaughter and her husband, T.W. and S.W. This is the oldest sign in Boston still on its original site, marking the location of the Red Lion Inn.

The **Paul Revere House,** at 19 North Square, is one of the oldest in the city, the housing having been purchased by Revere when it was almost a hundred years old. Revere owned it until 1800, bringing up sixteen children (not all of them living in it at the same time) by his two wives. Many of the furnishings belonged to the Reveres, and in the front yard is a Revere bell. Next door is the more prosperous-looking **Pierce-Hichborn House,** believed to be the oldest brick home in the city. Revere's home was built in 1676, just after one of the many great fires in Boston, and was the site of the home of the Reverend Increase Mather, who along with his son, Cotton, was among the most puritanical of Puritans. It was not far from here, on Moon Street, that in 1673 a sea captain was placed in the stocks for "lewd and unseeingly [sic] conduct": Having just returned from a long voyage, he had kissed his wife on the family doorstep.

Just beyond the Revere House is the **Mariners House,** where rooms were rented to sailors for $3.75 a night until 1997—an indication of how close the sea once was to this square. Also just off North Square is Garden Court Street, where John F. "Honey Fitz" Fitzgerald, congressman and mayor of Boston, lived and where Rose, his daughter and the mother of President John Fitzgerald Kennedy, was born—a reminder that the North End was at one time heavily Irish (at another time it was largely Jewish). Along Garden Court was the residence of Thomas Hutchinson, the royal governor whose opulent home was nearly destroyed by angry rioters protesting the Stamp Act in 1765.

Continuing along the Freedom Trail, notice the beautiful flower garden at **St. Leonard's,** the first Italian-built Catholic church in New England.

Almost across the street, at 383 Hanover Street, another era of political unrest in the country is recalled. It was from here, where the Langone Funeral Home once was located, that Nicola Sacco and Bartolomeo Vanzetti, accused of a 1920 robbery in nearby Braintree but caught up in a modern witch trail, were brought following their execution on August 23, 1927. Was justice served? Their trial is still debated.

Next is **St. Stephen's,** the only remaining Bulfinch church in Boston. Originally a Congregational church, it became Unitarian; then, as immigrants took over the area, the church became Catholic in 1849. In 1870 the building was raised 6 feet and moved back 16 feet to widen Hanover Street, and in 1964 Richard Cardinal Cushing gathered funds to restore it to its original appearance.

The church faces **The Prado,** or Paul Revere Mall, which has a gallant equestrian statue of Paul Revere at its entrance. The statue, by Cyrus E. Dallin (whose famed *Appeal to the Great Spirit* stands in front of the Museum of Fine Arts), was modeled in 1865 but not cast until 1940 when funds were found for it. The mall is considered the most European space in Boston, as it feels as though it was carved out of the urban scene around it. Like Europe it is an outdoor room walled in by the city and with the sky as its ceiling, and plenty of trees to provide shade. And it is a neighborhood room, as you will see people gathered to play checkers, babies in carriages, and strollers. Boston's legendary mayor James Michael Curley, who you may have visited with back in the park across from the Union Oyster House, created it in 1933 for the North Enders after seeing The Prado, the famed Spanish museum. Along its walls are bronze plaques telling of the people and places in this historic neighborhood.

The **Old North Church (Christ Church)** is just ahead. Being a Congregationalist, Paul Revere was not a member of this Anglican and now still-active Episcopal church. But he was very familiar with it, having at the age of fifteen been one of the ringers of what are said to be the sweetest bells in America (although the eight bells were cast in England). From its 191-foot steeple—perhaps the most famous in the land—were hung the lanterns that told, "One if by land, and two if by sea," thus advising Revere and Dawes of the British plans to march on Concord and Lexington. The steeple is not the original, having twice been toppled by hurricanes, in 1804 and 1954. From it also took place one of humankind's first flights: In 1757 one John Childs gave notice that he would fly from the steeple, firing two pistols. Although he survived, a law was quickly passed forbidding flying from church steeples.

The Old North Church, with its plain white interior, is well worth visiting. It is filled with memories and markers with the names of the original owners; General Thomas Gage, the British commander in chief in America, had pew sixty-two and used the steeple to witness the Battle of Bunker Hill. You can see the window through which Robert Newman, who lit the lanterns in 1775, escaped. The church, built in 1723, appears to have been inspired by the works of British architect Christopher Wren. Beneath the church are crypts that help support the buildings. In one are said to be the remains of Major Pitcairn, leader of the march on Lexington, who was killed at Bunker Hill; he was to have been buried at Westminster Abby but through a mistake lies here somewhere. (A body believed to be his was sent to Westminster Abby and just before burial was discovered to be that of an American soldier.) Services at the church have been attended by many U.S. presidents and by Queen Elizabeth. When Lafayette in his later years saw the bust of George Washington at the front of the church, he said, "Yes, this is the man I knew." Near the entranceway are twelve bricks in the wall, sent from Boston, England, from a cell used there to intern the Pilgrims.

If you have time, take the tour of the crypt and steeple. The crypt, while dark and dusty, offers another perspective on life in colonial days. While you cannot go to the top of the steeple, you can visit the area from which the bells are rung and see some memorabilia. Next door is a gift shop. You might also ask about the **Vinegar Bible,** now in storage, that was a gift of King George II. The book is so named because a page that should read "the Parable of the Vineyard" instead says "the Parable of the Vinegar."

A short walk up Hull Street to **Copp's Hill Burying Ground** offers both history and a good view, especially for shutterbugs, of the USS *Constitution* across the water in Charlestown. The most famous tomb here is of the Mather family, among the most influential church leaders in colonial times. Buried here also is Prince Hall, a black man who fought at Bunker Hill and established the first black Masonic lodge. The cemetery, being the highest point in the North End, was used to fire cannons at Bunker Hill. Redcoats also used it for target practice: The stone of Captain Daniel Malcom, stating that he was "a true son of liberty," was a favorite target.

North End Walk

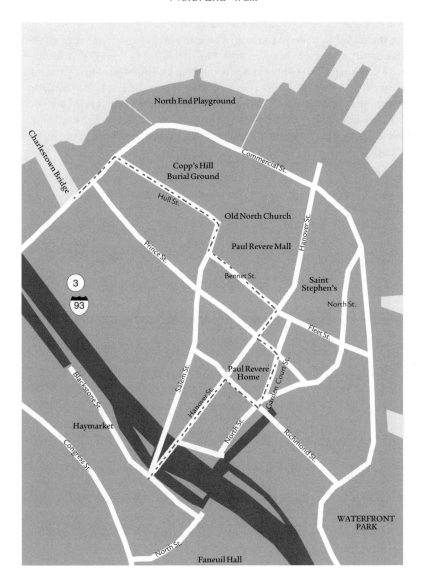

North End Playground

Charlestown Bridge

Commercial St.

Copp's Hill
Burial Ground

Hull St.

Old North Church

Prince St.

Paul Revere Mall

Hanover St.

Bennet St.

Saint
Stephen's

3

93

North St.

Fleet St.

Salem St.

Paul Revere
Home

Garden Court St.

Hanover St.

Blackstone St.

North St.

Richmond St.

Haymarket

Congress St.

WATERFRONT
PARK

North St.

Faneuil Hall

Before leaving the area, notice the house at **44 Hull Street.** At 10 feet wide, it is the narrowest in Boston and believed to have been built for spite, in the eighteenth century, to block the view of a neighbor.

It wasn't far from here that two of the more sticky situations of the twentieth century occurred. Just below the hill on January 15, 1919, a tank holding 2.2 million gallons of molasses collapsed, killing twenty-one persons and twenty horses, injuring 150 persons, and causing $1 million in property damage. And on January 17, 1950, the Brinks armored van company, then at 165 Prince Street, across from where the molasses tank was located, was held up in a crime that has now been retold in three movies, all with Brinks in their titles.

The Waterfront

L ike Back Bay, Boston's waterfront is primarily on filled-in land. For years it was a decaying area, blocked off from the rest of the city by the Central Artery, which is now gone. Today it is a lively district of restored and renovated warehouses that serve as expensive condominiums, offices, hotels, restaurants, and boating facilities.

Freighters and cruise ships still call on Boston, but not along this waterfront area. Freighters either continue past, heading up the Mystic River to Charlestown, or unload cargo, primarily containers, at Castle Island, some distance away. Cruise ships now have a port of their own, the Black Falcon Cruise Terminal, named in memory of longshoremen killed when the *Black Falcon,* a freighter, burned and sank at the South Boston pier.

You may begin the tour at the State Street MBTA station (Blue or Orange Line). If you follow the painted blue line down State Street—formerly King Street, the gateway to the sea—to the harbor, you can still see the name CUNARD on the building at **126 State Street.** With its bronze anchors, head of Neptune, and scroll that suggests waves, the building stands as a reminder that Boston, in the past, did attract much shipping. Although Samuel Cunard had chosen Boston as his American port when he began making transatlantic crossings in 1840, one winter a frozen Boston Harbor forced Cunard to use New York, and another chapter in Boston history came to an end. The **Richards Building** next door, at 114 State Street, has a cast-iron facade that was made in Italy and then bolted together here.

The harbor-front area is now more at home with pleasure craft, commuter boats, and ferries; in summer, not to take one of the sightseeing boats or lunch cruises (see chapter 2) is to miss a lot of Boston. Waterfront property has become among the most expensive in the city, with condominiums at Rowes Wharf going for many millions. If you own a boat, a berth along the waterfront can cost more than $3,000 a foot—a lot of money for a few months of pleasure, but try to find an available berth.

As of this writing in 2004, work continues on restoring the city with its waterfront. For more than twelve years, this was the site of the Big Dig project, at more than $14 billion the most expensive public-works project in the history of the United States. The massive project called for the tearing down of the Central Artery—route Interstate 93—that ran through the city connecting the north and south. For more than thirty years, this artery physically cut off the waterfront from the city. While there has been massive criticism of the project's cost, it is amazing that it was accomplished. Remember this was all filled-in land and the project required not only digging a tunnel underneath the overhead highway without stopping the thousands of vehicles a day that passed through it, but also the rerouting of water and sewer pipes as well as telephone and electrical lines.

To accomplish this with as few traffic woes as possible, engineers used a technique called slurry-wall, which involved (a) digging 4-foot-wide trenches on either side of the work zone as deep as 80 feet; (b) pumping into the trench a clay-and-water mix (slurry) to keep the earth from falling in; (c) pumping in concrete as the slurry is pumped out; and (d) building decks to hold up the artery while the earth—all filled-in land—is dug out. The technique had been used before in the building of the extended MBTA line through Harvard Square in Cambridge.

The project also included the building of a third Boston Harbor tunnel, named for legendary Red Sox player Ted Williams. The tunnel, which opened in 1995, now eases traffic coming from the Massachusetts Turnpike to Logan Airport in East Boston. The twenty-seven-acre site is now becoming a greenway with parks and, possibly, museums.

Boston has also completed another multibillion-dollar project to clean up the harbor. The project included a 9-mile tunnel into the ocean to send treated sewage out of the harbor. Residents in Greater Boston are paying a high price for this in increased water rates for home consumption. How bad was the pollution? An exhibit at the New England Aquarium showed that 5,000 gallons of poorly treated waste spilled into the harbor daily before the cleanup—that's 500 million gallons each day. The harbor is much improved.

Before crossing Atlantic Avenue to the waterfront, stop by the **Custom House,** which for more than fifty years was Boston's tallest building. Begun in 1847, the building was one of the costliest of its day, and in 1915, when its twenty-nine-floor tower was added to its Greek-temple base, it became the city's tallest structure. When the Custom House was first built, Walt Whitman called it the noblest piece of commercial architecture in the world. The building is now a Marriott hotel and time-share. The observation tower can still be visited.

As you arrive at the waterfront, the three sights that greet you are Christopher Columbus Park (to the left), Long Wharf, and the redbrick Boston Marriott Long Wharf. (The latter is the chain's busiest, almost constantly full.) **Long Wharf** is Boston's oldest wharf, dating from 1710, and at one time extended all the way to Dock Square just below the Old State House at Faneuil Hall, almost where you began this walk—a good example of how much filling in of land has occurred since colonial days. **Columbus Park,** with its cobblestone walk and playground, is a pleasant place to relax and a good spot for kids to enjoy themselves.

One of the busiest parts of the waterfront is this Long Wharf/Central Wharf area, the starting point for many harbor cruises.

This is also the home of the city's most popular attraction, the **New England Aquarium.** You might want to watch the seals at play in front of the aquarium, or take a lunch or refreshment break at one of the many spots along here. Better still is to go inside the aquarium and marvel at its four-story ocean tank. The aquarium also has a 3-D theater adjacent to it with films running about an hour in length.

Long and Central Wharves are side by side. The Marriott Long Wharf is at the front of that wharf, and the aquarium is on Central. On the other side of the Marriott are docks for ferry boats to Charlestown and other areas of the city, as well as Columbus Park, which offers benches, shade, and a playground for children.

Just beyond the Marriott on the wharf is the Chart House Restaurant, originally built in its simple brick style in 1763, and, beyond it, the granite Custom House block (built in 1845), where Nathaniel Hawthorne served as an inspector.

Walking along the shoreline past the I. M. Pei–designed Harbor Towers condominiums, you will arrive at the **Rowes Wharf** complex of hotel, offices, and condominiums, highlighted by a grand arch in its center. The complex has become one of the most photographed scenes along the waterfront, and from its landing pier one can take lunch and dinner cruises and harbor tours.

Leaving Atlantic Avenue, turn left onto Northern Avenue, where you might detour to **James Hook and Company** to see thousands of lobsters waiting for shipment to stores and restaurants. The Hook company now lies

Waterfront Walk

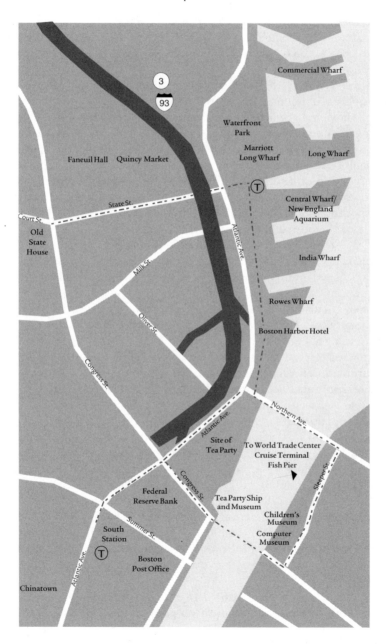

Commercial Wharf

Waterfront
Park

Marriott
Long Wharf

Long Wharf

Faneuil Hall   Quincy Market

State St.

Central Wharf/
New England
Aquarium

Court St.

Old
State
House

Atlantic Ave.

India Wharf

Milk St.

Oliver St.

Rowes Wharf

Boston Harbor Hotel

Congress St.

Northern Ave.

Atlantic Ave.

Site of
Tea Party

To World Trade Center
Cruise Terminal
Fish Pier

Congress St.

Sleeper St.

Federal
Reserve Bank

Tea Party Ship
and Museum

Children's
Museum

South
Station

Summer St.

Computer
Museum

Atlantic Ave.

Boston
Post Office

Chinatown

between a seventy-plus-year-old bridge to Northern Avenue and its replacement, the Evelyn Moakley Bridge. The city had been seeking someone to take the old bridge, but to date there have been no offers for the historic turn-style drawbridge. It's only open to foot traffic these days. To the left after crossing the bridge is **Fan Pier,** the site of the Joseph Moakley Federal Courthouse (Moakley was a former congressman from South Boston; the bridge is named for his wife). Along the pier is a Discovery Center for the harbor islands, and boats to Boston Light leave from here.

If you continue on Northern Avenue about a half mile, you will find the World Trade Center Boston on Commonwealth Pier, and, just beyond it, Fish Pier, where the catch of the day is still unloaded. Anthony's Pier 4, Jimmy's, and the No Name—three popular seafood restaurants—are along here. Across the way is the **Boston Convention & Exhibition Center.**

Turning right onto Sleeper Street, you will arrive at the **Children's Museum,** easily spotted with the giant wooden milk bottle in front. The museum is in a former warehouse, where leather and wool, for which this area was known, were stored.

The **Boston Tea Party Ship and Museum** is just beyond, on Congress Street, in the middle of Fort Point Channel. This is a good opportunity to learn more about the Boston Tea Party. The actual site of Griffin's Wharf, where the "party" occurred in 1773, is not far from here, at 470 Atlantic Avenue; a marker on the building locates the site.

Conclude your walk by continuing down Atlantic Avenue toward the massive granite **South Station,** the city's major railroad center; the Red Line of the subway is here as well. South Station was completely restored inside and out in the 1980s. It is now a grand place to stroll or to have lunch. There is a lively food court inside the spacious granite-enclosed structure that recalls the era when trains were the way to go. Many days there is live musical entertainment, making it a great place to stop whether you are boarding a train or not. On your way to South Station, you'll pass the new Federal Reserve Building (the white building with the hole in the middle), where tours are held to see the processing of checks and currency (see page 138).

DETOURS

From here you can take the subway back to your hotel, walk up Summer Street to Downtown Crossing, follow Congress Street back to the Old State House, or perhaps continue along the Surface Artery to Beach Street to enter Chinatown—one of the nation's largest—through its ceremonial gate. Or you could tour the Boston Harbor Islands, which are filled with history (see chapter 13), or take a cruise to Provincetown. Whale-watch and scenic cruises of Boston Harbor are also available.

Charlestown

Had the early Puritans not been thirsty for a good drink of water, Charlestown might have kept them instead of seeing them row across the Charles River to settle near the good spring of the Shawmut Peninsula.

Charlestown is a significant stop on the American history trail. Not only does it mark the site of the battle that turned the tide in the colonists' revolt against and separation from England, but it is also the home of the world's oldest battleship still in commission.

Charlestown Navy Yard is easy to reach. One can walk, following the painted or bricked red line of the Freedom Trail. Even easier is either to take the ferry to Charlestown from Long Wharf or to board a trolley tour that allows easy off-and-on access to the site.

THE USS *CONSTITUTION* AND THE CHARLESTOWN NAVY YARD

The best place to begin a visit to Charlestown is at the **Charlestown Navy Yard,** where the **USS** *Constitution,* the oldest battleship still in commission, can be visited. The forty-four-gun frigate was authorized in 1794 and launched from just across the water in the North End in 1797. It has fought in, and never lost, forty battles, including one in 1815 in which enemy fire

Charlestown Tour

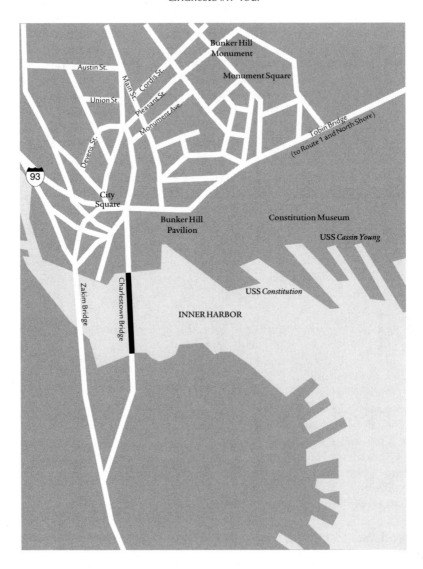

appeared to bounce off its sides, giving it the nickname "Old Ironsides." Although the ship's engagements took it around the world, its greatest days were during the War of 1812, when once again the enemy was Great Britain. At the Charlestown Navy Yard, crew members, all on active duty with the U.S. Navy, are dressed in 1812-style uniforms and guide visitors around the vessel, showing navy life as it was then. Each day at sunrise and sunset a cannon is fired.

Within a few feet of the vessel is the USS *Constitution* Museum, where you can "meet" the crew and learn how, in an era of no clocks, they could tell time; how the *Constitution* was built; and what life aboard the ship was like.

Moving to another era, visitors can board the USS *Cassin Young*, a destroyer built in 1943 and representing the 140 similar craft built at the Charlestown Navy Yard. A self-guided tour explains the workings of a destroyer.

In the know . . .

Many a Bostonian will smugly tell you that the Battle of Bunker Hill really took place on Breed's Hill. But I've never heard anyone explain why, if Breed's Hill was the setting, the battle has gone down in history as the Battle of Bunker Hill or why Breed's Hill contains a commanding obelisk called the Bunker Hill Monument. In 1775 Bunker Hill was the name given to the two heights of Charlestown. Breed's, a more recent name, referred to a lower ridge (62 feet, compared with Bunker Hill's 110-foot height), but since Breed's, being closer to the water than Bunker Hill, would prove to be more of a threat, the redoubts were placed there.

The Charlestown Navy Yard dates from 1800 and was used until 1974. During World War II, 50,000 persons were employed here, building and refitting ships for the war effort. The yard today is rapidly turning into a fashionable community of condominiums, shops, and marinas.

The yard's information center offers a slide show and exhibits. Among other sights are the Commandant's House, an exhibit by the Boston Marine Society, a dry dock, and Marine Corps barracks.

BUNKER HILL

Adjacent to the Charlestown Navy Yard is another prime attraction of Charlestown: Bunker Hill. Within the **Bunker Hill Pavilion** is *The Whites of*

Their Eyes, an excellent thirty-minute multimedia show re-creating the Battle of Bunker Hill and the events leading up to it. Lights flash, cannons roar, and "Paul Revere" narrates—providing an excellent introduction to a visit to Bunker Hill.

To reach the site of the battle, simply follow the red line of the Freedom Trail to Bunker Hill, about a fifteen-minute walk from Charlestown Navy Yard. The site is on trolley tours, and there is parking along the streets for those driving.

Although the Battle of Bunker Hill, which occurred on Saturday, June 17, 1775, was one the colonists eventually lost, it proved to be a turning point in the Revolution: His Majesty's troops, in their victory, suffered such a great loss of life—of the 2,200 British troops engaged, 1,054 were killed or wounded—that the win proved hollow, and the events that day sped up the British retreat from Boston.

If you have the energy, do take the fifteen-minute walk up to Bunker Hill. The 220-foot, 294-step monument can be climbed for a view of Boston and the surrounding area. The monument, designed by Solomon Willard in 1825, commemorates the battle at which Colonel William Prescott uttered the now-famous words "Don't . . . fire until you see the whites of their eyes." To build the monument, the nation's first railway was constructed, in Quincy to the south.

DETOURS

The **Warren Tavern** in Charlestown is where Paul Revere is known to have had a nip, as well as to have established a Masonic lodge; it is still open for lunch and dinner.

On the way to Charlestown, crossing the Charlestown Bridge, you will see to the left the **Colonel Richard Gridley Locks,** which control the water level in the Charles River Basin and keep it fresh. In colonial days, the river was a tidal one and ships would sail up it, as the British did. There are three locks here, as well as a fish passageway that allows the fish to swim unimpeded up the river to spawn. Within the Charles River Information Center are displays on the history of the area.

A New Symbol for Boston

The **Leonard P. Zakim Bunker Hill Bridge,** the sleek new bridge soaring over the Charles River, is a major connector in the Big Dig project linking Charlestown and areas north of the city with the downtown and areas south of the city. It is the widest cable-stayed bridge in the world. It is, however, relatively short for such a magnificent design.

Surprisingly, the $102 million for the bridge was spent not just to relieve traffic but also to leave no support columns in the river below, keeping it as open as possible to boaters and marine life. The Zakim bridge also has seventy diamond- and hexagonal-shaped holes all to allow light to filter through to the river just to prevent a shadow that, according to environmentalists, might have caused spawning alewife fishes to lose their way up the river.

A few facts: The bridge is 1,457 feet long and 330 feet at its highest point (the north tower; the south tower is just 295 feet high), has 215 miles of cables, is 185 feet wide, weighs 100,000 tons, and has six northbound and four southbound lanes.

How do you tell when you've reached the midpoint? Look at the cables. It is where those from the south tower end and those from the north tower begin.

And, just in case you were concerned, the bridge was designed to handle an earthquake of a magnitude up to 7.9 on the Richter scale and winds of up to 400 miles an hour.

Leonard P. Zakim, the bridge's namesake, was a civil rights activist and former head of the Anti-Defamation League who died of cancer in 1999 at the age of forty-six.

CHAPTER THIRTEEN

Boston Harbor Islands

It is amazing how far you can be from Boston yet still be so close to it on one of the islands of Boston Harbor. The islands offer all the beauty of more distant isles; they're full of history and wonderful tales of ghosts and pirates, as well as prominent Bostonians who once had lavish summer homes here that are remembered now only by an occasional foundation wall.

Best of all, the islands are easy to reach. From Long Wharf, next to the New England Aquarium, boat tours include a stop at George's Island, from which hardy explorers can obtain free water-taxi service to some of the other islands.

Although this chapter does not outline a specific walking tour of any of the islands, you will find much to do on a visit. You can camp, primitively, on some of the islands; swim (the harbor is far cleaner than it was a decade ago); hike; or relax far from the madding crowd, yet with Boston's magnificent skyline in view. And you can visit the nation's oldest lighthouse site—Boston Light, since 1716—where a pair of 1,000-watt bulbs shine a light visible for 27 miles out to sea.

The islands were formed more than 20,000 years ago, when melting glaciers raised the Atlantic Ocean's waters more than 300 feet. Some archaeologists say the islands have been a retreat for more than 7,000 years, but from colonial times to well past World War II, they were valued for strategic importance. Now they have been rediscovered.

The Boston Harbor Islands are now a National Park Area. The park consists of thirty islands ranging in size from less than an acre to more than 200 acres, totaling 1,200 acres in 50 square miles. The islands are from ¼ mile to 4 miles from the mainland. Seven of the islands are open to the public: George's, Grape, Lovell's, Bumpkin, Gallops, Little Brewster, and Spectacle. Entrance to the park is free. However, a charge is made for boat service to the islands.

In case you wondered . . .

Ghosts—Boston has a few. Touring the fort on George's Island, you might meet the Lady in Black. Or you could take a ride on the world's only streetcar to run right through a cemetery—the Red Line from Ashmont to Mattapan—since a ghost is said to haunt the section of track that runs through Cedar Grove Cemetery. As the story goes, the ghost is that of a caretaker who devoted his life to caring for the cemetery, was devastated when tracks were laid through it, and died a broken man. Trolley drivers have reported seeing his face on nights when the fog rolls in from the Neponset River. Thus, to scare off the ghost, the drivers now clang the trolley bell through this stretch of track.

Most popular and convenient of the islands is **George's Island,** where Fort Warren, built in the mid-nineteenth century, lies. The fort is famous as a prison for Confederate soldiers during the Civil War, though its massive fortifications have otherwise been little utilized. You can climb the fort, take in the view to Boston, watch the planes landing at Logan, participate in one of the many programs that now take place here, or use the island as a jumping-off point to take a free water taxi to islands where camping is permitted. Or you can enjoy the chills of the tale of the Lady in Black, who, disguised as a man, came to rescue her Confederate husband but killed him by mistake instead of the fort commander. Caught and sentenced to die, she chose to wear black, and for years guards at night would report seeing her ghostly presence. If you take the *Edward Rowe Snow* to the island, you might want to look up one of Snow's books, as the Lady in Black was a favorite story of this author, and he loved to hide a person in her supposed grave, having the person suddenly leap from cover at just the right moment.

Boston Harbor Islands

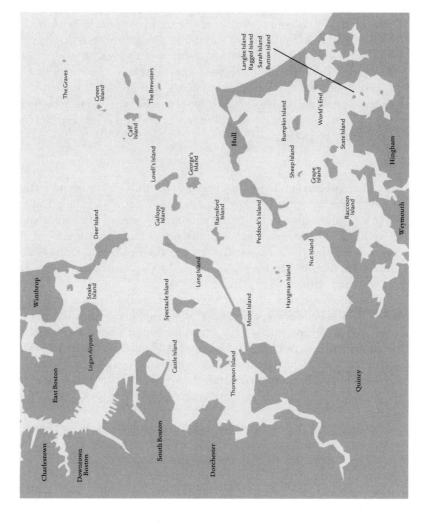

Charlestown

Downtown Boston

East Boston

Logan Airport

Winthrop

Snake Island

South Boston

Castle Island

Deer Island

Spectacle Island

Long Island

Thompson Island

Moon Island

Dorchester

Gallops Island

Rainsford Island

Hangman Island

Nut Island

Peddock's Island

Lovell's Island

George's Island

Calf Island

The Brewsters

Green Island

The Graves

Hull

Sheep Island

Bumpkin Island

Grape Island

Raccoon Island

World's End

State Island

Hingham

Weymouth

Quincy

Langlee Island
Ragged Island
Sarah Island
Button Island

In the know . . .

There is a wilderness adventure experience in view of the Boston skyline. Camping is available on Bumpkin, Grape, and Lovell's by permit only. Lovell's is free, while there is a charge on Grape and Bumpkin. Each island offers ten sites and one group area. The islands have toilet facilities, picnic areas, and piers, but no drinking water is available. There is free water-taxi service to the islands from George's, where water is available. George's Island is reached by boat from Long Wharf.

In 2004 **Spectacle Island** was opened to the public. The island features a marina, visitor center, two sandy beaches, and 5 miles of hiking trails that lead to a 157-foot-high hill, offering panoramic views of the harbor and the city. In the 1920s Boston began using the island as a dump, adding thirty acres to it. In the 1990s fill excavated from the Big Dig and Ted Williams Tunnel were used to cap the island. Then 2 to 5 feet of topsoil was laid to grow trees and shrubs.

Little Brewster, where Boston Light stands, is the farthest island. Other islands include **Peddock's,** where 1,800 Italian soldiers were interned during World War II; **Grape,** named for the vines found there in colonial days; **Bumpkin,** with its raspberry bushes and wild rabbits; **Great Brewster,** a rugged isle with views as far as Plymouth; and **Lovell's,** a favorite with migrating birds. **Thompson Island,** with hills, meadows, beaches, and a pristine salt marsh, is used as a conference center and for Outward Bound courses.

Boston Light, the nation's oldest lighthouse site and the last staffed by the U.S. Coast Guard, can be visited and climbed on weekends in season. The original light was built in 1713 but was destroyed by the British when they evacuated Boston in 1776. The present light dates from 1783, with a major renovation adding seventy-six spiral stairs to the lantern completed in 1844. At its base one can see the first "fog horn" in North America—a cannon. The boathouse has a museum with lighthouse memorabilia. Boston Harbor Light cruises are operated from Fan Pier and the John F. Kennedy Library.

Two other islands are accessible by land. **Deer Island,** which includes the city's new Treatment Plant, has 4.6 miles of trails and hills with great views of Boston. It is accessible through Winthrop. **Nut Island,** off Quincy, has walking trails and a fish pier. Also part of the park is World's End in Hingham, a 251-acre peninsula with 5 miles of carriage paths and trails and more magnificent views of Boston Harbor.

Since the park islands offer little shelter, visitors should be prepared for sudden squalls or wind and cool temperatures. Good walking shoes, hats, and sunscreen are recommended.

On some of the islands camping, although somewhat primitive, is allowed. There are island ranger programs ranging from historic theme walks to scavenger hunts. Picnicking is another activity on the islands. Bring your own food or purchase items on George's Island. On the second Thursday of July and August, free trips to George's Island are offered.

Boston Light tours are offered Saturday and Sunday from the Discovery Center in the Moakley Courthouse at Fan Pier. Thursday and Friday tours are offered from the John F. Kennedy Library.

Kayak tours of the Harbor Islands and Boston waterfront are offered for all skill levels. Rentals and instruction are available.

For information on the Harbor Islands, call 223-8666 or visit the information kiosk at Long Wharf near the New England Aquarium.

Ferry service to George's Island, 223-8666

Thompson Island information, 328-3900

World's End, (781) 740-7233

PART THREE

THE
ATTRACTIONS

What to See While in Boston

Boston's Attractions and Museums

Alexander Graham Bell Exhibit, Verizon Building, 185 Federal Street, Boston (across from the Langham Hotel). Open Monday through Friday from 8:30 A.M. to 5:00 P.M. On weekends, ask the guard, as he may allow you to enter the exhibit, which is located just inside the lobby entrance. Free. The birthplace of the telephone has been preserved not in its original location but near the spot in Boston where Alexander Graham Bell invented the phone. The attic room and laboratory, which were located at the present site of the John F. Kennedy Federal Office Building in Government Center, have been re-created—using the materials from Bell's laboratory—as an exhibit in the lobby of the Verizon Building. Even the view from Bell's original lab has been preserved. You can see his workbench and tools, the first switchboard, and replicas of the first telephones. (The setting is referred to as the garret, in case no one knows it as Bell's lab.)

Black Heritage Trail, Boston African American National Site, 14 Beacon Street, Boston. Telephone 725-0022. From Memorial Day through Labor Day, tours leave from the Robert Gould Shaw Memorial at Park and Beacon

Streets (across from the State House), at 10:00 A.M., noon, and 2:00 P.M. daily. Tours at other times by reservation. With its fourteen sights, primarily on Beacon Hill, the Black Heritage Trail presents an easy and informative way to discover blacks' contributions to Boston history. Included on the trail are the African Meeting House, at 8 Smith Court; the oldest black church building in America; and the Robert Gould Shaw and Fifty-fourth Regiment Memorial, a magnificent bas-relief by Augustus Saint-Gaudens, across from the State House.

Boston Athenaeum, 10½ Beacon Street, Boston. Telephone 227-0270. Tours are held on Tuesday and Thursday at 3:00 P.M. The Gallery on the second floor is open to the public and contains changing exhibitions. One of the oldest private libraries in the nation, it contains the books of George Washington. Its collection also includes distinguished books on literature, art, and early America.

Boston Common, America's oldest public park and the starting place of the Freedom Trail. Cows once roamed here, now a nice oasis in the heart of the city. Across from it is the Public Garden, home to the famed Swan Boats.

Boston Public Library, 700 Boylston Street, Copley Square, Boston. Telephone 536-5400. Open Monday through Thursday from 9:00 A.M. to 9:00 P.M., Friday and Saturday from 9:00 A.M. to 5:00 P.M., and Sunday from 1:00 to 5:00 P.M. (See page 86.)

Boston Tea Party Ship and Museum, Congress Street Bridge, Boston. Telephone 338-1773. Open daily from 9:00 A.M. to 6:00 P.M. Admission is $8.00 for adults, $7.00 for students and children ages four through twelve, and free for kids age three or younger. Here's your chance to toss some "tea" into Boston Harbor from a boat that is a replica of those used at the time. Shows are held every thirty minutes.

Bunker Hill Monument, Monument Square, Charlestown, on the Freedom Trail. Telephone 242-5641. Free. Take the 294 steps to the top of this monument, which commemorates the 1775 Battle of Bunker Hill. Open daily from 9:00 A.M. to 5:00 P.M.

Bunker Hill Pavilion, 55 Constitution Road, Charlestown. Telephone 241-7575. Offers a multimedia presentation titled *The Whites of Their Eyes.* Open daily from 9:30 A.M. to 4:30 P.M.; shows on the half-hour. Admission is $3.00 for adults, $1.50 for children sixteen and under, and $2.00 for senior citizens.

Children's Museum, Museum Wharf, 300 Congress Street, Boston. Telephone 426-8855 for the "What's Up?" line. Open daily from 10:00 A.M. to 5:00 P.M., Friday until 9:00 P.M. Admission is $9.00 for adults, $7.00 for seniors and children ages two through fifteen, and $2.00 for one-year-olds; admission Friday from 5:00 to 9:00 P.M. costs $1.00 for all ages. Definitely a

An alleyway on Beacon Hill

©2004 NOVA DEVELOPMENT

The Christian Science Center

©2004 NOVA DEVELOPMENT

The Hampshire House and Cheers pub ©DAVID NOBLE/PICTURES COLOUR LIBRARY

The State House ©DAVID NOBLE/PICTURES COLOUR LIBRARY

Quincy Market

A view of Back Bay

Newbury Street

John F. Kennedy Library

The Public Garden

Fenway Park

Bunker Hill Monument
©2004 NOVA DEVELOPMENT

The Prudential Center
©2004 NOVA DEVELOPMENT

Boston Harbor

Robert Gould Shaw Memorial, Beacon Hill

Statue of Paul Revere and the Old North Church
COURTESY GREATER BOSTON CONVENTION AND VISITORS BUREAU, INC.

Quick Draw

You can visit artists in their studios at the Fort Point Arts Community, just behind the Children's Museum. For information, call 423-4299. The office is at 300 Summer Street, South Boston.

hands-on place for little fingers. The young ones can visit "Grandparents' Attic" and try on period clothing; be on TV; explore Arthur's World; truck into the Construction Zone; tour a Japanese house brought piece by piece from Kyoto, Boston's sister city in Japan; test their skills on a giant Climbing Maze; or just blow bubbles. Outside the building there is a giant 40-foot milk bottle, which serves, as it once did along the Massachusetts highway, as a refreshment stand. Inside there is a McDonald's.

Chinatown, Boston. The nation's third-largest Chinatown is in a compact area just a couple of blocks from Downtown Crossing. Guarding Chinatown at its Beach Street entrance off the surface artery are four marble Chinese Foo dogs that sit at the base of a tile-and-marble gateway arch, gifts to the city from the people of Taiwan. The dogs protect the neighborhood.

Christian Science Center, Massachusetts Avenue by the Prudential Center, Boston. Telephone 450-7300. Home of the Mother Church of the First Church of Christ, Scientist. (See pages 132–33.)

Commonwealth Museum, Massachusetts Archives Building, 200 Morrissey Boulevard, Dorchester. Telephone 727-9268. Open Monday through Friday from 9:00 A.M. to 5:00 P.M. and the second and fourth Saturday of each month from 9:00 A.M. to 3:00 P.M. Free. The state's early charters, proclamations, and other colonial papers can be viewed in the Massachusetts Archives. The Commonwealth Museum offers changing exhibits on the people and history of Massachusetts.

Copp's Hill Burying Ground, Snowhill and Hull Streets in the North End, Boston. Established in the 1660s, buried here are Cotton Mather and Edward Hartt, builder of the USS *Constitution,* which can be seen from here. The British used the stones for a firing range.

Custom House, 3 McKinley Square, Boston. Telephone 310-6300. Once Boston's tallest building, it was used in the nineteenth century as a counting house. The Marriott Corporation has preserved the building and now uses it as a luxury hotel. Visit the twenty-sixth-floor open-air observation deck for fine views of Boston Harbor and the North End. Historical exhibits are found in the Rotunda Museum.

Dreams of Freedom Cultural Exhibit Center, 1 Milk Street, Boston. Telephone 338-6022. Located in the International Institute of Boston, this is also the site of Benjamin Franklin's birthplace. Open daily from 9:30 A.M. to 6:00 P.M. Admission is $7.50 for adults, $6.50 for senior citizens and college students, and $3.50 for children. The exhibit covers two floors and includes a map of the world illustrating the diversity of the people who have molded the face of Boston. Inside a replica of a ship are trunks and suitcases that can be opened to discover the secrets of their owners. There is also a multimedia show that retraces immigration to Boston from the Pilgrims to the present.

Faneuil Hall, Government Center on the Freedom Trail, Boston. Built in 1742, the scene of early meetings on the Revolution and still used for public gatherings. Open daily from 9:00 A.M. to 5:00 P.M. The Ancient and Honorable Artillery Company Museum on the fourth floor is closed weekends. (See page 65.)

Franklin Park Zoo, Franklin Park Road, Boston. Telephone 541–LION (541–5466). Open Monday through Friday from 10:00 A.M. to 5:00 P.M. and Saturday and Sunday from 10:00 A.M. to 6:00 P.M.; October through March 10:00 A.M. to 4:00 P.M. daily. Admission is $9.50 for adults, $8.00 for seniors, and $5.00 for children ages two through fifteen. The zoo houses the African Tropical Forest, the largest tropical forest in the United States, with more than 150 animals and fifty species, including gorillas. Also to be seen is Birds' World, Butterfly Landing ($1.00 additional charge), and Hoofs and Horns, with animals from camels to zebras. The children's zoo includes a New England farm-animal exhibit and contact barn.

Gibson House, 137 Beacon Street, Boston. Telephone 267-6338. Open for tours Saturday and Sunday at 1:00, 2:00, and 3:00 P.M. Admission $5.00. The home is filled with eighteenth-century furnishings. It is like stepping into the Victorian age. Complete with bells in the basement to summon the servants.

Granary Burying Ground, Tremont Street, Boston, on the Freedom Trail. This burial site is the final resting place of Paul Revere, Samuel Adams, John Hancock, Crispus Attucks, Benjamin Franklin's parents, and Mary Goose.

Harrison Gray Otis House, 141 Cambridge Street, Boston. Telephone 227-3956. Open Wednesday through Sunday from 11:00 A.M. to 4:00 P.M. Admission is $5.00 for adults, $4.00 for seniors, and $2.50 for students and children ages six through twelve; free to Boston residents. Built in 1796 by Charles Bulfinch, the house has classic architecture, elegant furnishings, and other features to highlight the Federal style of the eighteenth century. Headquarters of the Society for the Preservation of New England Antiquities.

Institute of Contemporary Art, 955 Boylston Street, Boston. Telephone 266-5152. Open Tuesday, Wednesday, and Friday from noon to 5:00 P.M., Saturday and Sunday from 11:00 A.M. to 5:00 P.M., Thursday from noon to 9:00 P.M. Admission is $7.00 for adults, $5.00 for seniors and students, and free for children under twelve. Admission on Thursday from 5:00 to 9:00 P.M. is free to all. Founded in 1936, this is the oldest institution in the country dedicated solely to the presentation of contemporary art. Changing exhibits devoted to twentieth-century art, video, and photography.

Isabella Stewart Gardner Museum, 280 The Fenway, Boston. Telephone 566–1401. Open Tuesday through Sunday from 11:00 A.M. to 5:00 P.M. Admission is $10.00 for adults ($11.00 Saturday and Sunday), $7.00 for seniors, $5.00 for students age eighteen or older with ID ($3.00 on Wednesday), and free for youths age seventeen or younger. Free to all with the first name Isabella. Guided tours Friday at 2:30 P.M. By T, Green Line to Museum of Fine Arts; then walk 1½ blocks north on Louis Prang Street. Certainly one of Boston's must-visit museums. Designed in the style of a fifteenth-century Venetian palace, the museum is filled with treasures and art from Europe, including paintings by Rembrandt and Titian, as well as by American painters Sargent and Whistler, friends of Mrs. Gardner. The museum stands as the personal expression of a woman whose prominence and individuality punctuated Boston society in the late 1800s. Since Mrs. Gardner left the museum to the city with the stipulation that the museum must remain as she left it with no painting sold or purchased, there are some blank spots on the walls marked with discreet cards. These spaces mark where some $200 million worth of art, including two Rembrandts and five works by Degas, were stolen in 1990 in a still-unsolved mystery.

John F. Kennedy Birthplace, 83 Beals Street, Brookline. Telephone 566–7937. Open May 12 to September 26, Wednesday through Sunday from 10:00 A.M. to 4:30 P.M. Admission is $3.00 for those age seventeen or older, free for sixteen or younger. The house has been restored to look as it did in 1917. Tours from downtown Boston are offered by Old Town Trolley.

John F. Kennedy Library and Museum, Columbia Point, Boston. Telephone 514–1600. Open from 9:00 A.M. to 5:00 P.M. daily. Admission is $10.00 for adults, $8.00 for seniors and students, $7.00 for youths age thirteen through seventeen, and free for children age twelve or younger. Free parking. By car, take the Southeast Expressway to exit 15 and follow the signs. By T, take the Red Line to JFK/UMass Station and then a free shuttle bus to the library. The story of the thirty-fifth American president is movingly told in a film and exhibits. Kennedy family memorabilia is included. From the striking I. M. Pei–designed building along the edge of Boston Harbor, striking views of the Boston skyline can be seen.

King's Chapel and Burying Ground, Tremont and School Streets on the Freedom Trail, Boston. Telephone 227–2155. Church is open Memorial Day to Veterans Day, Monday, Thursday, and Friday from 9:00 A.M. to 4:00 P.M. and Saturday all-year from 9:00 A.M. to 4:00 P.M. A donation of $2.00 is suggested. Classical music most Tuesdays at 12:15 P.M. (suggested donation of $3.00), Sundays at 5:00 P.M. (suggested donation of $12.00, $6.00 seniors and students). Buried in the adjacent cemetery are William Dawes, who, along with Revere, rode to Lexington; and Mary Chilton, the first Pilgrim to step upon Plymouth Rock.

Larz Anderson Auto Museum, 15 Newton Street, Brookline. Telephone 522-6547. Open Tuesday through Sunday from 10:00 A.M. to 5:00 P.M. Admission is $7.00 for adults; $5.00 for children ages six through sixteen, students, and seniors; and free for kids age five or younger. The museum is located in a grand old carriage house once part of the Larz Anderson estate. Inside are some of the oldest vehicles in the country, once owned by the Andersons. Also many changing automotive exhibits. In summer there are wonderful Lawn Shows featuring vehicles from Germany, Italy, and the United States.

Mugar Memorial Library, Boston University, 771 Commonwealth Avenue, Boston. Telephone 353-3696. The Howard Gotlieb Archival Research Center within the library contains personal papers and memorabilia of twentieth-century people, ranging from Theodore Roosevelt and Bette Davis to Martin Luther King Jr. Rotating exhibits throughout the building showcase the center's holdings from various collections. Open Monday through Friday 9:00 A.M. to 5:00 P.M.

Museum of Afro American History, 46 Joy Street, Boston. Telephone 725-0022. Open daily from 10:00 A.M. to 4:00 P.M. Free. Includes the African Meeting House, the oldest standing black church building in the United States, at 8 Smith Court. The museum was founded to study the social history of New England's African-American communities. Beacon Hill was once one of those.

Museum of Fine Arts, 465 Huntington Avenue, Boston. Telephone 267-9300. Open Saturday to Tuesday from 10:00 A.M. to 4:45 P.M., Wednesday through Friday from 10:00 A.M. to 9:45 P.M. (Thursday and Friday after 5:00 P.M., only West Wing is open). Admission is $15 for adults, $13 for students age eighteen or older and seniors, and free for youths age seventeen or younger; voluntary contribution Wednesday after 4:00 P.M., $2.00 discount Thursday and Friday after 5:00 P.M. Parking is available for a fee. By T, take the Green Line to Museum. The museum has extensive collections of European and American art, featuring forty-three Monets and paintings by Renoir, Rembrandt, Pissarro, Manet, Whistler, Sargent (the museum is the only place in the United States with murals by Sargent), and Hassam; twentieth-century artists include Motherwell, Picasso, Miró, Pollack, and Morris Louis. Its Egyptian collection is considered second only to the Cairo Museum's, partly the result of a forty-year, museum-sponsored expedition. The Boston museum has classical objects dating from 490 B.C. and Etruscan sarcophagi. Its Asiatic art collection is unmatched in the world and includes the Temple Room, with Buddhist deities. The collection of silver is vast and contains works by Paul Revere. Furnishings, decorative arts, and sculptures are among the treasures to be found here. Tenshin-En, the Garden of the Heart of Heaven, contains seventy species of plants of Japanese and American origin. Outside the museum's main entrance is a dramatic bronze statue, *Appeal to the Great Spirit,* by Cyrus E. Dallin; the statue received a gold medal at the Paris Salon of 1909. The museum contains three restaurants: the Galleria Cafe, a cafeteria, and the Fine Arts Restaurant. And don't leave without visiting the Museum Shop, which offers some extraordinary gifts and souvenirs.

Museum of Science, Science Park, Boston. Telephone 723-2500. Open Saturday through Thursday 9:00 A.M. to 7:00 P.M., Friday 9:00 A.M. to 9:00 P.M. Admission to exhibit halls is $14 adults, $12 seniors sixty and older, $11 children three to eleven. Tickets to the Mugar Omni Theater, Planetarium or Laser show are $8.50 adults, $7.50 seniors, $6.50 children. Combination tickets to the exhibit halls and a show or to two shows that cut the cost substantially are available. Parking is available for a fee in the museum garage. By T, take the Green Line (Lechmere) to Science Park Station. A world-renowned museum with something for everyone. Includes the Mugar Omni Theater, where films are shown on a giant domed screen that fills the auditorium with spectacular views and sound; the Hayden Planetarium, which features seasonal views; and a laser show. More than 600 exhibits and frequent traveling shows of significance. A hands-on museum with physical science demonstrations and computer exhibits. Also a food court and wonderful shop.

Museum of the Ancient and Honorable Artillery Company, Fourth Floor, Faneuil Hall, Boston. Telephone 227-1638. Open Monday through Friday from 9:00 A.M. to 3:30 P.M. Admission free. Contains memorabilia of the nation's oldest military organization, including a cannon used by the British at Yorktown in 1783.

Museum of the National Center of Afro-American Artists, 300 Walnut Avenue, Roxbury. Telephone 442-8014. Open Tuesday through Sunday from 1:00 to 5:00 P.M. Admission is $4.00 for adults, $3.00 for students and seniors, and free for children ages four or younger. Contains collections and exhibitions of black visual art heritage worldwide.

New England Aquarium, Central Wharf, Boston. Telephone 973-5200. Open Monday through Thursday 9:00 A.M. to 6:00 P.M. and Friday through Sunday 9:00 A.M. to 7:00 P.M. Admission is $15.95 adults, $13.95 seniors, $8.95 children three to eleven, free for children under three. Perhaps Boston's most popular attraction, located right on the waterfront. Has a huge four-story glass ocean tank that houses sharks, sea turtles, and a variety of fish.

There are coral displays and a hands-on area. Just outside the aquarium is the 3-D Simons IMAX Theatre; telephone (866) 815–IMAX (4629) for schedule and tickets. Admission to the IMAX show is $8.95 adults, $6.95 seniors and children three to eleven.

New England Historic Genealogical Society, 101 Newbury Street, Boston. Telephone 536–5740. The society is the nation's leading private institution dedicated to the collection, preservation, and publication of material relating to family and local history. The first-floor rotunda serves as the Orientation Center. A Family Treasures bookstore on the first floor carries a wide variety of genealogical publications.

Nichols House Museum, 55 Mt. Vernon Street, Boston. Telephone 227–6993. Open Tuesday through Saturday from 12:15 to 4:15 P.M. Admission $5.00; free to children ages eleven or younger. Rose Standish Nichols left this four-story town house—built in 1804 and designed by Charles Bulfinch—just as she had lived in it. Furnishings include works by Augustus Saint-Gaudens, a cousin.

The **Old Corner Bookstore building,** 1 School Street, Boston, on the Freedom Trail. Once the Old Corner Bookstore, this was the meeting place of eighteenth-century authors who made the city the "Athens of America."

Old North Church, Christ Church, 193 Salem Street, on the Freedom Trail, Boston. Telephone 523–6676. Boston's oldest church, built in 1729, it was from its steeple that lanterns were placed to warn Paul Revere if the British were traveling by land or sea. Open daily from 9:00 A.M. to 5:00 P.M. except during services Sunday at 9:00 and 11:00 A.M. Suggested donation is $3.00 Behind the Scenes tour includes a visit to the crypt and bell tower ($8.00 adults, $4.00 children). Services on Sunday at 9:00 and 11:00 A.M.

Old South Meeting House, 310 Washington Street, on the Freedom Trail, Boston. Telephone 482–6439. Open daily from 9:30 A.M. to 5:00 P.M. Admission is $5.00 for adults, $4.00 for seniors and students age eighteen or older with ID, $1.00 for youths ages six through seventeen, and free for children age five or younger. This is where the Tea Party began, where Benjamin Franklin was baptized, and where many of the fiery debates of the Revolution were housed. Offers interactive exhibits and has a nice shop with Boston souvenirs.

Old State House Museum, State and Washington Streets, on the Freedom Trail, Boston. Telephone 720–1713. Open daily from 9:00 A.M. to 6:00 P.M. Admission is $5.00 for adults, $4.00 for seniors and students, $1.00 for children six to eighteen, and free to children age five or younger, Boston seniors, and Massachusetts schoolchildren. The museum has a collection of items relating to the city's heritage, ship models, and Revolutionary War artifacts. Outside is the site of the Boston Massacre.

Park Street Church, 1 Park Street, Boston. Telephone 523–3383. Tours July and August. Services Sunday at 8:30 and 11:00 A.M. and 4:00 and 6:00 P.M. Tours Tuesday to Saturday 9:30 A.M. to 3:30 P.M. Built in 1809, this church is often called Brimstone Corner, not for its preaching but for the gunpowder that was stored inside during the War of 1812. It is from here that the first missionaries to Hawaii left and where the hymn "America" was first sung.

Paul Revere House, 19 North Square, on the Freedom Trail in the North End, Boston. Telephone 523–2328. Open from 9:30 A.M. to 5:15 P.M. Admission is $3.00 adults, $2.50 seniors and students, $1.00 children five to seventeen, and free for children age four or younger. Built in 1680, this is the oldest house in Boston. Paul Revere bought it in 1770 and raised sixteen children here (not all at the same time).

Pierce-Hichborn House, 19 North Square, adjacent to the Paul Revere House, Boston. Telephone 523–1676. Tours daily. Combination tickets with Revere house available. Built in 1711, it is one of the city's oldest brick structures and a fine example of Georgian architecture.

Prudential Skywalk Observation Deck, 800 Boylston Street, Boston. Telephone 859–0648. Open daily from 10:00 A.M. to 10:00 P.M. Admission is $9.50 for adults, $7.00 seniors, and $6.50 for children. The skywalk offers the only 360-degree view of Boston and beyond from its fiftieth floor. Great view of Fenway Park.

Sports Museum of New England, fifth- and sixth-floor premium seating levels, FleetCenter, Causeway Street, Boston. Telephone 624–1234. Open Tuesday through Saturday from 11:00 A.M. to 5:00 P.M., Sunday from noon to 5:00 P.M. Admission is $6.00 for adults, $4.00 for seniors and youths ages six through seventeen, and free for children age five or younger. Honors New England athletes and teams through artwork, video footage, memorabila, and interactive exhibits.

State House, opposite Boston Common, on the Freedom Trail, Boston. Telephone 727–3676. Free tours are offered Monday through Saturday from 10:00 A.M. to 3:30 P.M. Designed by Charles Bulfinch and completed in 1798, it features a twenty-three-karat gilded dome with an underlayer of copper installed by Paul Revere.

Swan Boats, the Public Garden, Boston. Telephone 522–1966. Seasonal. Open daily from 10:00 A.M. to 4:00 P.M. Admission is $2.50 for adults, $2.00 for seniors, and $1.00 for children ages two through fifteen; free for children under age two. You haven't seen Boston until you ride the Swan Boats. Since 1877 these swan-shaped boats have glided through the lagoon by pedal power only.

Trinity Church, Copley Square, Boston. Telephone 536-0944. Open daily. Sunday services at 7:45, 9:00, and 11:00 A.M. and 6:00 P.M. Magnificent choir. Designed by Henry Hobson Richardson, this church is considered one of the most beautiful in the United States. Built in 1877, its interior was decorated by John La Farge and includes five of his windows. Its ninth rector, Phillips Brooks, wrote the Christmas carol "O Little Town of Bethlehem." His statue, by Augustus Saint-Gaudens, is outside.

USS *Constitution,* Boston National Historic Park, Charlestown Navy Yard, on the Freedom Trail. Telephone 242-5671. Open Tuesday to Sunday 10:00 A.M. to 4:00 P.M. Free. The world's oldest commissioned warship. This fifty-two-gun frigate never lost a battle and is called "Old Ironsides" because cannonballs bounced off its oak sides.

USS *Constitution* Museum, Navy Yard, Charlestown. Telephone 426-1812. Open daily from 10:00 A.M. to 5:00 P.M. Admission free. Gallery tours on the half hour from 12:30 to 3:30 P.M. The museum contains artifacts and exhibits on the USS *Constitution* and claims the largest gift shop on the Freedom Trail.

Boston for Free

Many of the attractions listed in this chapter are free, either at all times or at designated times. In addition, consider the following:

Following the redbrick line, take the Freedom Trail walk (see chapter 7).

It's not the Panama Canal, but Boston has its locks that raise and lower boats into and out of the Charles River (see page 110).

What's a dry dock? Visit the Charlestown Navy Yard to find out (see page 109).

Check out the *Boston Globe*'s "Calendar" section on Thursday and the "Arts Etc." section on Sunday to learn about many free events. Look, too, for outstanding speakers and programs at area colleges; many are free and open to the public.

Go for a swim. Boston has lots of beaches, all free, and many with bathhouses (see pages 191–92).

Live vicariously: Do some window-shopping in Copley Place or along Newbury or Boylston Streets.

People-watch—sit on a bench at Faneuil Hall Marketplace (maybe join Mayor James Michael Curley or the great Celtics coach Red Auerbach on their bench) or the Public Garden watching children frolic on the *Make Way for Ducklings* statues.

Enjoy the street performers at Downtown Crossing or Faneuil Hall Marketplace.

MetroParks has happenings at its parks and beaches throughout Greater Boston. Call 727-5215 for information.

Ever want to play on a major roadway? Memorial Drive in Cambridge has a section closed on summer Sundays for just that purpose. You can bicycle, in-line skate, or stroll to your heart's content without worrying about car traffic.

Go gallery viewing along famed Newbury Street.

Join the fun of a summer street festival in the North End (see page 234).

Listen to a free faculty or student concert at Berklee College of Music or the New England Conservatory of Music (see page 169).

Picnic along Boston Harbor or the Charles River.

Walk anywhere in Boston; use the walks in this book for a day of fun.

Find out what takes place on Beacon Hill or in the chambers of New City Hall.

Go plaque hunting in Boston—it seems as if every other building has a historical marker.

Explore the Northeast's largest fortification open to the public, Fort Warren, on George's Island (see page 114).

Churches

Boston was founded by the Puritans for religious freedom, yet they themselves soon proved to be intolerant to those who did not believe as they did. Roger Williams, for one, soon left the colony for Rhode Island, where he founded the Baptist Church.

Unlike other cities, churches in Boston have figured prominently in events that have shaped the nation. From the steeple of **Old North Church (Christ Church)** were hung the lanterns to signal Paul Revere of the approach of

British Redcoats on their way to Concord and Lexington and the start of the War for Independence. The **Old South Meeting House** was once the church where Benjamin Franklin was baptized and the Boston Tea Party began (the church, the new Old South Church, has since moved to Copley Square), and **Park Street Church** became known for its early stand against slavery. It is also the site of the first Sunday school, where "America" ("My Country 'Tis of Thee") was first sung, and from which the first missionaries to Hawaii left. **King's Chapel,** built in 1749 from mail-order plans, has a simple beauty that hides the anger Puritans had at having an Anglican church in their community. British troops once used it as a stable. It later became the first Unitarian church in the country.

Other churches of historical interest include **Old West Church,** which lost its steeple when the British tore it down to prevent its use as a signal tower. John F. Kennedy voted here during his presidential campaign. **St. Stephen's Roman Catholic Church** is the only remaining church by Charles Bulfinch in Boston. **Trinity Church** in Copley Square, designed by famed architect H. H. Richardson, is considered one of the finest examples of church architecture in the United States. Trinity's first rector, Phillips Brooks, wrote the famed Christmas carol "O Little Town of Bethlehem."

For information on daily church services, including Sunday, see page 40, see your hotel concierge, or call. Most of these churches are open daily, particularly in summer, for visits. And note that many churches offer free concerts at noon; check newspaper listings for time and location.

On the Freedom Trail
King's Chapel, 64 Beacon Street; 523–1749
Old North Church, 193 Salem Street; 523–6676
Old South Meeting House, 310 Washington Street; 482–6439
Park Street Church, 1 Park Street; 523–3383
St. Stephen's Roman Catholic Church, 401 Salem Street; 523–1230

Other Locations
Old South Church, Copley Square; 536–1970
Old West Church, 131 Cambridge Street; 227–5088
Trinity Church, Copley Square; 536–0944

THE CHRISTIAN SCIENCE CENTER

The Christian Science Center near Copley Square is a testament to one woman's faith. Mary Baker Eddy founded the Christian Science Church in 1866. She was then age forty-five and frail. She turned to the New Testament for inspiration after suffering a fall near her home in Lynn. Eddy not only healed but also found many of her earlier illnesses cured. She continued her

Bible study and at the same time began to heal others. From this practice the Christian Science faith began, and Eddy, at the age of eighty-seven, founded the respected *Christian Science Monitor.* Her book, *Science and Health,* which teaches an approach to spirituality and health, has become one of the best-selling books of its kind ever published and recently has found new popularity, epecially in developing countries.

While membership in the Christian Science faith is small, the church has a huge presence in Boston. Covering more than fifteen acres adjacent to the Prudential Center, its world headquarters consists of the Mother Church, its publishing house, a large reflecting pool, and offices designed by renowned architect I. M. Pei.

Until 2002, the center's most notable attraction to tourists had been its Mapparium, a glass globe of the world built in 1935 and still displaying the nations of that era, many of which have disappeared. The **Mapparium** is now the centerpiece of the Mary Baker Eddy Library for the Betterment of Humanity, illustrating through sound, music, and lighting how ideas have traversed time and geography and changed the world.

The entire library is designed to explore the power of ideas that inspire individuals and change the world. Entering the library, visitors travel through the Hall of Ideas and view a fountain that serves as a wellspring of an ever-changing flow of quotations. On the second floor the Monitor Gallery overlooks the newsroom of the Pulitzer Prize–winning paper. The library also makes available for the first time the Mary Baker Eddy Collections, one of the largest by and about an American woman. There are interactive exhibits, a shop, and a cafe for refreshment.

Christian Scientists have been criticized for putting too much faith in church healers rather than medicine. The library holds promise of giving insight into the church, Eddy, and her beliefs. No matter what, the Mapparium is well worth a visit.

The Mary Baker Eddy Library for the Betterment of Humanity, which includes the Mapparium, is open Tuesday through Friday from 10:00 A.M. to 9:00 P.M., Saturday from 10:00 A.M. to 5:00 P.M., and Sunday from 11:00 A.M. to 7:00 P.M. Admission is $5.00 for adults; $3.00 for seniors, students, and children ages six through twelve; and free for children ages five or younger. Call 450-7300.

Parks and Recreation Areas

Maybe it was the openness of Boston Common that started it all, but one thing is sure: Boston has more open space and wilderness areas within and just beyond it than perhaps any other city in the nation.

The Emerald Necklace, designed by Frederick Law Olmsted (who also designed Central Park and the New York side of Niagara Falls) in 1887, is a classic example, extending for 5 miles from Franklin Park to downtown Boston. Along the way are a zoo, golf courses, riding trails, river walkways, a Victorian garden, and an internationally known arboretum. The final jewel in the necklace is Boston Common.

In 1892 Charles Eliot, who worked for the Olmsted architectural firm, proposed to create easily accessible open space to which people in a crowded urban area could escape. The Metropolitan Parks Commission, predecessor to today's Division of Urban Parks Recreation, was established in 1893 with 9,177 acres. At present, its domain continues to grow, with more parks being set aside as well as 13 miles of oceanfront and 56 miles of parkway.

The **Arnold Arboretum** in Jamaica Plain is along the Emerald Necklace. This 265-acre botanical garden with more than 14,000 plants, a particular delight in May when its many varieties of lilacs bloom, was designed by Olmsted and Sargent. It is administered by Harvard University. Free. For information, call 524-1717.

Walking tours of the **Emerald Necklace** are conducted by the Boston Park Rangers and focus on urban ecology, architecture, history, botany, and wildlife. For information, call 635-4505.

Frederick Law Olmsted National Historic Site, 99 Warren Street, Brookline. Telephone 566-1689. Open Friday through Sunday from 10:00 A.M. to 4:30 P.M. Free. The former home and office of America's first landscape architect, who designed not only Boston's Emerald Necklace but also countless parks elsewhere, such as New York City's Central Park and Niagara Falls, New York. The home is administered by the National Park Service, which Olmsted's son helped establish.

Sources of Information

Appalachian Mountain Club, 5 Joy Street, Boston. Telephone 523-0655. The AMC offers trips that include biking, hiking, canoeing, and camping; camping programs are even held near Boston.

Boston National Historical Park Visitor Center. See page 21. Also provides information on Dorchester Heights (really in South Boston), where in 1776 the American troops secretly moved cannons to the hilltop, aiming them at British ships in the harbor below. The British, seeing the cannons, decided it would be best to leave Boston. The event is recalled yearly as Evacuation Day, though the date also happens to be St. Patrick's Day. The National Park Service offers tours and opens the tower in summer for views of the city.

Division of Urban Parks and Recreation, 20 Somerset Street, Boston. Telephone 727-5114. Offers a complete listing of recreation programs at its many parks and beaches in and near Boston. Also maintains ice-skating and swimming facilities.

Places to Visit

Most areas listed below either are free or charge a low rate for parking or entrance. Many do not allow dogs, and some have restrictions on picnics.

Arnold Arboretum, 125 The Arborway, Jamaica Plain. Call 524-1717. Open daily from sunrise to sunset. The visitor center is open weekdays from 8:30 A.M. to 4:00 P.M. and weekends from 10:00 A.M. to 4:00 P.M.; guided tours are offered in spring and fall on Sunday at 2:00 P.M. Admission is free. By car from Boston, take Storrow Drive to the Route 1 South exit and follow Route 1 South along Brookline Avenue, first to the Riverway and then to the Jamaicaway; the main entrance is located 100 yards south of the junction of Routes 1 South and 203. By T, take the Orange Line to Forest Hills and walk 3 blocks northeast on the Arborway. Or take the Arborway bus from the Boston Public Library stop at Copley Square to the Monument stop in Jamaica Plain.

Plants and trees from around the world fill the 265 acres of one of America's oldest and most majestic parks. In spring the arboretum is particularly beautiful and fragrant with the hundreds of lilacs, as well as rhododendrons and azaleas, found here. Other attractions are the arboretum's collection of bonsai and its Chinese Path, where rare specimens from Asia are found. Its shop has the largest collection in New England of books on horticulture.

Belle Isle Marsh, East Boston. Call 727-5350 for information. Free parking; walkways. No picnics. No restrooms or drinking water available. Easy to reach on the T: Take the Blue Line to Suffolk Downs Station and you are there.

A protean wetland with wonderful views of Boston, Belle Isle Marsh is the largest remaining salt marsh in the city. In the 1630s, sheep grazed here and hay was harvested for winter fodder.

Castle Island, South Boston (located at the end of Day Boulevard). For tours of **Fort Independence,** call 268-5744. Food, a picnic area, a playground, and restrooms are available. By car from William J. Day Boulevard in South Boston, take the Southeast Expressway to the JFK Library exit and follow the beach to Castle Island at the end of the causeway. By T, take the Red

Line to Broadway Station and then take T bus number 9 (City Point) or 11 (Bay View) to City Point at the end of the line; from City Point, it's about a half-mile walk to Castle Island.

Castle Island's first fort was begun in 1634. When the British retreated from Boston during the Revolutionary War, they destroyed Castle William, which had been built there. New fortifications were built by Colonel Richard Gridley of Bunker Hill fame, and in 1799 Fort Independence was authorized and built of five-bastioned solid core. Positioned across from Fort Warren on George's Island, Fort Independence halted British naval attacks during the War of 1812 because of the cross-fire possibility. The present fort dates from 1834 and is part of an overall harbor defense system engineered by Colonel Sylvanus Thayer, Father of West Point. The site offers wonderful views of the harbor.

The **Esplanade,** Boston. Easiest access is by the Arthur Fiedler Footbridge, which crosses Storrow Drive at Beacon Street near Arlington Street. The Esplanade runs along the Charles River at the foot of Beacon Hill and continues up the river to around Boston University.

Unfortunately cut off from downtown Boston by Storrow Drive, the Esplanade is one of Boston's most enjoyable recreation areas. It's a place for walking, jogging, sunning, biking, sailing, and picnicking.

If you follow its bike path, you can ride for 17 miles all the way to Watertown and back on the other side of the Charles River. In summer the Boston Pops concerts are held here, and on July 4 the grass area from the Hatch Shell forward is covered with well over 100,000 people for the annual Pops concert and fireworks display. Among the more notable statues near the Hatch Shell is one of Arthur Fiedler that is made of aluminum and honors the Boston Pops conductor for his fifty years of leadership. The Lotta Fountain depicts a dog just above a drinking basin for animals and is the gift of Lotta Crabtree, the Shirley Temple of the Old West, who as a child so engaged miners that they threw silver dollars on the stage as she performed; Crabtree died in Boston in 1924, and her trust fund is used for animal causes. Also nearby is a statue of General George Patton Jr., the colorful commander of the Third Army in Europe during World War II. Patton was married to a Boston woman; their son, also an army general, retired to Hamilton on the North Shore.

Special Tours

If you have an interest in an organization, product, or company not listed in this section, look it up in the phone book and ask whether tours are available. Some companies offer tours as a company benefit; thus, if you know someone who works there, maybe he or she can arrange a look. Tours are generally free.

Boston Ballet, 19 Clarendon Street, Boston. Telephone 695–6950, extension 239. Tours given weekdays between 10:00 A.M. and 6:30 P.M. Call for reservations. Free. You'll tour the dance studios, music and dance libraries, and costume departments all in a grand South End setting. Depending on time and season, you may also see actual rehearsals of productions.

If your feet are made for walking . . .

Combine a visit to a park with a tour of historic sites in the area. Or take a tour of the Brookline home of Frederick Law Olmsted, master of the Emerald Necklace; get out a map and orient yourself for other nearby attractions.

Boston Beer Museum and Visitors Center (Samuel Adams Beer), 30 Germania Street, Jamaica Plain. Telephone 522–9080. Hour-long tours and tastings are offered Thursday and Friday at 2:00 P.M. and Saturday at noon and 1:00 and 2:00 P.M. Admission $2.00, which is donated to charity. By T, take the Orange Line to Stony Brook and walk 2 blocks. Samuel Adams beer is now being brewed in the old Haffenreffer Brewing building in Jamaica Plain. See the brewing process, learn about the history of Boston brewing, and walk through a 30-foot aging tank now filled with facts and myths about beer, some history about Samuel Adams, and, of course, a sample or two (if you're age twenty-one or older). The tour is open to people of all ages; soft drinks are served to those under the legal age.

Boston Globe **offices,** 135 Morrissey Boulevard, Dorchester. Telephone 929-2653. Participants must be at least twelve years old. See how a newspaper is put together by visiting the composing room and editorial and advertising offices. A good time to visit is on Friday, when the presses are rolling during the day.

Boston Stock Exchange, 100 Franklin Street, Boston. Visitor information telephone 235-2223. Self-guided visits from 9:00 A.M. to 4:00 P.M. Free but must be booked in advance. Visitors enter at either 210 Devonshire or 60 Arch Street. The Boston Stock Exchange is one of the oldest in the nation, having been founded in 1834. Visitors can see a display chronicling the history of trade in the city, get real-time financial data, and view the trading floor. Fidelity Investments, one of the largest fund companies in the nation, is headquartered in Boston. It also has offices in the city where you can check on your money. Call (800) 544-7558.

Federal Reserve Bank of Boston, 600 Atlantic Avenue, Boston. Telephone 973-3463. Public tours are usually given one Friday of the month between 10:30 and 11:30 A.M.; call to check on the date. Group tours only by appointment. Spend about ninety minutes seeing how coins are sorted and counted and checks are cleared. And yes, you can take home a souvenir—some shredded currency. Learn also that the dollars with an "A" on the seal or the figure "1" in the four corners are distributed from here.

Fenway Park, Yawkey Way, Boston. Telephone 236-6666. Seasonal. Tours are daily on the hour from 9:00 A.M. to 4:00 P.M. Tickets $10.00 adults, $9.00 seniors, $8.00 ages fourteen and under. Ticket purchases for same day only. Tours, all subject to availability, may include the dugouts, bullpens, the .406 Club, Hall of Fame Room, and the Green Monster (the high wall in left field), and, maybe, inside the famed scoreboard.

Harpoon Brewery Tours, 306 Northern Avenue, Boston. Telephone 574-9551. Tours offered Tuesday through Saturday at 11:00 A.M., 1:00 P.M., and 3:00 P.M. Tours last thirty to forty-five minutes. Free. See the mash mixer, brew kettle, and fermentation tanks used in the brewing process, and, of course, sample the brew (if you're age twenty-one or older). People of all ages are welcome to take the tour; soft drinks are served to those who are underage.

Massachusetts General Hospital, the Bulfinch Pavilion, 55 Fruit Street, Boston. Telephone 724-1754. Open daily from 9:00 A.M. to 5:00 P.M. A tour that includes sights of an Egyptian mummy; the Ether Dome, where the first use of ether in a surgical procedure occurred; and old surgical instruments—in a building designed by none other than Charles Bulfinch.

National Braille Press, 88 St. Stephen Street, Boston. Telephone 266-6160. Tours Monday to Friday at 10:30 A.M. and 2:30 P.M.; advance notice should be given. Free. You'll learn about Braille, how it was invented, and how it is produced as you tour the National Braille Press headquarters. Most of the workers here are visually impaired, so you'll also learn what it is like to be blind.

Symphony Hall, 301 Massachusetts Avenue, Boston. Telephone 638-9390. Free. Symphony Hall is home to the Boston Symphony and Boston Pops, and this tour takes you both backstage and onstage. You'll also learn the acoustics of the hall, which is considered one of the best in the world.

Whale Watching

Boston offers whale-watch tours from the heart of the city. There's no need to head to Cape Cod or some other distant location; just walk over to one of the city's wharves for a half- or full-day adventure.

Whale-watch season in Boston runs from April to October. Prices for trips range from $20 to $30, depending on age and line. Be sure to wear warm clothing (bring an extra jacket or sweater that you can take off if the sun is out) and sneakers or rubber-soled shoes. Bring lots of film for your camera, as well as a pair of sunglasses. Seas can be rough; be prepared.

Many boat owners claim up to a 98 percent sighting record. On your trip you just may see finback whales, which can reach a length of 70 feet and a weight of sixty-five tons, and humpback whales, known for their explosive leaps out of the sea ("breaching") and reaching a length of 50 feet and a weight of forty-five tons. Other whales include right whales and minkes. Most gather on Jeffreys Ledge and Stellwagen Bank, the major feeding grounds off the Massachusetts coast. Both Gloucester on the North Shore and Provincetown at the tip of Cape Cod claim to be the closest to whaling grounds and offer many half-day trips, both in the morning and in the afternoon.

In Boston contact the following:

A. C. Cruise Line, 290 Northern Avenue, near Jimmy's Harborside restaurant. Telephone 261–6633. Trips offered weekends. This company has been offering cruises for more than twenty-six years. Trips last about six hours. Adult fares include up to four children free.

Boston Harbor Cruises, Long Wharf. Telephone 227–4321. This line uses high-speed catamarans with three outside decks and in-cabin seating. Whale watches are three hours long and are narrated by a naturalist. Two sailings weekdays, five on weekends.

Massachusetts Bay Lines, Rowes Wharf. Telephone 542–8000. Offers a choice of a four- or five-hour trip. Vessels have multiple decks for extra viewing. Naturalist onboard. Offers one trip daily, two on weekends. Galley service.

New England Aquarium Whale Watch, Central Wharf by the aquarium. Telephone 973–5281. Naturalists offer history of Boston Harbor as well as information on whales. Onboard interactive laser-disk program displays photos and additional information. Main deck is wheelchair accessible. Trips last between four and five hours. Two sailings weekdays, five on weekends.

Accommodations

Boston hotels can be very pricey compared to hotels in many other cities in the country, but the accommodations are first-rate. Reasonable accommodations can also be found at bed-and-breakfast lodgings in the city and at hotels located just outside the city's core. Most of these, along with an excellent selection of hotels in towns and cities and along Interstates 93 and 95, which circle Greater Boston, are convenient to public transportation into the heart of the city.

Cambridge, which is separated from Boston by the Charles River, also has an excellent selection of hotels. Many of these are near MBTA stations. From Harvard Square to downtown Boston is but fifteen minutes by MBTA and no more than 5 miles by car. Many locations noted in Brookline are just a quick MBTA ride into the city.

Most hotels offer special weekend and other package rates, often lower than prices shown.

Hotels

IN BOSTON

Note: Most downtown hotels offer valet parking. An asterisk (*) indicates the hotel has its own garage, allowing easy access to one's vehicle. A double asterisk (**) indicates the hotel has luxury or concierge floors. A triple asterisk (***) indicates the hotel has its own garage and luxury or concierge floors.

All rates are for two people in high season. But note that hotel rates—like hairstyles and weather—are constantly changing. Call to get the current best rate.

$200 or More a Night

Beacon Hill Hotel and Bistro, 25 Charles Street; 723-7575 or (888) 959-2442. A converted town house that dates to 1830, this hotel is located at the foot of Beacon Hill near the Public Garden. Full restaurant and twenty-four-hour room service. Thirteen rooms.

Boston Harbor Hotel, 70 Rowes Wharf; 439-7000 or (800) 752-7077. This hotel is one of the best for service, facilities, dining, and views—it's right on the harbor. The Boston Harbor Hotel has an indoor pool, a spa service, health club, and award-winning restaurants. Sixteen floors, 230 rooms. ***

Boston Marriott Long Wharf Hotel, 296 State Street; 227-0800 or (800) 228-9290. An ideal family or business location right on the waterfront. Across from its entrance are the New England Aquarium and harbor excursion boats. Indoor pool overlooks the harbor. Seven floors, 400 rooms. ***

The Eliot Hotel, 370 Commonwealth Avenue; 267-1607 or (800) 443-5468. An intimate and quiet oasis with almost all suite accommodations. Very homelike; along Boston's grandest boulevard and adjacent to the Harvard Club. Ninety-five suites, nine stories.

Four Seasons Boston, 200 Boylston Street; 338-4400 or (800) 268-6282. This hotel is one of the best in the nation. Overlooking the Public Garden, the Four Seasons has an excellent location. Its Aujourd'hui restaurant is one of the finest in the country. From the hotel's indoor pool, you can look over the State House and the Public Garden. Fifteen floors, 288 rooms. ***

Hotel Commonwealth, 500 Commonwealth Avenue; 933-5000 or (866) 784-4000. An upscale hotel located in Kenmore Square. For Red Sox fans: a short walk to the park, or book a room that overlooks Fenway. All the amenities one could ask for, and excellent restaurants. 150 rooms.

Jurys Boston Hotel, 350 Stuart Street; 266-7200. A hotel with Irish traditions featuring original works of Irish art. Located in the former Boston Police Headquarters in the Back Bay. Ten floors, 217 rooms.

Langham, 250 Franklin Street; 451-1900. A hotel with unusual distinctions. Few of its rooms are the same, as the Langham was built within the old Federal Reserve Building, a historic landmark. Its Julien restaurant is elegant, as is its bar, with original Andrew Wyeth painting from the building's bank days. Indoor pool and health club. Nine stories, 326 rooms. *

The Lenox, 710 Boylston Street; 536-5300 or (800) 225-7676. An elegant small hotel. Its corner rooms have working fireplaces and are particularly good to book at Boston Marathon time as the race ends within feet of the hotel. A brief walk to Copley Square and the Prudential Center. Eleven stories, 212 rooms.

Nine Zero, 90 Tremont Street; 772-5800 or (866) 646-3937. This elegant, innovative, and contemporary hotel also offers traditional comfort. Located along the Freedom Trail. 190 rooms.

Omni Parker House, 60 School Street; 227-8600 or (800) 843-6664. A Boston institution and the oldest continuously operated hotel in the country. Located right on the Freedom Trail. Fourteen floors, 541 rooms.

Onyx, 155 Portland Street; 557-9955. A boutique hotel near the FleetCenter. Eleven floors, 112 rooms.

The Ritz-Carlton, Boston, 15 Arlington Street; 536-5700 or (800) 241-3333. One of the finest hotels anywhere, the Ritz-Carlton is old Boston, where jackets and ties are mandatory in the dining room. Across from the Public Garden and on the corner of Newbury Street, Boston's European-style shopping area. Hotel was completely renovated in 2002. Some suites with fireplaces. Fifteen stories, 278 rooms.

The Ritz-Carlton Boston Common, 10 Avery Street; 574-7100 or (800)241-3333. Contemporary luxury along with Ritz-Carlton traditions are the hallmarks of this, a second Ritz in the city. Twelve floors, 193 rooms (including suites).

The Westin Hotel, Copley Place, 10 Huntington Avenue; 262-9600 or (800) 228-3000. A large hotel located on Copley Square and within the Copley Place complex. Many rooms have sumptuous views of the city. Thirty-six stories, 804 rooms. ***

$150 to $199

Boston Marriott Hotel Copley Place, 110 Huntington Avenue; 236-5800 or (800) 228-9290. A convention-style hotel located within the Copley Place shopping complex. Indoor pool, health club, and sports bar. Thirty-nine floors, 1,147 rooms, and 77 suites. ***

The Boston Park Plaza Hotel & Towers, 50 Park Plaza at Arlington Street; 426-2000 or (800) 225-2008. A good central location. Excellent selection of restaurants and entertainment in the hotel. Fifteen floors, 960 rooms. **

Copley Square Hotel, 47 Huntington Avenue; 536–9000 or (800) 255–7062. This hotel, more than one hundred years old, is stylish, comfortable, and thoroughly up-to-date. Family rooms are available. Seven stories, 150 rooms.

Doubletree Hotel Downtown Boston, 821 Washington Street; 956–7900 or (800) 222–8733. Walking distance to Theater District, offers restaurant and sports complex. 268 rooms.

Fairmont Copley Plaza, 138 St. James Avenue; 267–5300 or (800) 527–4727. Boston's grande dame hotel, with an elegant lobby and hard-to-beat location in the heart of Copley Square. Its piano bar is a longtime Boston favorite. Seven stories, 394 rooms. **

Harborside Inn, 185 State Street; 723–7500. Handy to the waterfront and Faneuil Hall Marketplace. Nice touches throughout its fifty-four rooms; eight floors.

The Hilton Back Bay, 40 Dalton Street; 236–1100 or (800) 847–0663. Located just across from the Prudential Center, this soaring hotel offers graciously decorated rooms, an indoor pool, and a health club. Twenty-six floors, 335 rooms. ***

Hyatt Regency Boston, 1 Avenue de Lafayette; 912–1234 or (800) 621–9200. In the heart of downtown Boston. Has indoor pool and a health club. Twenty-two floors, 500 rooms. ***

Radisson Hotel, 200 Stuart Street; 482–1800 or (800) 333–3333. Handy to the Theater District. Has indoor pool. Twenty-four stories, 350 rooms. *

Seaport Hotel, 1 Seaport Lane; 385–4000. Located across from the World Trade Center and short walk to the new convention center in the Seaport District of the city. It has a pool and health club, and many rooms overlook the harbor. Eighteen floors, 427 rooms. ***

Sheraton Boston Hotel and Towers, 39 Dalton Street; 236–2000 or (800) 325–3535. Located within the Prudential Center and adjacent to the Hynes convention center. A Towers area offers 120 rooms and clublike atmosphere. Twenty-nine stories, 1,300 rooms.

The Tremont House, 275 Tremont Street; 426–1400 or (800) 331–9998. In the heart of the Theater District. Fifteen floors, 322 rooms.

Wyndham Boston, 89 Broad Street; 556–0006. Originally Boston's first Art Deco skyscraper in 1928, the building has been totally renovated and makes for a wonderful address. Handy to Faneuil Hall and waterfront. Fourteen floors, 362 rooms.

$100 to $149

Best Western Boston—The Inn at Longwood Medical, 342 Longwood Avenue; 731-4700 or (800) 438-2378. Adjacent to Children's, Beth Israel-Deaconess Hospitals. Six floors, 155 rooms.

Doubletree Club Hotel Bayside, 240 Mt. Vernon Street; 822-3600. Adjacent to Bayside Expo Center, convenient to T (four stops to downtown). Six floors, 195 rooms.

Holiday Inn Select—Government Center, 5 Blossom Street; 742-7630. Convenient location. Has health club. Shopping center adjacent to it. Fourteen floors, 303 rooms. *

Midtown Motel, 220 Huntington Avenue; 262-1000. A motel-style hotel just across from the Christian Science Center, Symphony Hall, and Prudential Center. Two floors, 159 rooms. *

Millennium Bostonian Hotel, Faneuil Hall Marketplace; 523-3600 or (800) 343-0922. An excellent downtown location overlooking Faneuil Hall Marketplace. Seven floors, 201 rooms.

GOOD VALUES

Doubletree Guest Suites, 400 Soldiers Field Road; 783-0090 or (800) 424-2900. On the Boston-Cambridge line just off the Massachusetts Turnpike at the Cambridge exit. An all-suite hotel overlooking the Charles River; offers two rooms for the price of one, with full breakfast included. Hotel features parking, an indoor pool, Scullers Jazz Club, and free transportation into the city. Children age seventeen or younger free. Fifteen stories, 310 suites.

Holiday Inn Boston–Brookline, 1200 Beacon Street, Brookline; 277-1200 or (800) 465-4329. Indoor pool, parking, MBTA service in front of hotel. Minutes to downtown. Six floors, 225 rooms.

Holiday Inn Boston–Somerville, 30 Washington Street, Somerville; 628-1000 or (800) 465-4329. Nine floors, 184 rooms.

Holiday Inn Express, just off I-93, exit 18; 287-9200. Near subway. Restaurant on-site. Six floors, 118 rooms.

Quality Inn, 900 Morrissey Boulevard, in the Dorchester section of Boston; (866) 866-8555. Free transportation to T. Five floors, 133 rooms.

Ramada Inn, 800 Morrissey Boulevard, 287-9100 or (866) 866-8449, in the Dorchester section of Boston. Free transportation to T. Outdoor pool. 174 rooms.

AROUND THE CITY

The following hotels and inns are within 20 miles of downtown Boston and offer easy access to the city.

At Logan Airport

Harborside Hyatt, 101 Harborside Drive, Logan International Airport; 568-1234. Water shuttle to downtown at its doorstep; indoor pool and health club. Fourteen stories.*

Hilton Boston Logan Airport, 85 Terminal Road, Logan International Airport; 568-6700. Has direct connections to Terminals A and E (international) via movable walkways to terminal; shuttle service also. This hotel would fit in any downtown location with all its amenities. Indoor pool and health club, restaurants, soundproof rooms, wheelchair accessible. Has 600 rooms, some with Boston skyline views, and ten stories.

Near Logan Airport

Comfort Inn & Suites Boston/Airport, 85 American Legion Highway, 3 miles north of Logan Airport; (781) 485-3600. Has indoor pool, restaurant. Eight floors, 208 rooms.

Holiday Inn Boston–Logan Airport, 225 McClellan Highway, 1.5 miles north of Logan Airport; 569-5250. Twelve floors, 356 rooms.

Wyndham Chelsea, 201 Everett Avenue, 884-2900. Has indoor pool, restaurant. Seven floors, 179 rooms.

North of Boston

Just off Route 128, I–95

Radisson Hotel, 15 Middlesex Canal Park Road, Woburn; (781) 935-8760 or (800) 333-3333. Four floors, 198 rooms.

Sheraton Colonial, 427 Walnut Street, Lynnfield; (781) 245-9300. Has golf course, indoor pool. Eleven floors, 280 rooms.

Off I–95

Sheraton Ferncroft Resort, 50 Ferncroft Road, Danvers; (978) 777-2500. Has golf course. Eight floors, 360 rooms.

Off I–93

Courtyard by Marriott, River Road, off I-93 at exit 45; (978) 794-0700. Indoor pool; 134 rooms and 12 one-bedroom suites; three floors.

Other North Locations

Hawthorne Hotel, on the Common, Salem; (978) 744-4080 or (800) 315-7557. Six floors, 93 rooms.

New Englander Motor Court, 551 Broadway, Malden; (781) 321-0505. Two floors, 21 rooms.

South of Boston

Just off Route 128, I–95

Fairfield Inn by Marriott, 235 Elm Street, Dedham; (781) 326-6700. Three floors, 150 rooms.

Hampton Inn Braintree, 215 Wood Road, Braintree; (781) 380-3300. Indoor pool. Four floors, 103 rooms.

Hilton at Dedham Place, 25 Allied Drive, Dedham; (781) 329-7900 or (800) HILTONS (800-445-8667). Four floors, 257 rooms.

Holiday Inn Dedham, 55 Ariadne Road, Dedham; (781) 329-1000 or (800) HOLIDAY (800-465-4329). Eight floors, 837 rooms.

Holiday Inn Randolph, 1374 North Main Street, Randolph; (781) 961-1000 or (800) HOLIDAY (800-465-4329). Four floors, 158 rooms.

Sheraton Braintree Hotel, 37 Forbes Road, Braintree; (781) 848-0600. Indoor pool. Six floors, 376 rooms.

West of Boston

Along Route 128, I–95

Boston Marriott Newton, 2345 Commonwealth Avenue, Newton; (617) 969-1000 or (800) 228-9290. Seven floors, 430 rooms.

Doubletree Guest Suites Waltham, 550 Winter Street, Waltham; (781) 890-6767 or (800) 803-2582. Eight floors, 275 rooms.

Holiday Inn Newton, 399 Grove Street, Newton; 969-5300 or (800) HOLIDAY (800-465-4329). Near MBTA station into Boston. Seven floors, 192 rooms.

The Sheraton Needham Hotel, 100 Cabot Street, Needham; (781) 444-1110. Five floors, 260 rooms.

Other West Locations

Best Western at Historic Concord, 740 Elm Street, Concord; (978) 369-6100. Two floors, 106 rooms.

Best Western TLC Hotel, 477 Trotten Pond Road, Waltham; (781) 890–7800. Six floors, 100 rooms.

Colonial Inn, 48 Monument Square, Concord; (978) 369–9200 or (800) 370–9200. Three floors, 56 rooms.

Natick Travelodge, 1350 Worcester Road, Natick; (508) 655–2222. 68 rooms.

Sheraton Newton, 320 Washington Street, Newton; 969–3010. Sits over the Massachusetts Turnpike. Twelve floors, 280 rooms.

Summerfield Suites by Wyndham–Boston/Burlington, Wayside Road off I-95 at exit 33A; (781) 270–0800. 151 units, some with kitchens, outdoor pool.

Just off the Massachusetts Turnpike

Hampton Inn, 319 Speen Street, Natick; (508) 653–5000 or (800) HAMPTON (800-426-7866). Seven floors, 190 rooms.

Red Roof Inn, 650 Cochituate Road, Framingham; (508) 872–4499 or (800) THE ROOF (800-843-7663). Two floors, 180 rooms.

Sheraton Framingham, 1657 Worcester Road, Framingham; (508) 879–7200. Six floors, 373 rooms.

Bed-and-Breakfast Reservation Services

Bed & Breakfast Agency of Boston, 47 Commercial Wharf; 720–3540 or (800) 248–9262. Offers accommodations from Victorian town houses to waterfront lofts.

Bed & Breakfast Associates Bay Colony, P.O. Box 57166, Boston 02457; 720–0520 or (888) 429–7596. Offers accommodations in Boston, Cambridge, and surrounding towns, as well the North and South Shores of the city and Cape Cod.

Budget Accommodations and Hostels

Berkeley Residence/Boston YWCA, 40 Berkeley Street; 482–8850; fax 482–9692.

Boston Irish Embassy International Tourist Hotel, 232 Friend Street; 973–4841. Includes kitchens, laundry, bar, and restaurant.

College accommodations are offered in summer at *Emerson College,* 824–8554; *Fisher College,* 236–8828; *Northeastern University,* 373–2814; and *Artists Residence @ MassArt,* 879–5105.

Constitution Inn, 150 Second Avenue, Charlestown; 241–8400 or (800) 495–9622. A YMCA conference facility near the USS *Constitution.*

Hostelling International Boston, 12 Hemenway Street; 536–9455. Dormitory-style rooms with two to six beds. Kitchen and self-service laundry.

Guest Houses, Inns

Anthony's Town House, 1085 Beacon Street, Brookline; 566–3972.

Beech Tree Inn, 83 Longwood Avenue, Brookline; 277–1620 or (800) 544–9660. Handy to hospitals.

Cappella Suites, 290 North Street; 523–9020. Steps from the Freedom Trail. Some rooms with balconies.

The College Club, 44 Commonwealth Avenue; 536–9510. Six rooms with private baths and fireplaces. Six single rooms with shared baths. All in the Back Bay.

Clarendon Square Inn, 198 West Brookline Street; 536–2229.

Copley House, 239 West Newton Street; 236–8300 or (800) 331–1318.

Copley Inn, 19 Garrison Street; 236–0300 or (800) 232–0306.

The John Jeffries House, 14 David G. Mugar Way; 367–1866.

Oasis Guest House, 22 Edgerly Road; 267–2262.

Reservation Services

Reservation services are free and are a good source of accommodations when rooms are scarce.

The Greater Boston Convention and Visitors Bureau offers a free reservation service: Call 561-4100 or (888) 733-2678.

For visitors driving into Boston from out of state, there is a tourist information center with a reservation service along the Massachusetts Turnpike at Charlton (the first service area after entering from Interstate 84 from Connecticut); this resource features many unadvertised values for accommodations. Information also at Natick East Plaza on the turnpike (the last rest area on the Pike). An information center is also available on I-95 east in the Mansfield area (shortly before the Interstate 495 intersection) to assist travelers arriving from Rhode Island and beyond.

Weekend Packages

Friday, Saturday, and Sunday nights are bargain times in Boston's hotels, many cutting room rates by 50 percent and throwing in such extras as parking or a breakfast or dinner.

You might also take advantage of one of the many weekend packages rates offered in January and February, which are slow months at Boston and area hotels. Call the Boston Convention Bureau for a weekend hotel package guide, 561-4100 or (888) SEE-BOSTON (888-733-2678).

For information on special packages for families, see pages 217-19.

If a romantic weekend is in your plans, the Boston Harbor Hotel offers standout views, service, and rooms. The Ritz-Carlton on Arlington Street, with its quiet elegance, has many suites containing working fireplaces, and the views of the Public Garden are magnificent. The Millennium Bostonian is intimate; its beautiful views of historic Faneuil Hall are complemented by balconies overlooking the city, and some rooms have fireplaces. The Four Seasons features equally beautiful views of the Public Garden and superb rooms (its Four Season Rooms offer a small suite for slightly more than the regular room rate). From its upper floors, the Westin Hotel at Copley Place offers views of the entire city; once in the hotel, you can shop, dine, and swim without ever going outdoors. Less costly, but with corner rooms containing working fireplaces and Victorian elegance, is the Lenox Hotel. The Langham is a favorite; on weekends its businesslike atmosphere disappears, and it becomes an oasis of hospitality in the heart of the city, offering dancing, superior dining, loft rooms, a cozy health club, and quiet spots. The Seaport Hotel, along the waterfront, has wonderful views of the city and the harbor. It's quiet, elegant, and loaded with amenities. For the best views of the city, just cross the Charles River to Cambridge where the Hyatt Regency's and the Royal Sonesta's rooms overlook the river and the Boston skyline.

Dining

B oston may be "the home of the bean and the cod," but in recent years its appetite for dining has taken a turn toward international fare. Rave reviews are given its new cuisine. With more than 2,000 restaurants in the city, there is something somewhere to please everyone's palate and pocketbook.

No visit to the city would be complete without at least sampling the dishes or establishments thought of as "Boston's own." Nor would any visit be complete without discovering one of the many ethnic delights that are finding their way into the city. In years past, who would have expected to find Ethiopian and other ethnic restaurants in the heart of the city? And whereas the feasts of Chinatown beckon from near downtown Boston, nothing, next to being in Italy, could be finer than to dine in the North End. Thai, vegetarian, Vietnamese, Mexican, Japanese, and other international dining delights are also well represented throughout the metropolitan area.

Seafood, though, is Boston's specialty. (And if you don't believe this, just head for the State House, where the Sacred Cod stands guard over the House of Representatives.) One favorite dish offers a confusing spelling for visitors. *Scrod* or *schrod* is the name used by fishermen for cod, haddock, or pollack fillets. Why two spellings? If it's *scrod,* it's young cod; if it's *schrod,* it's haddock (I've not heard an explanation as to what happens if it's pollack, but no matter—it's all very good). And if you ask for clam chowder, which you should, don't expect to see any red—that's Manhattan style, with a tomato base. In Boston you can expect a rich, cream-based chowder. Show up at Harborfest in July and you can sample Boston's best chowder and cast your vote for your favorite. Other popular seafoods are flounder, scallops, bluefish, mussels, oysters and cherrystones, and, of course, lobster.

Maryland has crab cakes, but Boston has fish cakes. At Durgin Park, where fish cakes are a staple, they usually come with beans, offering a contrasting salty and molasses-flavored sweet taste. "Finnan haddie" is another strange-sounding phrase, referring to smoked haddock served with potatoes and deriving its name from Findon in Scotland, where it was first made. Lobster, along with steamed clams, is a treat to be savored with melted butter used as a dip. Fried clams are a popular choice for a sit-down meal or to be enjoyed from one of the many roadside stands offering them. Fried clams were "discovered" in Ipswich, on the North Shore, and "Ipswich fried clams" means they're cooked just like the originals.

To add to an appreciation of dining in Boston, consider that Massachusetts is one of the nation's top cranberry-producing areas (the red berries in bogs near Plymouth are one of fall's colorful sights) and a leader in fruit production, offering in-season apples, raspberries, strawberries, and blueberries from some 200 orchards. The state's 7,500 farmers also produce corn and other fresh vegetables, poultry, eggs, and dairy products. It's no wonder that strawberry shortcake and fresh apple pie are favorite desserts. One place to sample the culinary fare of Boston and more is in the food court at Quincy Market in the Faneuil Hall historic area (a great place to buy a lunch to enjoy along the nearby waterfront).

At the Omni Parker House on the Freedom Trail, two other Boston favorites were conceived: Parker House rolls and Boston cream pie. And another old New England staple for dessert is Indian pudding, a combination of molasses and cornmeal, flavored with cinnamon and nutmeg.

Even wine making has taken a slight hold, with seven wineries and thirty-five vineyards in the commonwealth.

Listed in this chapter are just a few of the hundreds of restaurants Boston has to offer. More ideas are found weekly in the restaurant reviews in the Thursday "Calendar" section of the *Boston Globe;* for visitors looking for a less expensive way to eat out, a companion column suggests "Cheap Eats." And for meals with a show, see chapter 17 of this book.

Dining in Boston will cost at least $25 for a party of two without wine, more for the name establishments. As a guide, restaurants where two can dine for $40 or less are designated as $; for more than $40 but less than $50, $$; and for $50 or more, $$$. Many restaurants offer a lunch menu that is far less expensive.

Finally, a tip or two: Call first to make sure you can be seated and to find out whether credit cards are accepted and, should you be driving, whether parking is available or a reduced rate is offered at a nearby lot (Boston is tight on parking spaces, and expensive at that). You might also want to check on the dress code—the Ritz-Carlton on Arlington Street, for example, refuses entry to its dining room without a jacket and tie. Tipping is the standard 18 to 20 percent, and Massachusetts adds a 5 percent meal tax to the bill.

You Haven't Eaten in Boston Until You've Eaten at . . .

Durgin Park, 340 Faneuil Hall; 227-2038. This restaurant has been a tradition in Boston since 1827, with huge portions of New England fare (prime rib, baked beans, Indian pudding) served at long tables by a waitstaff you won't forget. $–$$

Jacob Wirth, 31 Stuart Street; 338-8586. Built in 1886, Jake's reminds you of a beer hall with its simple furnishings and grand bar. While there's still wurst, schnitzel, sauerkraut, and more, you'll also find salmon, Brie, and grilled chicken. $–$$

Locke-Ober, 3 Winter Place; 542-1340. Once a male bastion, this restaurant has been around since 1875; women have been allowed in since 1968. Hidden in an alleyway near Downtown Crossing, it is still a very proper Boston experience. While it still offers some old favorites, it's been given a culinary update by new owner Lydia Shire (Biba) and her chef Jacky Robert. $$$

Parker's Restaurant, in the Omni Parker House, 60 School Street; 227-8600. It's been a landmark and one of the most innovative dining rooms since it opened in 1856. It was the first American hotel restaurant to separate the room charge from the meal to provide better quality and service. It's also the home of the Parker House rolls, Boston cream pie (the official Massachusetts dessert), and scrod (meaning the phrase "the catch of the day" was coined here). Today you'll also find traditional New England fare such as New England clam chowder, Jonah crab cakes, and baked Boston scrod. Oh yes, Ho Chi Minh worked in the kitchen once, as did Malcolm Little, later known as Malcolm X, and diners have ranged from Henry Wadsworth Longfellow to John F. Kennedy and Bill Clinton. $–$$$

Ritz-Carlton Dining Room, 15 Arlington Street; 536-5700. It's very expensive, but very much a part of Boston. There may be more "in" restaurants in Boston today, but few come with such style or quality. $$$

Union Oyster House, 41 Union Street; 227-2750. This restaurant started serving diners when John Quincy Adams was president. Louis Philippe, king of France from 1830 to 1848, practically lived here. The restaurant has a great raw bar—for oysters, of course—and, for diners who don't like an old atmosphere, more than one dining room. $-$$

In-the-Know Establishments

Blackfin Chop House & Raw Bar, 116 Huntington Avenue; 247-2400. A fine restaurant with simple offerings—steak with mashed potatoes or seafood. Its raw/sushi bar is one of the best around. $$$

Clio, 370A Commonwealth Avenue (actually around the corner on Massachusetts Avenue); 536-7200. The ambience of this restaurant is matched by its cuisine. $$$

Davios, 75 Arlington Street; 357-4810. Northern Italian dishes with interesting touches. Guests can catch the kitchen show from the bar. A stylish yet casual spot popular with celebrities. $$$

Federalist Restaurant, 15 Beacon Street; 670-2515. Here you'll find a luxurious dining room with the service and food to match. $$$

Grill 23 & Bar, 161 Berkeley Street; 542-2255. This is an elegant place to have an elegant steak. $$-$$$

Hamersley's Bistro, 553 Tremont Street; 423-2700. Located in the South End, it has a casual ambience and superb tastes. A favorite with Julia Child when she was in town. $$-$$$

Hampshire House, 84 Beacon Street; 227-9600. This is a genuine town house that offers a quiet retreat from the Bull & Finch Pub (Cheers) below. It offers live jazz, friendly service, even fireplaces. $-$$

Icarus Restaurant, 3 Appleton Street; 426-1790. For innovative American dishes with great seasonal ingredients, this is it. $$

L, 234 Berkeley Street; 266-4680. Set within the elegant Louis Boston clothing store, L is a reincarnation of the former Cafe Louis restaurant with a minimalist look and a stylish, modern cuisine. $$$

L'Espalier, 30 Gloucester Street; 262-3023. For an evening to remember, this restaurant offers elegant dining in three small rooms of a nineteenth-century town house. Chef-owned and superb. $$$

Mantra, 52 Temple Place; 542-8111. Try this—it's the talk of Boston: contemporary French cuisine with exotic Indian accents, all in a stunning setting. $$$

McCormick & Schmick's seafood restaurant, 34 Columbus Avenue; 482-3999. In the Boston Park Plaza Hotel & Towers, an upscale national chain with more than forty varieties of fish, along with meat, chicken, and pasta. $$-$$$

Mistral, 221 Columbus Avenue; 867-9300. Dining here is like being on center stage. It's energetic, and the food is great. $$-$$$

Morton's of Chicago, 1 Exeter Plaza; 266-5858. This eastern offshoot of a Windy City classic offers superb steak. $$-$$$

No. 9 Park, 9 Park Street; 742-9991. Dine here on contemporary European fare within view of the State House. $$-$$$

Plaza III, 101 South Market Building, Faneuil Hall Marketplace; 720-1626. There's a Kansas City flair to this steak house. Great beef with all the trimmings. $$-$$$

Radius, 8 High Street; 426-1234. This restaurant features contemporary cuisine served with flair. $$-$$$

75 Chestnut, 75 Chestnut Street; 227-2175. Creative American dishes are served in a romantic Beacon Hill setting. $$-$$$

Sonsie, 327 Newbury Street; 351-2500. This is the place to be seen. Wonderful tastes, drinks. $-$$

Spire, 90 Tremont Street; 772-0202. In the Nine Zero Hotel featuring California-influenced dishes. The dining room is separated from the kitchen by a shimmering veil. $$$

29 Newbury, 29 Newbury Street; 536-0290. A good place to find nourishment while celebrity watching. $$

The Vault, 105 Water Street, Liberty Square; 292-9966. Set in a former bank, the Vault offers an eclectic menu that's not to be missed. $-$$

And then there's Todd English—no, that's not a restaurant but the celebrity chef who started in Boston and now has an empire across the country. Even in Boston it's getting hard to keep up with his tastes. Try *Olives* with its bold flavors, his first restaurant, 10 City Square, Charleston; 242-1999 (closed Sunday); $$-$$$. *Todd English Rustic Kitchen* offers a wide-ranging menu, 200 Quincy Market, Faneuil Hall Marketplace; 523-6334; $-$$. For great pizza, try his *Figs,* 42 Charles Street; 742-3447; or 67 Main Street, Charlestown; 242-2229; both $. *Bonfire* is a Latin steak house, 50 Park Plaza in the Park Plaza Hotel; 262-3473; $$-$$$.

Hotel Restaurants

Aujourd'hui, in the Four Seasons, facing the Public Garden, 200 Boylston Street; 351-2071. Here is one of the best dining experiences in Boston and the nation. $$$

Aura, Seaport Hotel, 1 Seaport Lane; 385-4300. This restaurant features Boston classics with dedicated local ingredients. The tip is included in the price. $$$

Jer-Ne, in the Ritz-Carlton downtown, 12 Avery Street; 574-7176. Seafood and local dishes with an Asian touch dominate the menu here. Formal service in a contemporary setting—wear your Sunday best. $$$

Julien at Langham, 250 Franklin Street; 451-1900. This is one of the most impressive dining rooms in the city in both style and cuisine. $$$

Oak Room, Fairmont Copley Plaza, 138 St. James Avenue; 267-5300. Tenderloin is the signature dish, but everything is delicious. First-class service. A grand room in Boston's grande dame hotel. $$$

Ritz-Carlton Dining Room, see page 155.

Rowes Wharf Restaurant, Boston Harbor Hotel, 70 Rowes Wharf; 439-3995. Chef Daniel Bruce has been tempting Bostonians for years with his delightful dishes. His cuisine also reflects his love of mushrooms. Overlooks Boston Harbor. $$-$$$

Seasons, in the Millennium Bostonian Hotel at Faneuil Hall Marketplace; 523-4119. As the name implies, each season brings something new to the menu. Nice view of the Faneuil Hall area, too. $$$

Restaurants with a View

Anthony's Pier 4, on the waterfront, 140 Northern Avenue; 423-6363. This place is very touristy and very, very popular. $-$$$

Spinnaker, at the top of the Hyatt Regency in Cambridge; 492-1234. It is the area's only revolving restaurant for a panoramic view of Boston. $-$$

Top of the Hub, on the fifty-second floor of the Prudential Center, 800 Boylston Street; 536-1775. The New American menu here is as spectacular as the far-ranging view. Live jazz nightly. $$-$$$

Seafood Restaurants

You haven't experienced Boston until you've dined on the freshest seafood in the world.

Anthony's Pier 4. See above.

Barking Crab, 88 Sleeper Street; 426-2722. A fish shack right on the edge of downtown and on the waterfront. Offers very casual fare with picnic-table dining. When the weather's fine there's outdoor dining. $

Daily Catch, 323 Hanover Street, North End; 523-8567. Don't let the setting deceive you, the seafood is exquisite, served with red sauce and garlic on top of pasta. $-$$

Jimmy's Harbor Side, 242 Northern Avenue; 423-1000. Located next to the Fish Pier, Jimmy's is another Boston tradition and a favorite with politicians and celebrities. Find out why Jimmy is called the Chowder King. $-$$

Legal Sea Foods, 26 Park Square; 426-4444. Also at Long Wharf, Prudential Center, Copley Place, and Kendall Square in Cambridge. From a humble beginning in Cambridge's Inman Square, Legal has spread across the state and the country, with every location stressing the freshest of fresh fish. It also offers nonseafood selections and a great wine list. No reservations, however. $-$$

No Name, 15½ Fish Pier; 338-7539. This favorite with real Bostonians now offers a broiled- as well as fried-fish menu. $-$$

Skipjack's, 199 Clarendon Street; 536-3500. Seafood, three-pound lobsters— you name it, Skipjack's has it. Live music during Sunday brunch. Lively bar. $-$$

Turner's, in the Westin Hotel; 424-7425. Here you'll have an enjoyable experience with nice surroundings. Turner's is the winner of numerous Harborfest clam chowder tastings. $-$$

Union Oyster House, see page 156.

Places in the North End

For a little bit of Italy in the heart of old Boston, the choices in the North End are many, and the prices reasonable.

Antico Forno, 93 Salem Street; 723-6733. The "old oven" features rustic dishes and brick-oven pizza. $–$$

Bricco, 241 Hanover Street; 248-6800. Classic Italian dishes. $$$

The Daily Catch, 323 Hanover Street; 523-8567. Wait until you try the seafood in red sauce and garlic served on pasta still in the pan. $–$$

Euno, 119 Salem Street; 573-9406. Like Sicily, Euno has a menu that reflects many nations while upholding the Italian tradition. $–$$

5 North Square; 720-1050. Almost next to the Paul Revere House, you'll find a neighborhood feel to this eatery. $–$$

Giacomo's, 355 Hanover Street; 523-9206. This family-run establishment provides ample dishes. $

Lucca, 226 Hanover Street; 742-9200. From the freshest ingredients to an emphasis on service, this is a true North End experience. $$

Mamma Maria, 3 North Square; 523-0077. You'll find some of the best Italian here. $–$$

Pizzeria Regina, 11½ Thatcher Street; 227-0765. Many say this is the place for the best pizza in town. $

Ristorante Fiore, 250 Hanover Street; 371-1176. Great choices in Italian dishes. A roof deck adds to the pleasure. $$–$$$

Sage, 69 Prince Street; 248-8814. Chef Anthony Susi is getting national attention with his rich Italian and French cuisine. $$

Terramia, 98 Salem Street; 523-3112. Now offering the new wave of Italian cuisine. $$–$$$

Restaurants in Chinatown

It's hard to go wrong in one of the nation's largest Chinatowns. Most restaurants are along Hudson, Tyler, Harrison, and Beach Streets, but you'll also find some now on Washington Street. Some, like Dynasty, stay open until 4:00 A.M.

Buddha's Delight, 3 Beach Street, second floor; 451-2396. This is the place for vegetarians with treats that will fool meat lovers. $-$$

Chau Chow City, 83 Essex Street; 338-8158. This is the place for dim sum. Choose from trays full of food brought right to your table. $

China Pearl, 9 Tyler Street; 426-4388. Dim sum is on the menu all day. Popular with the Chinatown neighborhood. $

Dynasty, 33 Edinboro Street; 350-7777. This is a lavish restaurant with a lavish menu. $-$$

East Ocean City, 27 Beach Street; 542-2504. Great seafood and Peking duck. $

Imperial Seafood House, 70 Beach Street; 426-8439. It's found just inside the China gate. $-$$

Jumbo Seafood, 7 Hudson Street; 542-2823. This is the place for exotic fare, and if you sit near the aquarium tanks, you can watch your food being caught. $-$$

New Shanghai, 21 Hudson Street; 338-6688. Delicacies not found elsewhere are a specialty, as well as Shanghai vegetables. $-$$

Ocean Wealth, 8 Tyler Street; 423-1338. Hong Kong-style seafood and more are featured at this chopsticks-only restaurant. $-$$

Pho Pasteur, 682 Washington Street; 482-7467. This restaurant is well worth a visit. $

Taiwan Café, 34 Oxford Street; 426-8181. Popular place for Taiwanese-style food. Nothing fancy but the food is great, and there's hardly a wait for it to arrive from the kitchen. $-$$

Just for Fun

And the food is good and reasonable, too.

Bob the Chef's, 604 Columbus Avenue; 536-6204. This restaurant serves great soul food including Bob's famed chicken—glorifried, baked, or BBQ-style. $

Dick's Last Resort, 55 Huntington Avenue; 267-8080. This is the place for American dishes. Lots of fun. $-$$

Division 16, 995 Boylston Street; 353-0870. The kitchen stays open late here. $

Fajitas & Ritas, 25 West Street; 426–1222. This is a fun restaurant and bar with Tex-Mex cuisine. $

FiRE + iCE, 205 Berkeley Street; 482–3473. Here you can create your own dish with a choice of twenty meats and seafoods and fifteen sauces, cooked before your eyes on a 25-foot grill. $–$$

Hard Rock Cafe, 131 Clarendon Street; 424–7625. If you're a rock fan, this memorabilia-filled spot is for you. $–$$

Marche Movenpick, 800 Boylston Street in the Prudential Plaza; 578–9700. It offers a feast for all the senses in a European market–style setting. $–$$

Metropolis Cafe, 584 Tremont Street; 247–2931. This place is reminiscent of an old ice cream parlor with its tin ceiling, wooden booths, and stools at the counter. $

Mike's City Diner, 1714 Washington Street; 267–9393. Mike's is a great place to hang out for comfort food and stick-to-your ribs cooking. $

The Rack, 24 Clinton Street; 725–1051. This spot in the Faneuil Hall Marketplace also offers lots of pool tables and live music. $

Vinny Testa's, 867 Boylston Street; 262–6699. Italian-American dishes generously served family-style. $$

Ethnic Delights

Sample the diversity of dining the city has to offer.

Addis Red Sea, 544 Tremont Street; 426–8727. This restaurant offers exotic Ethiopian dining. $

Bomboa, 35 Stanhope Street; 236–6363. Try a taste of Brazil with a lively scene. $–$$

Ginza Japanese Restaurant, 16 Hudson Street; 338–2261. Anytime, even up to 4:00 A.M. on weekends, this is the place for Japanese dishes, especially sushi. $–$$

Gyuhama of Japan, 827 Boylston Street; 437–0188. This restaurant is very popular for sushi, sashimi, and teriyaki. $–$$

Istanbul Cafe, 17 Bowdoin Street; 227–3434. This spot is a Turkish delight. $

Kashmire, 279 Newbury Street; 536–1695. This restaurant features Indian dishes cooked in a pitcher-shaped oven. $–$$

Lala Rokh, 97 Mount Vernon Street; 720-5511. Here is a relaxing place for Eastern Mediterranean/Persian dishes. $-$$

M. J. O'Connor's Irish Pub, 27 Columbus Avenue, Park Plaza Hotel; 482-2255. This eatery offers Harp beer-battered fish and chips and more, along with Irish entertainment. $-$$

Steve's Greek Cuisine, 316 Newbury Street; 267-1817. Here you'll find authentic Greek cuisine and great gyros. $

The Sultan's Kitchen, 72 Broad Street; 728-2828. This is Boston's oldest Turkish restaurant. $

Tapeo Restaurant & Tapas Bar, 266 Newbury Street; 267-4799. This restaurant offers innovative Spanish food and drink in a colorful atmosphere. $-$$

Tiger Lily, 8 Westland Avenue; 267-8881. Here you'll find Malaysian dishes at their best. $-$$

Entertainment

For complete, up-to-date listings, see the *Boston Globe*'s Thursday "Calendar" section or the *Boston Phoenix,* published each Friday. Also check out the telephone listings in chapter 2 of this book for various events lines. *Please note:* Fleet Bank has merged with Bank of America and will change its name in 2005. Name changes for the FleetCenter and Fleet Pavilion are sure to follow. As we go to press, such changes have yet to be finalized.

Ideas for Tickets

(See also page 39.)

BosTix (482–BTIX or 482–2849 for recorded information) offers half-price, day-of-show tickets. Tickets go on sale at 11:00 A.M. Locations at Copley Square and Faneuil Hall. Hours are 10:00 A.M. to 6:00 P.M. Tuesday through Saturday and 11:00 A.M. to 4:00 P.M. Sunday. Copley Square is also open Monday from 10:00 A.M. to 6:00 P.M. Also serves as a full-service box office and Ticketmaster outlet (charge cards accepted). Offers Arts/Boston Coupon Book with discounts to sixty museums and attractions. Has trolley tours, maps and guides, and MBTA Visitor Passports. Cash only for day-of-show tickets.

SPECIAL EVENTS

FleetCenter, Causeway Street at North Station, telephone 931–2000. Boston's home for shows such as the Ringling Brothers & Barnum and Bailey Circus, ice shows, and major rock concerts. Seats up to 20,000, depending on event. See page 186.

Bank of America Pavilion, 290 Northern Avenue, telephone 931–2000 for tickets; 728–1600 for information. Top stars perform under the harborside tent.

Theater

Boston's Theater District has expanded and offers lively, year-round fare ranging from Broadway shows to repertory-company productions, many staged in theaters that are as majestic as the performances onstage.

WITHIN THE THEATER DISTRICT

Charles Playhouse (just behind the Shubert), 74–76 Warrenton Street; 426–6912. Seats 550 and 280. Home to the long-running, perhaps never-ending *Shear Madness,* in which the audience gets into the act. Also *Blue Man Group,* the hit off-Broadway show.

Colonial, 106 Boylston Street; 426–9366. Seats 1,600. One of Boston's most beautiful legitimate theaters.

Cutler Majestic Theatre, 219 Tremont; (800) 233–3123. Part of the Emerson College complex and the home of many theater companies.

Opera House, 539 Washington Street; 482–8616. After being dark for years, it has reemerged as an architectural jewel and one of the finest theaters in New England.

Paramount Theatre, 549 Washington Street. While its commanding sign and marquee are once again bright, the theater remains dark. Built at the beginning of the "talkie" era of movies, plans for the theater's use are still in the works.

Shubert Theater, 265 Tremont Street; 482–5829. Seats 1,650. Home to many a Broadway tryout.

Wang Center for the Performing Arts, 268 Tremont Street; 482–9393. Seats 4,200. A former movie palace of grand proportions and huge seating capacity. Home to the Boston Ballet and major Broadway productions.

Wilbur Theater, 246 Tremont Street; 423–4008. Seats 699. A smaller, more intimate theater than its Wang Center and Shubert Theater neighbors.

SMALLER AREA THEATERS

There are many choices for the theatergoer in Boston and Cambridge:
Actor's Workshop, 40 Boylston Street, Boston; (781) 891–1188.

American Repertory Theatre, 64 Brattle Street, Cambridge; 547–8300.

Berklee Performance Center, 136 Massachusetts Avenue, Boston; 266–7455.

Boston Center for the Arts, 539 Tremont Street, Boston; 426–2787.

Boston Playwrights' Theater, 949 Commonwealth Avenue, Boston; 491–2026.

Copley Theater, 225 Clarendon Street, Boston; 266–7660.

Huntington Theater, 264 Huntington Avenue, Boston; 266–0800.

ICA Theater, 955 Boylston Street, Boston; (978) 369–5776.

Improvboston Theater, 1253 Cambridge Street, Cambridge; 576–1253.

John Hancock Hall, 180 Berkley Street, Boston; 572–7777.

Lyric Stage Company of Boston, 140 Clarendon Street, Boston; 437–7172.

Market Theater, Harvard Square, Cambridge; 576–0808.

Puppet Showplace Theater, 32 Station Street, Brookline; 731–6400.

Stuart Street Playhouse, 200 Stuart Street, Boston; 426–4499.

Tremont Theatre, 276 Tremont Street, Boston; 542–4599.

Meet Me At . . .

Boston's Theater District contains a nice mix of new restaurants and nightspots for before- and after-the-show dining and entertainment, all located just steps away from the box office. Here are some to try for dining:

Jacob Wirth (see page 155) is a wonderful Boston tradition. The sawdust has gone from the floor, but the waiters are still dressed in tuxes and the bar is one of the grandest in the city. German meals are a specialty.

Two nearby hotels have pre- and postdinner specials: **Aujourd'hui** in the Four Seasons (see page 158) offers a fixed-course menu from 5:30 to 6:30 P.M. in an elegant setting; later, on Thursday through Saturday, a Viennese dessert table containing twenty-four items is found until midnight in the hotel's Bristol Lounge. The **Cafe in the Ritz-Carlton** on Arlington Street (see page 155) offers a forty-five-minute predinner menu and until midnight a light supper menu.

If you're heading for the theater, go first or last to the **Back Lot,** a movie-themed bar with specialty martinis and great appetizers. It overlooks Boston Common above the Loews Theater in the Ritz-Carlton on Boston Common.

Nearby for steaks is the **57 Restaurant** at 200 Stuart Street (423-5700), and for fish, **Legal Sea Foods** (see page 159) at 26 Park Plaza.

For Symphony Hall performances, the Colonnade Hotel's restaurant offers pre- and postsymphony or Pops meals. Or end the night with a bit of jazz in the lounge. It's just a short walk to Symphony Hall. The hotel has indoor parking also. In the Prudential Center take a trip around the world at the self-service **Marche** (578-9700), a Swiss import. **P.F. Chang's China Bistro** at 8 Park Plaza (573-0821) offers traditional Chinese fare in the heart of the Theater District.

Dinner Theaters

Medieval Manor, at 246 East Berkeley Street, Boston, is a fun place for a "knight on the town." Medieval Manor combines a dinner with lively entertainment set in a royal hall, with entertainers playing the royal hosts, diners becoming the lords and ladies, and all eating without the benefit of modern silverware. A popular and fun time that's been around for more than twenty years. Call 423-4900.

Mystery Cafe Dinner Theater, at 290 Congress Street, Boston. Offers comedy-mystery spoofs. Call 426-1999.

Concerts

The **Boston Pops** plays at Symphony Hall, 301 Massachusetts Avenue, from April through June. Getting a table at a Pops concert and enjoying food and drink along with classical and popular music are a Boston tradition. In July free Pops concerts are held at the Hatch Shell on the Esplanade; bring a blanket and fixings for a picnic (no alcoholic beverages allowed) and make an evening of it. Tickets are $14 to $55. Call 266-1492.

Boston Symphony Orchestra performs at Symphony Hall from September through April. In July and August the orchestra moves to

Tanglewood in the Berkshires, a three-hour drive from Boston. Symphony Hall tickets are $27 to $90. Rush tickets, only one to a person sold on day of performance, are $8.00. Call 266-1200.

The **Handel & Haydn Society** performs baroque and classical repertoire with the instruments, techniques, and performing forces available to the composers in their time. Concerts are given at Symphony Hall, Jordan Hall, and the Old South Church. H&H gave the American premieres of Bach's Mass in B Minor in 1887 and Handel's *Messiah* in 1818, and the society still performs these pieces annually to sell-out audiences. Call 262-1815 or e-mail info@handelandhaydn.org.

Concerts, many free, are also given at the following:

Berklee College of Music, Berklee Performance Center, 136 Massachusetts Avenue, Boston; 747-8890. Music here has a popular and jazz emphasis, with a wide range of expression, considering that the college's 3,000 students are from more than sixty countries.

Boston College, 536-3356.

Boston University, 353-3345.

Emmanuel Church, 15 Newbury Street, Boston; 536-3355. Features the music of Bach at Sunday services.

Isabella Stewart Gardner Museum (see page 125). Offers chamber music and soloists on Tuesday at 6:00 P.M., Thursday at 12:15 P.M., and Sunday at 3:00 P.M. except in July and August. A donation is suggested.

Jordan Hall, 290 Huntington Avenue; tickets 536-2412, New England Conservatory Concert Line 585-1122. An acoustically superb hall that has more than 200 free concerts by students plus noted performers.

King's Chapel (see page 75). Many concerts given at lunchtime.

New England Conservatory of Music, 290 Huntington Avenue, Boston; 585-1122.

Film

MOVIE HOUSES AND OTHER VENUES

For visitors to Boston, theaters convenient to major hotels in Boston include:

Loews Boston Common, 176 Tremont Street; 423-3499. This complex has fourteen screens, with digital sound and stadium seats. Love seats are available.

Loews Copley Place, 100 Huntington Avenue; 266–1300. Set in the center of the lavish Copley Place, this venue has six screens.

The Reely Big Screen

Mugar Omni Theater, in the Boston Museum of Science at 723–2500. This theater presents special-interest films that wrap around your field of vision on a six-story screen along with 27,000 watts of sound power.

Simons Imax 3D Theatre, in the New England Aquarium at Central Wharf; (866) 815–4629. The newest huge screen also features three-dimensional films.

For visitors seeking foreign films, oldies, art, or just the unusual in film fare, these theaters should fit the bill:

In Boston

Hatch Shell, Charles River Esplanade. Popular and classic films shown on the outdoor stage where the Boston Pops celebrates the Fourth of July each year, featuring Friday Flicks. Screenings, which are free, are seasonal, of course.

Museum of Fine Arts, 465 Huntington Avenue (267–9300), shows films on occasion. Foreign, art, classics.

Wang Center, 268 Tremont Street (482–9393), is a classic 1920s movie palace turned performance center. Film classics are shown on the big, big screen.

In Cambridge

All these theaters are easily reached on the Red Line of the T.
Brattle Theatre, 40 Brattle Street, Harvard Square; 876–6837.

Harvard Film Archive, 24 Quincy Street; 495–4700.

Landmark's Kendall Square, 1 Kendall Square; 499–1996.

Loews Harvard Square Theatre, 10 Church Street; 864–4580.

In Brookline

Coolidge Corner Theatre, 290 Harvard Street (734–2500), offers one of the last big screens in the area. Easily reached by the Cleveland Circle branch of the T's Green Line. Classics, art films.

LIBRARIES OFFERING FILMS

Boston Public Library (536-5400, extension 317) has big-screen flicks for free.

The French Library, at 53 Marlborough Street in Boston (266-4351), shows—you guessed it—French films.

Goethe Institute, at 170 Beacon Street in Boston (262-6050), screens German classics.

Comedy Clubs

Beantown Comedy Vault, Remington's, 124 Boylston Street; 482-0110.

Comedy Connection, Faneuil Hall Marketplace, Middle Building; 248-9700.

Improv Asylum, 216 Hanover Street and 75 Warrenton Street; 263-6887.

Jimmy Tingle's Off-Broadway Theater, 255 Elm Street, Somerville; (617) 591-1616.

Nick's Comedy Stop, 100 Warrenton Street; 423-2900.

Nightspots

Throughout the city there are wonderful places for enjoying the night. Two areas where clubs are concentrated are Lansdowne Street, beside Fenway Park, and Boylston Place, across from Boston Common.

On Lansdowne Street

Avalon, 15 Lansdowne Street (262-2437), features one of the best sound systems in the city, along with a plush, ballroom-style atmosphere. Home of Avaland nightclub.

Axis, 13 Lansdowne Street (262-2437), features an eclectic set, with live music and disc jockeys. A rock-and-roll atmosphere.

Bill's Bar, 5½ Lansdowne Street (247-1222), offers a funky, relaxed atmosphere with a 1960s retro feel.

Boston Billiard Club, 126 Brookline Avenue, near Kenmore Square and Lansdowne Street (536-7665), has been rated by *Billiards Digest* as "the hands-down finest room in the country."

Jake Ivory's, 1 Lansdowne Street; 247-1222. Dueling pianos and lots of fun.

Matrix, 275 Tremont Street; 542-4077. Live music with experimental talent appealing to young audiences.

Rumor, 101 Warrenton Street; 536-0898. A cradle of hipster nightlife.

For Games and More

Boston Billiards, 126 Brookline Avenue; 536-7665. Gets great marks from billiard fans. Full bar.

Jillian's, 145 Ipswich Street (at the end of Lansdowne); 437-0300. High-tech games, pool tables, flight simulators, giant video wall, six bars, and now bowling as well.

King's Boston, 50 Dalton Street; 266-2695. Nightspot that features bowling and pool right next to the Prudential Center. Call ahead to check on wait.

The Rack, 24 Clinton Street; 725-1051. Near Faneuil Hall, this spot features slate tables, music, and good food.

Irish Fun

Black Rose, 160 State Street; 742-2286. Near Faneuil Hall.

The Green Dragon Tavern, 11 Marshall Street; 367-0055. Claims a history dating to Revolutionary times. Live bands and DJ.

Kinsale Irish Pub & Restaurant, across from City Hall; 742-5577. The pub and restaurant were built in Ireland and shipped to Boston.

M. J. O'Connor's Irish Pub, 27 Columbus Avenue, at Park Plaza; 482-2255. Traditional Irish music Wednesday evening.

McGann's of Boston, 197 Portland Street; 227-4059. More than twenty-six beers on tap. Features bands from Ireland.

Purple Shamrock, 1 Union Street; 227-2060. Lively spot near Faneuil Hall. Also features traditional Irish breakfast Saturday and Sunday.

Solas, 710 Boylston Street; 933-4803. A place for comfort (*solas* in Gaelic). It's in the Lenox Hotel.

Other Ideas

Dick's Last Resort, 55 Huntington Avenue; 267-8080. A fun place with live music.

Green Dragon Tavern, 11 Marshall Street; 367-0055. Entertainment, usually Irish music, from 9:30 P.M. Huge Irish breakfast on weekends.

Hard Rock Cafe, 131 Clarendon Street; 353-1400. Loud music, great hamburgers. The bar is shaped like a Fender Stratocaster guitar.

Jose McIntyre's, 160 Milk Street; 451-7400. Irish-Mexican bar with two floors of fun.

Dance Clubs

Avalon, see previous Lansdowne Street section.

Roxy, 279 Tremont Street, in the Tremont Hotel; 338-7699. Great sound, laser effects, and lighting. Music varies.

Sophia's, 1270 Boylston Street; 351-7001. The international crowd heads to this four-story Latin restaurant and nightclub. In season it features the roof deck Sky Bar.

Jazz and Blues Clubs

Harper's Ferry, 158 Brighton Avenue, Allston; 254-9743. The area's anchor club for blues and R&B.

Johnny D's, 17 Holland Street, Somerville; 776-2004. Blues, folk, roots, jazz, and international along with American and vegetarian dishes.

Regattabar, 1 Bennett Street, in the Charles Hotel, Cambridge; 661-5000. Great jazz.

Ryles, 212 Hampshire Street, Cambridge; 876-9330. Great jazz along with Latin, salsa, and merengue.

Scullers Jazz Club, 400 Soldiers Field Road, in the Doubletree Guest Suites Hotel, Boston; 562-4111. More great jazz sounds.

Music Clubs

Club Passim, 47 Palmer Street, Cambridge; 492-7679. The oldest folk club in the country, featuring nightly live music. Sorry, no alcohol, but a good spot for vegetarian pizza and more.

Middle East, 472 Massachusetts Avenue, Cambridge; 492-0576. Offers two restaurants along with two nightclubs featuring acoustic and live music.

Paradise Rock Club, 967 Commonwealth Avenue, Boston; 423-6398. Top local and national bands perform here.

Very Bostonian

The Roof Restaurant at the Ritz-Carlton, 15 Arlington Street, Boston; 536-5700. A Boston tradition begun in the 1930s, this venue offers a wonderful evening under the stars with great music and food. Open May through September.

At Boylston Place

The Big Easy, 1 Boylston Place (351-7000). A New Orleans-style bar that features top bands and has billiards.

The Sugar Shack, 1 Boylston Place (351-7000). It's a year-round Mardi Gras party with a DJ playing everything from the classics to funk.

Sweetwater Cafe, 2 Boylston Place (351-2515). Classic bar, live music, and DJs nightly. Also outdoor patio.

SPORTS BARS

The Baseball Tavern, 1306 Boylston Street; 437-1644. With Fenway Park across the street, this is a haven for Sox fans.

Cask 'N Flagon, 62 Brookline Street; 536-4840. A hangout for Red Sox fans just across from Fenway Park.

Champions, 110 Huntington Avenue, in the Boston Marriott Copley Place; 578-5800. Many TVs both small and large, fed by three satellites. Full menu of food until 1:00 A.M.

The Dockside Restaurant & Sports Bar, 183 State Street; 723-7050. Inexpensive eats, central location.

Four's Restaurant & Sports Bar, 166 Canal Street; 720-4455. Near FleetCenter and North Station. Has lots of sports memorabilia.

The Harp, 85 Causeway Street, near the FleetCenter; 742-1010. Live entertainment.

Porter's Bar, 173 Portland Street; 742-7678. Popular after games at nearby FleetCenter.

Who's on First, 19 Yawkey Way; 247-3353. Right on Red Sox turf, but you can get in without a ticket on game days by entering from an alley at 110 Brookline Avenue.

BEER

Boston and beer make a good combination. Although microbreweries and pub brewhouses are popping up across the country, I don't think there is anywhere in the country that can compare to Boston for a beer.

The Boston-beer connection goes back nearly four centuries. Although the Pilgrims did not settle Boston, there is a story that the reason they decided to cut their journey short and settle in Plymouth is they had run out of beer. Growing up in Boston we were never told that story, believing only that the Pilgrims were so pious a group that they did not indulge in such vices.

Even the early colonial patriots held many of their meetings in taverns, and if they were not drinking beer, it certainly wasn't tea—just look what they did to that stuff, dumping it in the harbor! Samuel Adams—whose name now graces one of the best beers in the country—was, in addition to one of the leaders and prime movers of the Revolution, also a beer maker.

In our time, the city has become world-famous all because of a TV beer pub set in Boston—**Cheers,** otherwise known as the Bull & Finch (for famed architect Charles Bulfinch, whose magnificent State House is just up the street), at 84 Beacon Street (227-9605). This touristy spot is still haunted by the ghosts of *Cheers.* Crowds still line up to get into the pub, and the series continues not in prime time but in reruns around the world. Is it popular? You bet. It's still one of the most visited sites in the city.

Beer lovers can have a feast within the Boston area. See chapter 20 for a complete listing of brewhouses in Cambridge.

Bell in Hand, 45 Union Street; 227-2098. It's the oldest tavern in the United States.

Black Rose, 160 State Street; 742-2286. A true Irish pub that, needless to say, features Irish music. In the Faneuil Hall area.

Cornwall's, 654 Beacon Street, Kenmore Square; 262-3749. An English tavern with twenty-four brews on tap.

Doyle's Cafe, 3484 Washington Street; 524-2345. Located in the Jamaica Plain area, this old-fashioned bar is a bit out of town, but the atmosphere is genuine. Doyle's has been used as a set for many a film shot in Boston.

Jacob Wirth, 31 Stuart Street; 338-8586. Features its own dark brew at a bar that is a landmark in the city. Restaurant specializes in German food and is one of the oldest in Boston.

Three Cheers Restaurant and Bar, 290 Congress Street; 423-6166. No, this is not the setting for *Cheers,* although its bar looks more like the one on TV than the original at Bull & Finch.

21st Amendment, 148 Bowdoin Street; 227-7100. Named after the amendment that repealed Prohibition.

Microbrewery Pubs

Boston Beer Works, 61 Brookline Avenue; 536-2337. Great beers, handy to Fenway Park and Lansdowne Street. Here, visitors are surrounded by brewing kettles. Always on tap are at least eight beers and ales, including their Boston Burton Ale, named the "Best of Boston" in 1995. A wide range of foods is also offered. Has a second location at 112 Canal Street (896-2337).

Beer Brewing Tours

Harpoon Ale, Mass. Bay Brewing Company, 306 Northern Avenue; 574-9551. Located on the waterfront. Free tours and samples.

Sam Adams Beer, Boston Beer Company, 30 Germania Street; 368-5221. Free tours, free samples. In the Jamaica Plain section of the city. Don't miss Doyle's Café nearby.

A Good Spot for a Drink and Conversation

The Oak Bar, at the Fairmont Copley Plaza, 138 St. James Avenue (267-5300), has long been a favorite with Bostonians. The **Bar at the Ritz-Carlton Hotel,** 15 Arlington Street (536-5700) is a classy place for a drink; overlooks the Public Garden. Offers a clublike setting for the perfect martini or other drink, with a pianist in the background. The **Bay Tower Room,** 60 State Street (723-1666), offers a high and spectacular view of the waterfront; **Julien Bar** in the Langham Hotel, 250 Franklin Street (451-1900), retains the Wyeth murals from the days when the hotel was the site of the Federal Reserve Bank. Nice piano music as well. The **Bristol Lounge** at the Four Seasons Hotel, 200 Boylston Street (338-1900)—a popular place for celebrity-watching. Very comfortable, great service. The **Atrium Cafe** in the Millenium Bostonian Hotel, Faneuil Hall (523-3600), provides a nice quiet setting for escaping the crowds across the way in the marketplace. The **Top of the Hub**, fifty-two stories above the city in the Prudential Tower, 800 Boylston Street (536-1775), is now a grand place to sip, talk, and enjoy the music and the views. **Whiskey Park in the Boston Park Plaza Hotel** (542-1482) offers a sexy setting with its leather loveseats, faux-mink fur couches, and two mahogany bars. The **Last Hurrah** in the Omni Parker House (227-8600) is adorned with political icons as its just steps away from the State House. The **Back Lot** in the Ritz-Carlton, Boston Common, is casual, lively, and with its movie theme drinks and appetizers, a great place to meet. Just above the entrance to Loews Theatres on Boylston Street. **The Ruby Room** at the Onyx Hotel is swank and has the feel of a New York lounge. **Sanctuary** at 189 State Street, near the Quincy Marketplace, offers a relaxing atmosphere and humorously named martinis.

Casinos

Although there is no gambling allowed in Massachusetts, there are regular motor-coach tours to the Indian casinos of Connecticut, about 1½ to 2 hours from Boston.

Foxwoods Resort Casino, Mashantucket, Connecticut; (800) 369-9663. The largest casino in the Western Hemisphere, it features top entertainment, dining rooms, and games. Also has an excellent Native American museum.

Mohegan Sun Casino, Uncasville, Connecticut; (888) 226-7711. Besides top entertainment, twenty-nine eateries, thirty shops, and a huge gaming area, Mohegan features Casino in the Sky, a planetarium that rises over the casino. Its Wombi Rock has a three-level lounge and dance floor.

CHAPTER EIGHTEEN

Shopping

The city is a haven for shoppers. Boston is home to six distinctive shopping districts, each with its own appeal. In addition, museum and souvenir shops offer unusual gifts.

Unlike many cities in the country, Boston offers many and varied shopping opportunities. Stepping out of a hotel downtown, one will find more than 2,000 shops of all descriptions—not just souvenir types—but real shops, some, like Filene's Basement, with real value.

Unlike many cities where the downtown has become empty canyons surrounded by office buildings that close by 6:00 P.M., Boston has retained its downtown fairly well. People not only work but also live and shop here.

Downtown Crossing, once Boston's hub for shopping, with major department stores and specialty shops, is still lively and still offers many reasons to go there for purchases. Less than a few blocks toward the harbor, one will find the Faneuil Hall Marketplace, a former warehouse area that has become the liveliest part of Boston day and night. Heading west about a mile is Copley Square, where the luxurious indoor Copley Place shopping area has top names in fashion, jewelry, and specialty items. Extending from it is the covered walkway to the Shops at the Prudential, where Saks Fifth Avenue heads up a long list of specialty merchants.

On the way to Copley Square, one can walk along Boylston Street, with its grand array of distinctive shops, or detour—and you should—over to Newbury Street, one of the classiest shopping streets in the United States. Top European designers, trendy outdoor cafes and restaurants, wonderful art galleries, and superb jewelers all line a street with a definite European feel.

And did we mention the shops on Charles Street at the foot of Beacon Hill? Here you'll find antiques shops and trendy boutiques.

So, which way do you go?

DOWNTOWN CROSSING

Downtown Crossing is anchored by **Macy's** and **Filene's** department stores. Beneath Filene's is the world-famous **Filene's Basement,** where items are automatically marked down and, if not sold within fifty-six days, are given to charity. Every piece has a price tag with the date it hit the selling floor. After fourteen days the price is discounted 25 percent, after twenty-eight days, 50 percent, and after forty-two days, 75 percent. Remember these items were already discounted to begin with.

Along Washington Street, which passes in front of both stores, there are no cars but lots of pushcarts brimming with bargains, and street entertainers. Here, too, is the **Jewelers Building,** long known for its great buys. I bought a wedding ring here.

Lots of specialty stores are along the way, and do explore the side streets. At 9 West Street is the **Brattle Book Shop,** a heavenly place for old books and maps. More than 150,000 books can be found on its three floors at prices from $1.00 up. At 50 Temple you'll find **Stoddard's,** the country's oldest cutlery shop, dating from the 1800s.

To reach this shopping area, take the Red Line to Downtown Crossing. Filene's and Macy's have subway entrances. You could also take the Red or Green Line to Park Street and stroll down the block of stores on Winter Street that hooks up to Washington Street.

FANEUIL HALL MARKETPLACE

When Ben Franklin was growing up in Boston, most of this area was waterfront. Then it was filled in during the early 1800s and became a warehouse area with the present 535-foot-long **Quincy Market** buildings fronting Boston Harbor. In 1976 the area was restored, filling the former warehouse buildings with hundreds of specialty shops inside and out. There's also a lively street scene, and music fills the air.

Wear comfortable shoes, as the cobblestones of the past still make up the walkways here. To get to Faneuil Hall Marketplace, take the T's Green Line to Government Center and walk to the complex.

Whether you are looking for a souvenir or a gift, the shops in the Faneuil Hall Marketplace are sure to please. The **Boston Pewter Company** has a huge selection of American-made pewter. If you run, head to **Bill Rodgers Running Center.** Rodgers (Boston's Marathon Man) has everything from shoes to accessories. **The Museum of Fine Arts** has wonderful items from reproduction posters to teacups. Other shops feature Celtic wear, charms of Boston, handicrafts, and more.

The area is brimming with dining and drinking spots. Inside the Quincy Market is a huge food court with Boston specialties, seafood, and tastes from India, Greece, Japan, and even Philadelphia. **Durgin Park** is a restaurant that is as Boston as can be, the **Union Oyster House** is the country's oldest dining place, and **Bell in Hand Tavern** is the country's oldest bar.

Faneuil Hall has been a marketplace for more than 250 years. Here Bostonians protested the British taxation policies of the 1760s, eventually leading to the American Revolution.

If you are taking the Freedom Trail to the area, stop by the **Old Corner Bookstore building,** a Boston literary landmark. You'll find a good selection of books on Boston, famous front pages of the century-plus-old paper, and other Boston souvenirs.

NEWBURY STREET

This street, parallel to Boylston, is one of the classiest shopping streets of any city. Its brownstones have become elegant shops for Burberry, Brooks Brothers, Cartier, and many European names. Newbury is where the international set heads for fashions. A standout at the corner of Berkeley Street is **Louis Boston** in the former Museum of Natural History building. Here you'll find high fashion and a delightful cafe. Newbury is also known for its beauty salons and spas. If you are looking for works by John James Audubon or antique maps, head to the **Haley & Steele Gallery,** or for the latest in high tech, high design, set your sights on **Bang & Olufsen.** For a change of scene, try **Gargoyles, Grotesques, and Chimeras,** a gallery filled with gargoyles and religious statuary that just might fit into your home's design. As many galleries are located on the second floor, do look up. You'll also find such wonderful galleries as the Society of Arts and Crafts, the Copley Society, Vose Galleries, and Robert Klein. Sidewalk cafes, too, dot the landscape along this street, which begins at the Public Garden and the original Ritz-Carlton Hotel and continues for a half mile, ending with the giant **Virgin Records Shop** at Massachusetts Avenue. (To get to Newbury Street, take the Green Line to Arlington or Copley Station. Newbury Street is a block away.)

BOYLSTON STREET

This street is making its mark with its unusual and interesting stores. The street makes a delightful walk between downtown and Copley Square. Along the way you'll discover **Aquascutum of London,** outfitters to British royalty, with its sole U.S. location; **Hermes** (where a beach towel can cost in the hundreds); **Escada** (only the second one in the United States for this Munich-based firm); and on to **Shreve, Crump & Low,** reportedly America's oldest jewelry store (see "Souvenirs" on the next page). There's also **Cigar Masters** with a walk-in humidor filled with finely aged tobacco. Lest you think this is just an expensive shopping area, you'll also find a **Marshall's** for off-price clothing.

COPLEY PLACE AND THE PRUDENTIAL CENTER

Boston's upscale indoor mall, **Copley Place,** is set on nine and a half acres of land over the Massachusetts Turnpike and is home to Neiman-Marcus, Tiffany, Gucci, Ralph Lauren, and a hundred other premier shops. On two levels, the complex is anchored by the Westin and Boston Marriott Hotels, and within it are nine movie theaters, a waterfall, many restaurants, and offices. (To reach Copley Place, take the Green Line to Copley Station. Walk across Copley Square from the T station, passing the Boston Public Library. Enter the center through the Westin Hotel entrance, which leads directly into the shopping area. Or take the Orange Line to Back Bay Station; Copley Place is right across the street.)

The **Shops at Prudential** are connected to Copley Place via a glass-enclosed walkway across Huntington Avenue. Along its walkway you'll find Saks Fifth Avenue, along with lots of specialty shops, and even a chapel to find some solitude.

Here you can also soar above the city to take in its surroundings from the fifty-second floor of the **Prudential Tower.** There's lots of good dining here, from Legal Seafoods to fun places like Dick's Last Resort. For fine dining, the Top of the Hub can't be beat—nor can its view. There's also a food court and Marche Movenpick, a three-floor food feast that's well worth discovering. Krispy Kreme and Dunkin Donuts are here to tempt you, too.

You can reach the Prudential Center by taking the Green Line to the Convention Center/ICA station.

CHARLES STREET

Located at the foot of Beacon Hill, Charles Street offers a nice collection of antiques shops and restaurants. Among shops to check out are **Period Furniture Hardware Company** (123 Charles), with reproductions of hardware items from the eighteenth century and on; **Helen's Leather** (110 Charles), with a wooden boot outside to catch your eye and, inside, an exotic collection of handmade boots along with briefcases and backpacks; **Elegant Findings** offers fine European porcelain, while **Polly Latham Antiques** specializes in Chinese and Japanese export porcelains, and those are but a few of the shops. Don't fear getting hungry here as there are many choices including the **Paramount** for a great meal any time of the day. Or stop by **DeLuca's Market,** a Beacon Hill institution, to pick up the makings for your own picnic on nearby Boston Common or the Public Garden.

MUSEUM SHOPS

For some uncommon gifts for all ages, Boston's museum shops can answer one's prayers. Look to the shops at the Museum of Fine Arts, the Museum of Science, the Children's Museum, the New England Aquarium, the USS *Constitution* Museum, the John F. Kennedy Library, Paul Revere House, Museum of Afro American History, Isabella Stewart Gardner Museum, Bostonian Society Museum Shop, and the Tea Party Ship and Museum.

SOUVENIRS

Some of my favorite gifts for family come from, of all places, **Shreve, Crump & Low,** the nation's oldest jewelry shop—and a Boston tradition. Despite its elegant and expensive look, Shreve's also offers lovely Boston charms and pins, especially ones featuring the famed ducks of the Public Garden, at prices beginning around $30. Perhaps their most unusual souvenirs are the Gurgling Cod water pitchers. The cod is so well regarded in Boston that a replica of one hangs in the House of Representatives in the State House. These custom-made pitchers from England actually gurgle as water is poured. Best of all, they are priced from $35 to $50. Shreve, Crump & Low is at 440 Boylston Street; telephone 267-9100 or (800) 324-0222.

Finally, don't go home without trying lobster. Lobsters are even available at Logan Airport, packed for the trip home—a wonderful way to savor your Boston visit.

CHAPTER NINETEEN

Sports and Recreation

Boston is a sports town. What else can you say about the city that is home to a basketball team, the Celtics, who have won more championships than any other NBA team? Or a hockey team, the Bruins, who have made it to the Stanley Cup play-offs more than seventeen times? Or a baseball team, the Red Sox, who finally achieved the impossible dream, winning the 2004 World Series after 86 years of trying? Or even the New England Patriots, who toss the pigskin some 25 miles south of town, and after years of disappointment surprised the nation with their unbelievable 2001 season that culminated in the Super Bowl championship, and then went on for another championship season? The team now has a spectacular state-of-the-art stadium, Gillette Field in Foxborough. The New England Revolution brings professional soccer action to the area.

What's the score? Call the *Boston Globe*'s recorded score line, 265-6600. You might also want to visit the Sports Museum of New England, described later in this chapter.

THE PROS AND WHERE THEY PLAY

Boston Bruins, FleetCenter, Causeway Street; 624-1900. Tickets can also be purchased through Ticketmaster at 931-2222.

Boston Celtics, FleetCenter, Causeway Street; 533-3030. Tickets can also be purchased through Ticketmaster at 931-2222.

Boston Red Sox, Fenway Park (Yawkey Way and Lansdowne Street), Boston. For ticket information, call 384–4378 or (877) REDSOX–9.

New England Revolution, Gillette Stadium, Foxborough; (877) GET–REVS.

New England Patriots, Gillette Stadium, Foxborough; (800) 543–1776.

Fenway Park, built in 1917, is the oldest and smallest park in the major leagues. Most visitors would also agree that it is one of the nicest ballparks. Fenway has added many seats from luxury boxes high above the grand stand to ones atop the famed left-field green wall—the Green Monster, with its ancient scoreboard below—that still defies batters. If you can't get tickets to a game, look into taking a tour, which are offered daily.

Across from the Fenway ticket office on Yawkey Way is the Souvenir Shop, which, Boston being the sports town it is, claims to be the world's largest sports souvenir store.

FleetCenter, completed in 1995, replaced the ancient and honorable Boston Garden. Here the Boston Celtics and Boston Bruins have their home games, and events ranging from rock concerts and Ringling Brothers and Barnum & Bailey Circus to the Democratic National Convention in 2004 are showcased. Unlike its predecessor, the FleetCenter has no obstructed views and is air-conditioned, so never again will a Celtics game be called because moisture seeping from the ice rink under the parquet floor made the court too slippery to play on. Visitors will also find a great selection of food choices inside as well as at the many fast-food and sports bars just outside along Causeway, Canal, Friend, and Portland Streets. For persons driving to an event, there is ample parking in the area as well as at the 1,300-car MBTA Parking facility under the center.

Gillette Stadium, the home of Super Bowl champions the New England Patriots, is a state-of-the-art stadium with 68,000 seats that opened in 2002. The $325 million open-air stadium covers seventeen acres; has plenty of parking (train service from Back Bay and South Station is available at a cost); includes eighty luxury suites and two three-story-high club lounges; and offers lots of good food choices, more than enough bathrooms (unlike the old stadium now torn down), and a park for pregame picnics. Gillette is also the home to the New England Revolution soccer team.

WHERE COLLEGE TEAMS PLAY

Boston College Alumni Stadium, Brookline; 552–3000, extension 3000.

Boston University Nickerson Field, Babcock Street, Boston; 353–2000.

Harvard University Stadium, North Harvard Street and Soldiers Field Road, Allston; 495–2212.

Major Sports Events

The **Boston Marathon,** held annually on Patriots' Day in April, is a holiday weekend in Massachusetts. The run begins in Hopkinton, continues for 26 miles and 385 yards, and ends at Copley Square in Boston. Thousands of runners from around the world compete. There is excellent viewing all along the route, and corner rooms in the Lenox Hotel overlook the finish line. The Boston Athletic Association sponsors the event. You can contact them at 40 Trinity Place; 236–1652.

Head of the Charles Regatta, held in October, involves more than 800 boats and 3,000 participants with teams from around the world: a grand social event, as there is no head-to-head competition, with boats leaving every ten seconds from the Boston University Boathouse. By T, take the Green Line Boston College branch to Boston University or the Red Line to Harvard Square and then walk over to the Charles.

Sports and Recreational Activities

Looking for sports and fitness activities? The *Boston Globe* on Friday offers in its sports section a "What's Happening" page that lists activities ranging from auto racing to yoga. The Thursday "Calendar" section has extensive listings of outdoor activities for the week.

BICYCLING

In Boston and along the Charles River, the **Dr. Paul Dudley White Charles River Bike Path** goes from the Museum of Science along both sides of the Charles to Watertown Square; it is also open to joggers, roller skaters, and persons out for a stroll. The entire circuit is 17.7 miles.

In Cambridge, a section of **Memorial Drive** from Mount Auburn Hospital to the Harvard Square area is closed on summer Sunday afternoons for bike riding, jogging . . . you name it.

Blue Hills Reservation offers mountain biking. For maps and information, call reservation headquarters at 698–1802.

Organizations for Bike Riders

Appalachian Mountain Club, at 5 Joy Street in Boston (523-0636), sponsors rides throughout southeastern Massachusetts and New England. It offers individual, family, and senior citizen memberships.

Worldwide Hostel Info Line, at 1020 Commonwealth Avenue in Boston (731-5430), features evening and weekend rides as well as weekend trips. It offers individual, family, and senior citizen memberships.

Bike Rentals

Biking along the Charles River is a delight. Call the shops first about available rentals, age limits, and cash or credit card policies.

Boston Bike Tours and Rentals, on Boston Common; 308-5902. Also offers guided sightseeing tours of Boston, Cambridge, and other areas.

Community Bicycle Supply, 490 Tremont Street; 542-8623.

International Bicycle Centers, 89 Brighton Avenue; 783-5804.

The Hyatt and Royal Sonesta hotels in Cambridge, which front the river and the bike path, offer bikes to their guests.

BOATING

Boston Sailing Center, 54 Lewis Wharf, 227-4198, offers lessons for all ability levels. Open year-round.

Community Boating, located at 21 David Mugar Way at the Hatch Shell on the Charles River, offers reasonable rates on sailing lessons, and membership includes the use of sailboats. The organization offers a program for persons age eleven and up. Even short courses are available for visitors. Call 523-1038.

Jamaica Pond Project, at 507 Jamaicaway in Boston (635-4505), offers boat rentals.

CANOEING/KAYAKING

Charles River Canoe and Kayak, 2401 Commonwealth Avenue, Newton; 965-5110. Has a green-roofed kiosk along Soldiers Field Road, 200 yards past Eliot Bridge. Parking nearby. Within walking distance of Harvard Square.

DOG RACING

Wonderland Greyhound Park, 190 VFW Parkway, Revere, near Wonderland T stop on the Blue Line; (781) 284-1300. Racing all year; nightly at 7:30 P.M. and matinees Tuesday at 4:30 and 6:30 P.M. Has a dining room overlooking the track and a sports bar.

FISHING

Ponds near and in Boston stocked with trout include Jamaica Pond in Jamaica Plain, Lake Cochituate in Wayland, and Walden Pond State Reservation in Concord. Ponds stocked with northern pike include Ponkapog Pond in Canton and Hammond Pond in Brookline. Lake Cochituate is also known for tiger muskie. For information on fishing and fishing regulations, call (800) 275-3474. Boston Harbor Cruises offers deep-sea fishing.

GOLF

Many golf courses, both public and private, lie within the Greater Boston area. The 1988 U.S. Open was held at the Country Club in Brookline, but don't expect to play at this exclusive club unless you know someone. For information on golf courses, contact the Massachusetts Golf Association at 300 Arnold Palmer Boulevard, Norton; (800) 356-2201. The office is open weekdays from 8:00 A.M. to 5:00 P.M. The Massachusetts Golf Museum, which includes a replica of the Francis Oulmet Library, is open weekdays 10:00 A.M. to 5:00 P.M. Free. For information, call (774) 430-9100. The private eighteen-hole Tournament Players Club of Boston, operated by the PGA, is adjacent.

Public Courses

Ferncroft Country Club, 50 Ferncroft Road, Danvers; (978) 777-5614. A private eighteen-hole Robert Trent Jones course open to those staying at the Sheraton Ferncroft Resort. Handy to Boston.

Franklin Park Golf Course, Franklin Park, Boston; 265-4085. Minutes from downtown Boston, this is the second-oldest course in America and a part of the Emerald Necklace.

George Wright Golf Course, 420 West Street, Hyde Park; 364-2300. An eighteen-hole Donald Ross course within the city of Boston.

Granite Links Golf Club at Quarry Hills, 100 Quarry Hills Drive, Quincy;
296-7600. Seven miles from Boston featuring twenty-seven holes
designed by John Sanford. Great views of Boston and its harbor.

Sheraton Colonial Hotel and Golf Club, 1 Audubon Road, Wakefield; (781)
245-9300. Has an eighteen-hole PGA-certified course. Handy to Boston.

HORSE RACING

Suffolk Downs, Route 1A, East Boston, near T stop; 567-3900.
Thoroughbred racing afternoons except Thursdays; first race is at noon.
Admission to the grandstand is free! Dining room overlooks the finish line.
Take the Blue Line to the Suffolk Downs T stop.

RUNNING AND JOGGING

Most Boston hotels have a map of the best jogging routes in their area—just
ask. The Esplanade, though, is always a delight.

NATURE TRAILS AND BIRDING TOURS

The **Massachusetts Audubon Society** offers a number of areas for nature
walks, including tours from the Trailside Museum in the Blue Hills just outside Boston in Canton and Milton; Drumlin Farm Sanctuary in Lincoln;
Ipswich River Wildlife Sanctuary; and Moose Hill Sanctuary in Sharon.

Some of the best birding sites within 30 miles of Boston include the
Arnold Arboretum, Blue Hills and Fowl Meadows, Boston Harbor islands,
Mount Auburn Cemetery, Crane Beach Reservation in Ipswich, Plum Island
in Newburyport, Drumlin Farm Sanctuary, and Great Meadows National
Wildlife Refuge. For information, call the Audubon Society at (781)
259-9500.

ROLLER SKATING/IN-LINE SKATING

The Esplanade is ideal for this sport. Also, on Sunday in summer, a portion
of Memorial Drive in Cambridge is closed for roller skating/in-line skating
and other forms of recreation.

For rentals, contact **Beacon Hill Skate Shop,** 135 Charles Street;
482-7400.

SKIING

Although most skiing activities take place outside the Boston area, the *Boston
Globe* sponsors free downhill and cross-country ski clinics each January. For
information and dates, call 929-2000. Clinics are held at various ski areas.

Downhill Skiing

Blue Hills Ski Area, Canton; (781) 828-7300. Located 9 miles south of the city. Has snowmaking, limited slopes, night skiing. Great area for learning.

Wachusett Mountain Ski Area, 499 Mountain Road, Princeton; (800) 754-1234. Located about an hour west of Boston, just off Route 2. Has eighteen trails, night skiing, 100 percent snowmaking.

Waterville Valley, Waterville Valley, New Hampshire; (800) 468-2553. Superb New England skiing with fifty-three trails, full resort facilities, two hours from Boston. Cross-country skiing is also offered.

Cross-Country Skiing

Wachusett Mountain Ski Area, 499 Mountain Road, Princeton; (800) 754-1234.

Weston Ski Track, 200 Park Road, Weston; (781) 891-6575. Weston is less than a half hour from downtown Boston.

SWIMMING AND SUNNING

Boston is fortunate in having beaches all easily reached by public transportation and within 5 miles of the heart of the city. Unfortunately, all are within Boston Harbor, which until recently was the most polluted waterway in the country. While conditions are improving with the completed construction of a 9-mile outlet pipe into the ocean for treated water, I still would urge caution in swimming at one of the beaches. The beaches include **Malibu Beach** and **Tenean Beach** in Dorchester, **Constitution Beach** in East Boston, and **Castle Island, Pleasure Bay, L Street,** and **Carson Beaches** in South Boston.

In the **Boston Harbor Islands** (see chapter 13), facilities are as follows:

Bumpkin Island: tours, picnicking, trails, fishing piers, no lifeguards.

Gallops Island: swimming, picnicking, no lifeguards.

Grape Island: picnicking, trails, fishing piers, no lifeguards.

Lovell's Island: picnicking, tours, trails, camping, and lifeguards.

Spectacle Island: swimming, picnicking, trails, no lifeguards.

Parking is free at Boston area beaches. Most have bathhouses. Water temperature ranges from about 58 degrees in spring to perhaps 70 degrees in August. (August tends to be greenhead-fly season: Bring along insect repellent.)

Provincetown, at the tip of Cape Cod, offers some wonderful beaches and can be reached by boat from downtown Boston.

Revere Beach, just north of the city and on the Atlantic, is easily reached via the T's Blue Line to Revere Station.

Many clean, popular seaside spots on the north and south shores are easily accessible by public transportation. Contact the MBTA for information.

TENNIS

Longwood Cricket Club, at 564 Hammond Street in Brookline (731–2900), holds the U.S. Championship yearly. Don't be fooled by the club's name, as tennis is the game here.

SPORTS MUSEUM

The **Sports Museum of New England,** FleetCenter (624–1235), honors New England athletes and teams through art, video, memorabilia, and interactive exhibits. Call ahead to confirm hours. Admission is $6.00 for adults and $4.00 for youths age sixteen or younger and seniors.

PART FOUR

GETTING TO KNOW CAMBRIDGE

Cambridge Tour and Attractions

If Boston is considered the most European of American cities, then Cambridge, less than 3 miles away, must rank as the most international. Both cities, of course, are very much American, but when you take thousands of students from around the world, spending four or more years within the tight confines of a city that is only 6.25 square miles, the multiplicity of cultures is bound to have an effect. And indeed it does, creating a livelier, fun atmosphere that you can feel just stepping into Harvard Square.

Harvard Square, more triangular than square, with Harvard University forming one side and commerce the others, is the place to begin an exploration of Cambridge, for Harvard Square not only is where the city began but is still its heart.

And nowhere does Cambridge's diversity come together more than in Harvard Square. There are many other squares in Cambridge with lives all their own. Inman Square, a short walk from Harvard, is slower paced and smaller. It has the neighborhood feel but with shops stocked with gift items from every continent and classic restaurants like the S&S, which has been a landmark there since 1919. Central Square, just down Massachusetts Avenue, is the location of City Hall. But the liveliest action takes place around Harvard. For most visitors Harvard Square is a people-watching place. Grab some coffee and a muffin and just sit outside the Au Bon Pain that faces Harvard Yard from across Massachusetts Avenue for a wonderful show of street performers and passersby in all sorts of dress speaking a multitude of languages. If you get tired of watching, just take a few steps over to the Out of Town newsstand in the middle of the square. Here you can pick up publications from around the world.

Harvard Square is also for history and shopping. Early colonists once thought of making this the capital of the Massachusetts colony, and it is where George Washington took command of the Continental army. Some wonderful little shops can be found on both the main streets and side alleys. The square is also a book lover's haven, with more bookstores per square foot than just about anywhere in the country. Although some complain that the square is becoming too gentrified and losing its appeal, the visitor likely will not be bothered. There is just too much to see and do.

The square is filled with lots of delightful restaurants to experience new tastes, and there's a full array of nightlife to enjoy. There are great clubs; classic films can be seen at the Brattle Theater; and there are lots of cultural happenings, many sponsored by Harvard University.

Harvard Square is easily reached from downtown Boston, just a fifteen-minute T ride on the Red Line. You could easily fill a day or more just browsing through the shops, museums, and historical attractions and then while away your evening in one of the many folk, jazz, or blues clubs.

Beyond Harvard Square, you'll find lots of ethnic restaurants and music clubs in Central, Porter, and Inman Squares, all reachable by public transportation.

Two of my favorite places to stay in the Boston area are both in Cambridge along the Charles River, providing grand and sweeping views of downtown Boston. Both the Royal Sonesta and Hyatt Regency have easy access to jogging and walking trails along the river as well. The Hyatt has a revolving restaurant with superb views.

Gaining more attention these days is the CambridgeSide Galleria, just across from the Royal Sonesta. Here, besides shopping the mall's stores, you can catch a boat ride along the Charles or through the locks into Boston Harbor.

No matter where you are in Cambridge, you are never far from the Charles River. Sit or walk along the Charles and watch the rowers on the river. You'll see both shells (long racing boats with outrigged oars) and sculls (light racing boats propelled by an oar or a pair of oars), piloted by students from Harvard, Radcliffe, and M.I.T. Each October one of the greatest rowing events in the world, the Head of the Charles Regatta, takes place on the river. More than 250,000 people line the shores to partake in what has also been called the "world's largest picnic."

Tourist Information and Visitor Services

Cambridge Office for Tourism, 4 Brattle Street; 441–2884 or (800) 862–5678. A helpful source of information on sightseeing and on food and lodging in and around Cambridge.

Visitor Information Booth, located at the Harvard Square subway entrance. Here one will find walking tours of the square and Cambridge as well as maps and books. Open year-round from 9:00 A.M. to 5:00 P.M. Monday through Saturday and 1:00 to 5:00 P.M. Sunday.

Information Line, 441–2884 or www.cambridge-usa.org.

Harvard University Information Center, 1350 Massachusetts Avenue, in the Holyoke Center (next to Au Bon Pain); 495–1573. Free tours of the university are offered by Harvard students Monday through Saturday. Guided tours (free) leave the Holyoke Center Monday through Saturday at 10:00 and 11:15 A.M. and 2:00 and 3:15 P.M.

Other Tours

By Foot

For a detailed walking tour of Cambridge, buy a copy of John Harris's *The Boston Globe Historic Walks in Old Boston.*

ESL Walks and Talks, 264–8844. Fun ninety-minute tours for non-native English speakers.

Walking tours of Harvard Yard, free, see above.

By Boat

From the CambridgeSide Galleria Mall, a short walk from the Boston Museum of Science, the **Charles Riverboat Co.** offers fifty-five-minute narrated tours of the lower Charles River basin on weekends in April, May, and September. Tours depart daily, on the hour, noon to 5:00 P.M. June through August. Call 621–3001. Also cruises through the river's locks into Boston Harbor.

On Wheels

Accurate Tours (233–8471) offers hotel pickups. Covers Harvard and M.I.T as well as Boston.

By car, take the Grand Tour by Car in chapter 3.

Double Decker Bus Company (679–0031). New England's only double-decker buses leave from CambridgeSide Galleria. Tours cover historic sites and Harvard and M.I.T.

Old Town Trolley Tours of Cambridge (269–7150) offers eighty-minute tours of the city. Visitors can get on and off at various sites.

TRANSPORTATION

Cambridge is easily reached from Boston. The distance from downtown Boston to Harvard Square is just about 3 miles, or ten minutes by the T.

The T's Red Line runs through Cambridge from the heart of Boston, stopping at Kendall Square, Central Square, Harvard Square, and continuing on to Alewife. For those traveling from the north, coming into the city via Route 2, Alewife is a good place to board the T for a Boston visit. Because of Cambridge's convenience to Boston, it is also a good place to stay. Accommodations can be found near the Alewife, Harvard, and Kendall stations.

By car, Cambridge is easily reached from downtown Boston by taking Massachusetts Avenue across the Harvard Bridge (by M.I.T.) and on into Central and Harvard Squares. From the Government Center area, take Cambridge Street across the Longfellow Bridge into Kendall Square. Or from Interstate 93 take the Storrow Drive exit and take one of the many exits that lead to Kendall, Central, or Harvard Square. The Massachusetts Turnpike has a Cambridge exit just before its final toll booth. Route 2 from the western part of Massachusetts runs through Cambridge, and Interstate 95 from the north provides an exit into Cambridge.

Taxi Companies

Ambassador Brattle Taxi, 492-1100
Cambridge Cab, 354-5005
Checker Cab of Cambridge, 497-9000
Yellow Cab Company of Cambridge, 547-3000

MEDICAL

Mount Auburn Hospital, near Harvard Square; 492-3500, emergencies 499-5025.

CVS, Porter Square (Somerville, near the Cambridge line); open twenty-four hours; 876-4037, pharmacy 876-5519.

CURRENCY EXCHANGE

Bank of America, Harvard Square, 1414 Massachusetts Avenue; 788-5000.

GOOD DEALS

Boston CityPass includes admission to Harvard Museum of Natural History. See page 22.

The **Go Boston Card** offers discounts on tours and attractions in Cambridge as well as Boston. See page 23.

Harvard Box Office, Holyoke Center Arcade, 1350 Massachusetts Avenue; 482-2849. Offers half-price, day-of-show tickets to theater, dance, music, and more in the Boston area.

The **Harvard Hot Ticket** offers admission to six Harvard museums. It is good for up to one year, allowing plenty of time to take in all the museums. Available at the museums or the Harvard Collections store at the Holyoke Center. Adults $10.00, seniors and students $8.00.

A Walking Tour of Harvard Square

Cambridge began life as Newtown in 1630. It was here, for safety's sake, far up the Charles River—then a tidal river easily navigated—that the Massachusetts Bay Colony set up its seat of government within a protected area. Fears of Indian attacks and of invasions by the French or others were soon dispelled, and the government moved to Boston—but not entirely before the colony established the first college in the land here in 1636. The college was later named for a young Charlestown minister, John Harvard, who died in 1638, leaving his library of 400 volumes to the institution. That same year the town was renamed for the English university from which so many of the Puritan leaders had graduated: Cambridge.

Since that time, Cambridge has grown, filling in land along the Charles, some of which in 1916 became home to Massachusetts Institute of Technology, which, like Harvard, has become an international center of learning, with students from about a hundred nations attending its classes. Between these two universities alone are more than 34,000 undergraduate and graduate students.

Perhaps owing to the presence of two major institutions that are also major employers in the city, Cambridge retains a lively mix of professors, students, blue-collar workers, and scientists. It is a city that blends history, education, commerce, entertainment, and culture as perhaps nowhere else. The city is known as "The People's Republic of Cambridge" because of its independent and sometimes somewhat radical ideas and politics. Although close to Boston, the views expressed in Cambridge are quite different.

Cambridge is also where George Washington took command of the Continental army. It offers the literary shrine of Henry Wadsworth Longfellow's home (even George Washington once lived there) and is a bib-

Harvard Square Walk

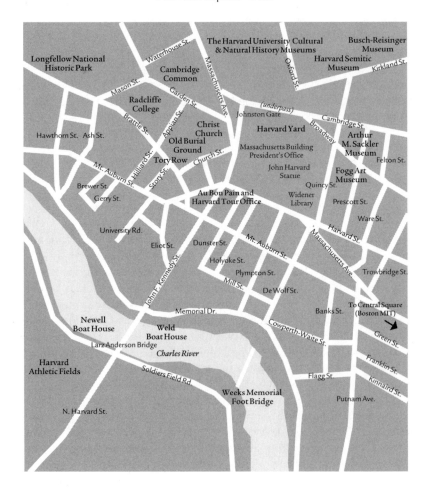

liophile's paradise, with its vast collection of bookstores. In Cambridge are the classic mansions of Tory Row, as well as three-decker houses. As the home of M.I.T., the city has been, and continues to be, the birthplace of many technological innovations. It is also a food lover's paradise, cooking up everything from ethnic treats to haute cuisine. Julia Child lived here for years. It offers theater, nightlife, and street performers, and its museums are filled with world treasures, even some remarkable flowers made of glass. Many motion pictures have been filmed here. One, *Good Will Hunting,* introduced native sons Ben Affleck and Matt Damon to the world. Both visit often. The author Robert Parker, of the popular Spenser detective series, lives here.

Our walking tour of Cambridge is designed to catch the flavor of old Cambridge and Harvard via a short walk that can easily be broken up with stops at any of the many small restaurants in the Harvard Square area. The tour offers a look at the historic, commercial, and university aspects of Cambridge and provides a couple of alternatives to add to the exploration.

From the T station in **Harvard Square,** you might first stop at the Cambridge Discovery booth, located at the T entrance, for additional maps, brochures, and ideas for your visit; Cambridge Discovery also offers low-cost walking tours in season.

Heading toward the **Harvard Cooperative Society ("the Coop,"** which you will probably want to visit at some point for shopping), walk to the gray church seen just ahead to the right. This **Unitarian church** was built in 1833 and until 1873 was the site of Harvard commencements. Now pass **God's Acre,** an ancient cemetery containing the remains of Harvard presidents, patriots, and others, and note the mile marker that indicates 8 miles to Boston—a distance shortened after 1793 with the construction of the West Boston Bridge, site of the present Longfellow Bridge.

Christ Church, just ahead, was built in 1761. It was designed by Peter Harrison, the country's first trained architect, who also designed King's Chapel in Boston; both churches were Anglican at the time. George and Martha Washington worshiped here, and as you enter, you will see a reminder of more violent times: a bullet hole. The church was used as a barracks during the Revolution.

Nearby is a **Congregational church,** the members of which split from the Unitarian church you saw earlier, over the question of the Trinity. The Congregational church is distinguished by a rooster weather vane, designed by Shem Drowne, who made the grasshopper atop Faneuil Hall. From here, you could continue to Appian Way and stroll through **Radcliffe Yard**— Radcliffe College, once an independent woman's college, is now part of Harvard University (its Library of the History of Women in America is worth a visit). From here, it is easy to continue on to Brattle Street—perhaps stopping for a snack at the **Blacksmith House,** at 56 Brattle, the home of a village smithy made famous by a Longfellow poem—past the **Loeb Drama Center,** and on to the **Longfellow house,** which is less than a half mile from Harvard Square. You will be walking along **Tory Row,** so named because the great houses along here once belonged to persons loyal to King George. At the outbreak of the Revolution, their owners fled to New Brunswick, Nova Scotia, and elsewhere. Markers in front of the homes give a brief history.

Across from Christ Church is **Cambridge Common.** Here a small, fenced-in area marks the spot where, on July 3, 1775, George Washington took command of the Continental army.

Now return toward Harvard Square, stopping first at **Dawes Island,** where you can read about Cambridge history and see bronze horseshoes in the sidewalk, a gift from William Dawes's descendants to mark his ride through Harvard Square on the way to Lexington to warn, "The British are coming." Dawes, unlike Paul Revere, completed the ride, but Longfellow made Revere the hero, ignoring Dawes.

Cross the street near the seated statue of Charles Sumner, who is best remembered for his antislavery speeches in the U.S. Senate and who was once beaten almost senseless by a South Carolina senator. Despite Sumner's incapacity to resume his senatorial duties for almost three years, Massachusetts reelected him. The statue was meant for Boston, but upon hearing that the winning design in an anonymous competition was by a woman, Anne Whitney, the committee there awarded the work to a man. It wasn't until 1903, when Whitney was eighty years old, that her 1875 design was unveiled before her and the public in Cambridge.

Enter Harvard Yard through the Johnson Gate, passing on the right Massachusetts Hall, the oldest building (1718) on campus and the office of the president. To the left is Harvard Hall, built in 1774 to replace an earlier building that housed all of Harvard's library at the time but was destroyed in a fire, leaving only one of the original 400 books given by John Harvard, and the other books out on loan. Next to Harvard Hall is Stoughton Hall, designed by Harvard graduate Charles Bulfinch, who was paid $300 for designing and supervising the work. One thing you will not see in this Ivy League college is ivy; on the Bulfinch building, note the iron supports for ivy that at one time graced the wall before it was learned that ivy and brick do not mix.

Across the way is University Hall, also designed by Bulfinch, this time using Chelmsford granite. Here you will see a statue by Daniel Chester French of John Harvard. The statue is known for its three "lies": (a) It is not a likeness of Harvard; (b) it claims he was the founder of the college (he was not); and (c) it states the date of the college's founding as 1638 (it was 1636).

Going around the building, you'll come next to the **Widener Library,** which is the largest university library in the world and was named for and given by the family Harry Elkins Widener, who went down with the *Titanic.* (Two gift stipulations were that students had to pass a swimming test, and no alterations to the building were allowed—to get to a new wing, one must step through a window.) Step inside and see dioramas of what Cambridge looked like in the past.

Just across from the library is Sever Hall, designed by H. H. Richardson and considered one of the finest examples of his work. If there are three of you touring, step just inside the entrance archway, positioning one person in each corner and the third in the center. The two people in the corner may now whisper to each other quite clearly without the center person hearing a thing!

Leave Harvard Yard to the right of Sever Hall, stepping onto Quincy Street, where you will come upon the **Fogg Museum,** the Corbusier-designed **Carpenter Center for the Visual Arts,** and the **Arthur M. Sackler Museum.** (From here, it is a short walk to the **Harvard University Museums,** where among other displays are the famed glass flowers.) Continue down Quincy Street to Massachusetts Avenue, crossing it and heading down Bow Street to Mount Auburn, where you can view the whimsical "face" of the **Harvard Lampoon** building. Then continue along Mount Auburn until you come to Winthrop Square, the colonial marketplace of Cambridge, which even had boats pulling up to it.

Follow Winthrop Street to the intersection of Brattle and Eliot Streets; to the left you will see **Charles Square** and a walkway to the **Kennedy Park.** This is the site of the Charles Hotel and a number of interesting shops. This was to be the site of the John F. Kennedy Library, but residents fought the location for fear of traffic and congestion. (The library found a home in Dorchester.) Now, just behind the hotel is a lovely park in Kennedy's memory; notice the water basin, along which are carved words by JFK.

Detour

Mount Auburn Cemetery (580 Mount Auburn Street; 547-7105), about 2 miles from Harvard Square, is America's first garden cemetery, very reminiscent of Père Lachaise in Paris. When it opened in 1831, it changed the way cemeteries in the country were viewed, prompting many a colonial cemetery to be cleaned up (and in the process, stones were placed not above a person's grave but in a neat, orderly manner). The cemetery became a sensation, with visitors from around the world seeking it out. Within it lie the remains of some of Boston's most notable figures: Henry Wadsworth Longfellow; Mary Baker Eddy, founder of Christian Science; Charles Bulfinch;

Oliver Wendell Holmes; and Julia Ward Howe. Even the publishers Little and Brown lie side by side. The cemetery contains superb statues and magnificent shrubs, trees, and flowers; it's a popular spot for bird sightings. You'll enter by an Egyptian gate and find an Americanized Sphinx as part of a Civil War monument. From the cemetery's Norman tower, you can take in Boston and Cambridge. Stop first at the office for a map and a list of who's who. The cemetery is open daily until dusk (4:30 P.M. in winter).

Reflections, an audiotape driving tour of the famed cemetery, is now available for rent at the entrance gate or main office from 8:30 A.M. to 3:30 P.M. or through the Friends of Mount Auburn, 580 Mount Auburn Street, Cambridge 02138; 547-7105.

What to See While in Cambridge

MUSEUMS

Arthur & Elizabeth Schlesinger Library on the History of Women in America, 10 Garden Street; 495-8647. Open Monday through Friday from 9:00 A.M. to 5:00 P.M. On the former Radcliffe campus, it contains books, manuscripts, and periodicals on women's history. Also contains the largest culinary-books collection as well as the archives of Radcliffe College.

The Arthur M. Sackler Museum, 485 Broadway, includes the world's finest collection of Chinese jades, Korean ceramics, and Chinese cave temple paintings and sculpture. It also holds one of America's most important collection of Chinese bronzes, Greek and Roman sculpture and vases, and ancient coins.

The Botanical Museum has been the home since the 1800s to perhaps Harvard's most popular attraction, its glass flowers. These amazingly realistic flowers were created for the study of botany.

Busch-Reisinger Museum, 29 Kirkland Street, covers the arts of central and northern Europe with an emphasis on the German-speaking countries. It has notable collections of Austrian secession art; German expressionism; Bauhaus material; late medieval, Renaissance, and baroque sculpture; sixteenth-century paintings; eighteenth-century porcelain; and contemporary art from German-speaking Europe.

Fogg Art Museum, 32 Quincy Street, is Harvard's oldest art museum, opened in 1895, and has galleries illustrating the history of Western art from the Middle Ages to the present. It also has on the the finest collections of impressionist and postimpressionist work, and contains the Boston area's most important collection of works by Picasso. The museum has an Italian Renaissance courtyard based on a sixth-century facade from Italy.

Hart Nautical Collection, just a short walk back at 77 Massachusetts Avenue, documents the history of naval architecture and design. Some wonderful ship models. Free.

The Harvard Museum of Natural History (26 Oxford Street; 495-3045) includes three museums: the Botanical Museum, the Mineralogical and Geological Museum, and the Museum of Comparative Zoology. The museums are open daily from 9:00 A.M. to 5:00 P.M. Admission is $7.50 adults, $6.00 non-Harvard students and senior citizens, $5.00 children three to eighteen. Harvard ID holders and one guest are admitted free. Free to all Wednesday 3:00 to 5:00 P.M. September through May and year-round Sunday 9:00 A.M. to noon.

Harvard Semitic Museum, 6 Divinity Avenue; 495-4631. Open Monday through Friday from 10:00 A.M. to 4:00 P.M., Sunday from 1:00 to 4:00 P.M. Admission free. The museum has two exhibits open to the public. One from ancient Cyprus and the other from the ancient city of Nuzi, located in Iraq. An exhibit on the Sphinx and the Pyramids has closed, but images can be found in an archived exhibit link.

In case you wondered . . .

If you arrive in Cambridge by T, you will have traveled over the Longfellow Bridge, which spans the Charles River between Boston (Charles Street Station) and Cambridge (Kendall Station). The 1906 bridge, with its ornate turrets, was said to have been copied from a "celebrated bridge in Prague," but it gets its name from the poet Henry Wadsworth Longfellow, who used its predecessor many times on his literary journeys to Boston and began his poem "The Bridge," "I stood on the bridge at midnight. . . ."

Harvard University Art Museums, 32 Quincy Street and 485 Broadway; 495-9400. Comprises the Fogg Art Museum, Busch-Reisinger Museum, and Arthur M. Sackler Museum. Three museums with more than 160,000 objects of art from antiquity to the present. Open Monday to Saturday 10:00 A.M. to 5:00 P.M. and Sunday from 1:00 to 5:00 P.M. Admission is $6.50 adults, $5.00 seniors and students. Free for children under eighteen and on Saturday from 10:00 A.M. to noon. The museums are all within a short walk of each other.

M.I.T. Compton Gallery, under the big dome in the heart of the campus. A changing exhibition space where creativity in fields from science to art are highlighted. Open only during the school year.

M.I.T. List Visual Arts Center, 20 Ames Street; 253–4680. Offers changing exhibits throughout the year that explore the cutting edge of paintings, video, installation art, photography, and sculpture.

M.I.T. Museum, 265 Massachusetts Avenue; 253–4444. Open Tuesday through Friday from 10:00 A.M. to 5:00 P.M. and Saturday and Sunday from noon to 5:00 P.M. Admission is $5.00 adults; $2.00 students, seniors, and children five to eighteen; children under five and M.I.T. ID holders (plus one guest) free. The museum is free the third Sunday of each month. The museum offers more than 150 years of exploration in science, technology, and engineering all presented in interesting exhibits. For example, you'll see robots that once roamed M.I.T. labs and mechanical inventions that were built solely to entertain. The museum is designed to represent the importance of scientific and technological innovation.

The Mineralogical and Geological Museum houses exhibits ranging from samples of the earth's crust to meteorites and extraterrestrial rocks. The collection, first begun in 1784, ranks among the world's finest.

The Museum of Comparative Zoology features the Harvard mastodon, a giant sea serpent, whale skeletons, the largest turtle shell ever found, and the world's oldest reptile egg.

The Peabody Museum of Archaeology and Ethnology, 11 Divinity Avenue; 496–1027. Open daily 9:00 A.M. to 5:00 P.M. Admission is $7.50 adults, $6.00 seniors and students, $5.00 children three to eighteen. Free admission Sunday 9:00 A.M. to noon and, September through May, Wednesday 3:00 to 5:00 P.M. The Peabody is the world's oldest museum devoted to anthropology and houses one of the most comprehensive records of human cultural history in the Western Hemisphere.

OTHER ATTRACTIONS

American Repertory Theater, 64 Brattle Street, Cambridge; 495–2668. Tours by appointment; call the theater and ask for the Audience Development Department. Forty-five-minute tours are offered for groups of ten to twenty, high-school age and up. Take a walk onstage; go backstage; see the costume area, set design, and lighting; and learn how everything and everyone are coordinated at showtime.

Christ Church, Zero Garden Street (facing Cambridge Common); 876–0200. Open daily. Services are held at 8:00 and 10:00 A.M. and at 1:00 and 5:00 P.M. Free. (See page 201.)

Harvard University also offers a collection of historical scientific instruments at 1 Oxford Street in the Science Center basement; 495–2248.

Hooper-Lee Nichols House, 159 Brattle Street; 547–4252. Open Tuesday and Thursday from 2:00 to 5:00 P.M. A 1685 farmhouse remodeled in 1742 as a Tory Row mansion. Home of the Cambridge Historical Society. Admission is $5.00 for adults and $3.00 for children and seniors.

Longfellow National Historic Site, 105 Brattle Street; 876–4491. Open Wednesday through Sunday from 10:00 A.M. to 4:30 P.M. Tours are given at 10:30 and 11:30 A.M. and 1:00, 2:00, 3:00, and 4:00 P.M. Tours are $3.00 for anyone age seventeen or older and free for children age sixteen or younger. The home has been completely restored and features original furnishings and artwork from around the world. It is an outstanding example of a historic site representing the themes of arts and literature. For almost a half century (1837–82), this was the home of one of the world's foremost poets, scholars, and educators, Henry Wadsworth Longfellow. The home was also where then general George Washington, commander in chief of the newly formed Continental army, headquartered and planned the Siege of Boston between July 1775 and April 1776.

Massachusetts Institute of Technology, Information Office, 77 Massachusetts Avenue; 253–4795. Offers free guided tours Monday through Friday at 10:45 A.M. and 2:45 P.M. The university's outdoor sculpture collection contains works by Calder, Picasso, and Moore. Whereas the main buildings employ a neoclassical style, the campus has some outstanding examples of modern architecture. The newest, the Stata Center, by Frank Gehry, will certainly catch your attention with its with its wild curves and angles (see page 209). Also to be seen are the Kresge Auditorium, considered the finest twentieth-century auditorium in the Boston area, and the Kresge Chapel, built as a small brick cylinder with a moat around it that reflects light inside. The buildings are a short walk from the Information Office. Be sure to see the Hart Nautical Galleries, also at 77 Massachusetts Avenue (free), with their collection of ship models and displays of marine engineering.

Radcliffe College, 10 Garden Street; 495–8601. Radcliffe College, the former independent women's college, has merged with Harvard University. It has been replaced by the Radcliffe Institute, which offers advanced studies with a continuing commitment in the study of women, gender, and society. The Schlesinger Library is on its former campus.

Accommodations

Prices are the lowest shown for two at the time of writing. Rooms at these prices may be limited. Depending on season, could be higher. Cambridge is but ten minutes to downtown Boston via the T.

$150 or More a Night

Boston Marriott Cambridge, 2 Cambridge Center; 494–6600. In the Kendall Square area, also very convenient to Boston, with public transportation at the door. Health club, pool, and parking.

Charles Hotel, 1 Bennett Street; 864–1200. One of the best hotels in the Boston area. Superb accommodations, dining. Health club, spa, pool, parking. In Harvard Square.

Hotel @ M.I.T, 20 Sydney Street; 577–0200 or (800) 222–8733. Has 210 rooms, exercise rooms, and a roof garden. Free high-speed Internet access. Parking.

The Inn at Harvard, 1201 Massachusettts Avenue; 491–2222 or (800) 458–5886. A very elegant place to stay. Right in Harvard Square.

The Kendall Hotel, 350 Main Street; 577–1300. Built within a renovated 1895 Victorian Firehouse, along with a new seven-story tower. Offers sixty-five rooms with underground parking. Filled with firehouse memorabilia. Fully nonsmoking hotel.

Radisson Cambridge, 777 Memorial Drive; 492–7777 or (800) 333–3333. Has 205 rooms overlooking the Charles River and the Boston skyline. Has indoor pool, parking.

Royal Sonesta Hotel, 5 Cambridge Parkway; 491–3600. On the Charles River overlooking Boston. Has indoor pool, health club, restaurant. Shopping mall across the street. Wonderful family programs in summer.

$100 to $149

Best Western Hotel Tria, 220 Alewife Brook Parkway; 491–8000. Recently renovated with sixty-nine guest rooms. Indoor pool, parking.

Doubletree Guest Suites, 400 Soldiers Field Road; 783–0090 or (800) 222–TREE. Overlooking the Charles River on the Boston side, near the Mass Turnpike entrance. An all-suite hotel just half a mile from Harvard Square. Home to award-winning Scullers Jazz Club. Parking.

Harvard Square Hotel, 110 Mount Auburn Street; 864–5200. Right in the heart of Harvard Square.

Holiday Inn Express, 250 Monsignor O'Brien Highway; 577–7600. Has 112 rooms, parking.

What Is It?

That's the first thought looking at this building filled with amazing angles and curves. No, it's not a demolition project gone wrong. This is architect Frank Gehry's creation at Massachusetts Institute of Technology. Gehry, who won fame for the Guggenheim Museum in Bilbao, Spain, and the Walt Disney Hall in Los Angles, now offers the **Ray and Maria Stata Center for Computer, Information and Intelligence Sciences building,** a far contrast from the building it replaced—a World War II plain-Jane temporary structure that lasted for fifty-five years. The building's fanciful design offers a metaphor for the cutting-edge innovations that, it is hoped, will occur within its labs, offices, and classrooms. Inside, the lower floors have an open feeling to them with more private spaces on the top floors where private labs are named for donors Bill Gates and Alexander Dreyfoos. While the Stata Center may seem far apart from the rest of M.I.T., it is connected to the rest of the campus by bridges and corridors. And this may not be the last Gehry work in the area. Harvard University has signed him up for work on its Allston campus across the river.

The Stata Center, 32 Vassar Street, Cambridge, is open for ground-floor visits daily 10:00 A.M. to 5:00 P.M. A walking guide is available at the information booth. Entrance is at the Gates Tower at the intersection of Main Street and Vassar Street, near the Kendall Square T station.

Hotel Marlowe, 25 Edwin H. Land Boulevard; 867–8000. Hip hotel with 236 rooms just a short walk to Museum of Science and CambridgeSide shopping center. Parking.

Hyatt Regency Cambridge, 575 Memorial Drive; 492–1234. Has revolving rooftop lounge. Beautiful views of Boston overlooking the Charles. Has health club, large indoor pool, parking. In summer bikes are available to ride along the Charles.

Sheraton Commander, 16 Garden Street; 547–4800. Overlooking Cambridge Common just off Harvard Square. Has full service with 175 rooms.

Inns, $100 a Night or More

A Cambridge House, 2218 Massachusetts Avenue; 491–6300. An 1892 house listed on the National Register of Historic Places. Private baths, canopy beds.

Harvard Square Hotel, 110 Mount Auburn Street; 864–5200. Right in the heart of Harvard Square.

Irving House, 24 Irving Street; 547–4600. Has rooms with shared and private baths. Harvard Square area.

The Mary Prentiss Inn, 6 Prentiss Street; 661–2929. A charming 1843 Greek Revival inn. Handy to Harvard Square. All rooms have private bath.

Bed & Breakfasts, Inns Under $100 a Night

A Bed & Breakfast in Cambridge, 1657 Cambridge Street; 868–7082 or (877) 994–0844. An 1897 colonial revival house just 2 blocks from Harvard Yard.

Cambridge Bed and Muffin, 267 Putnam Avenue; 576–3166. Fifteen-minute walk to Harvard Square.

A Cambridge House Bed & Breakfast Inn, 2218 Massachusetts Avenue; 491–6300. An 1892 Victorian home featuring many rooms with canopy beds or working fireplaces. On-site parking

A Friendly Inn at Harvard, 1673 Cambridge Street; 547–7851. A Queen Anne–style house with seventeen rooms, all with private baths. Two blocks from Harvard.

The Monastery Guesthouse, 980 Memorial Drive; 876–3037. Built in the 1920s as a home for the brothers of the Society of Saint John the Evangelist. Experience the monastic life of reflection just two minutes from Harvard Square. In-room sink, shared bath. $60 a person with meals.

Dining

Restaurants in Cambridge run from the reasonably priced to expensive. As a guide, restaurants where two can dine for $40 or less are designated as $; for more than $40 but less than $50, $$; and for $50 or more, $$$. Many restaurants offer a lunch menu that is far less expensive. All prices are exclusive of alcohol.

Atasca, 50 Hampshire Street; 621-6991. A fine Portuguese restaurant that offers small plates for sampling many tastes. $-$$

Blue Room, 1 Kendall Square; 494-9034. Wood grilling is a specialty. $-$$

Casablanca, 40 Brattle Street; 876-0999. A fixture in Harvard Square, this restaurant is known for its Mediterranean flavors. $-$$

East Coast Grill & Raw Bar, 1271 Cambridge Street, Inman Square; 491-6568. Catch the show from the open kitchen of live fire and meat and fish dishes, or enjoy a pulled-pork sandwich. A fun place with great food. $-$$

Grendel's Den, 89 Winthrop Street; 491-1160. This is a great place for comfort food and meeting friends; a landmark in Harvard Square. $

Harvest, 44 Brattle Street; 868-2255. This very upscale restaurant serves interesting dishes and has an outdoor garden terrace. $-$$

Henrietta's Table, in the Charles Hotel, 1 Bennett Street; 661-5005. American fare is served in a farmhouse setting in this establishment that's popular with families. $-$$

Jasper White's Summer Shack, 149 Alewife Brook Parkway; 520-9500. Here you'll find great grilled fish and oysters galore. $-$$

Magnolia's Southern Cuisine, 1193 Cambridge Street; 576-1971. Southern specialties are prepared by a chef-owner here. $-$$

Middle East, 472 Massachusetts Avenue; 492-9181. This is a fun place for everything from couscous and falafel to burgers. $

Ole Mexican Grill, 11 Springfield Street; 492-4495. True Mexican dishes with an allegiance to the Veracruz and Oaxaca regions. Its guacamole is famous. $

Oleana, 134 Hampshire Street; 661-0505. Here you can taste the flavors of the Mediterranean. $-$$

Rialto, in the Charles Hotel, 1 Bennett Street; 661–5050. Outstanding Mediterranean food is served in an elegant and striking setting. $$–$$$

S & S Restaurant & Deli, 1334 Cambridge Street; 354–0777. For more than seventy-five years, this Inman Square landmark has been serving up dishes that are tasty and inexpensive. $

Salts, 798 Main Street; 876–8444. Eastern European fare is served with imagination. $$–$$$

Sandrine's, 8 Holyoke Street; 497–5300. You'll feel you are in the Alsatian region of France. $$–$$$

Zephyr on the Charles, Hyatt Regency Hotel, 576 Memorial Drive; 441–6510. This restaurant features an ecletic and fun menu. $–$$

BREW HOUSES

Cambridge Brewing Company, 1 Kendall Square, Building 100; 494–1994. Brews four beers along with seasonal specials, all on premises. Full restaurant featuring everything from fries to grilled salmon. Moderate prices.

John Harvard's Brew House, 33 Dunster Street; 868–3585. In the heart of Harvard Square. Grilled, baked, and barbecued foods, with a large selection of fresh brewed beers and ales. Also features jazz and Irish music on Monday and Tuesday evenings.

Entertainment

HARVARD SQUARE

Club Passim, 47 Palmer Street; 492–7679. The famed folk club.

Regattabar, Charles Hotel, 1 Bennett Street; 661–5000. Outstanding local and national performers in a club atmosphere. Its Jazz Festival, January through March, is one of the best in the country. (Concertix in Cambridge sells tickets for the Regattabar jazz performances and other events. Call 876–7777.)

Toad, 1912 Massachusetts Avenue; 497–4950. Near Porter Square. No-nonsense country rock.

CENTRAL SQUARE

Middle East Cafe, 472 Massachusetts Avenue; 864–3278. Music ranges from rock to reggae to folk.

Phoenix Landing, 512 Massachusetts Avenue; 576–6260. Irish pub that also becomes a nineteen-plus place some nights with a cozy rave and lounge scene.

River Gods, 125 River Street; 576–1881. Great DJs every night.

Ryles, 212 Hampshire Street, Inman Square; 876–9330. One of the top jazz clubs.

T.T. the Bears, 10 Brookline Street; 492–2327.

Western Front, 343 Western Avenue (near Central Square); 492–7772. Lots of local musicians, dancing.

MOVIE HOUSES

Brattle Theatre, 40 Brattle Street; 876–6837. The area's original classic movie house.

Harvard Film Archive, Carpenter Center for Visual Arts, Harvard University, 24 Quincy Street; 495–4700. Best to call for performances, shows.

Kendall Square Cinema, 1 Kendall Square; 494–9800. Art, foreign, and independent films on large screens.

Loews Harvard Square, 10 Church Street; 864–4580. Friday and Saturday, when *The Rocky Horror Picture Show* is screened, the audience can be more fun than the show.

Theater

American Repertory Theater, at the Loeb Drama Center, 64 Brattle Street; 495–2668. One of the country's top resident theaters presents a classic mix of drama, music, comedy, and more

ImprovBoston, 1253 Cambridge Street; 576–1253. Innovative improvisational theater.

Golf

Thomas P. O'Neill Jr. Municipal Golf Course at Fresh Pond, 681 Huron Avenue;
349-6282. A nine-hole course that was voted no. 1 public golf course in
Boston area. Named for former speaker of the House of Representatives.

Shopping

HARVARD SQUARE

You don't have to have crimson blood to shop at the Harvard Cooperative
Society ("The Coop"), which sits smack in the center of Harvard Square, just
across from the subway entrance. The Coop is a complete department store
that just happens to have three floors of books. There are, in fact, more bookstores per foot in Harvard Square than perhaps anywhere else in the country.
Also to be found in the square are gourmet food shops, record shops, and
clothing stores with the Harvard look. Harvard Square's popularity is changing its local-merchants look to one of trendy shops to serve the day-trippers
and yuppies with lots of cash to spend. Some things remain. Leavitt & Peirce,
a tobacco shop, is still in its original location after 120 years. They also spe-
cialize in chess sets and board games. (To get here, take the Red Line to
Harvard Station.)

CAMBRIDGESIDE GALLERIA

An indoor mall in East Cambridge opposite the Royal Sonesta Hotel and
next to the Hotel Marlowe. CambridgeSide contains more than 120 specialty
boutiques plus Best Buy, Borders, Sears, Filene's, and the Apple Store. It's
right along the Charles River and offers boat tours on the Charles as well as
summertime concerts. A large food center along with restaurants are found
here as well. (To reach CambridgeSide, take the Green Line to Lechmere
Station.)

OTHER SHOPPING HIGHLIGHTS

Check out the gift shops of the **Peabody Museum** (see page 206), with craft
items from around the world. If you're into antiques, the **Cambridge
Antique Market,** 201 Msgr. O'Brien Highway (868-9655), features more
than 150 dealers in one location.

ACTIVITIES OF SPECIAL INTEREST

Family Outings

Boston, you could say, is just a ducky place for families. Where else can you find statues (that kids can sit on) honoring a family of ducks? Or a city that's featured in a book about a swan that took a room at the ritzy Ritz-Carlton? Or swan boats? Or the grave of Mother Goose? Or even a tour that ducks into the Charles River as part of its exploration of the city? And there are lots of other "animals" and creatures of the sea easily found along the city streets to fascinate the kids. Boston is a child-friendly city, but one in which grown-ups will feel equally at home.

Accommodations for Families

For starters on a family outing to Boston, choose family-friendly accommodations. Most hotels offer indoor swimming pools and free accommodations for children under a certain age (check first, as the age limit ranges from twelve to eighteen).

Check with the Boston Convention and Visitors Bureau (888-SEE-BOSTON or www.bostonusa.com) for the latest in family fun packages. While many offer discounted Family Friendly Passes and tickets to area attractions, some include more. For example, the Embassy Suites Boston at Logan Airport has a family suite, along with toys, cooked-to-order-breakfast, and free Internet access. The Omni Parker House, right on the Freedom Trail, provides a coloring book telling the story of the country's oldest continuously operating hotel, and the Marriott Long Wharf, right on the waterfront, has an indoor pool overlooking the harbor as well as a game room for the kids. The Ritz-Carlton on Arlington Street has a family suite with a separate room just for the young set that's snug and safe and complete with small-size furnishings—even the bathroom is designed just for kids—along with games and a video on *The Trumpet of the Swan,* the E. B. White story about Louis, the swan who stayed at the hotel. Just across the Charles River, the Cambridge Royal Sonesta offers a summer-long family fest that includes free bikes to ride along the river just in front of the hotel, free ice cream, and a lot more. The Langham Hotel offers two rooms along with museum tickets and a limousine ride to your favorite Boston destination. Older kids might like to stay in the Britney Spears room at the Onyx Hotel.

Ask also for a copy of the *Kids Love Boston* guidebook available at visitor centers.

Another fun idea is to stay at a bed-and-breakfast where guests can experience a Boston home that might include one on Beacon Hill or on the waterfront. There are also yachts and sailboats being used as bed-and-breakfasts.

While many Boston hotels may seem to be out of many a family's budget, keep in mind the added value the hotel packages may include from free parking, tickets, or discounts for attractions, to amenities such as free meals. There's also the matter of convenience. Little ones can tire easily, so it's nice to be near "home" for a rest break.

Staying outside the city can save money. Reasonably priced accommodations are found in cities and towns just outside Boston. Quincy, Braintree, Cambridge, Newton, and Brookline are attractive, as accommodations can be found near T lines running into the city (see chapter 15). The T offers a visitor's pass that cuts the cost of using the transportation system.

Boston calls itself "America's Walking City" and for good reason—it's fairly compact, so going from one end of the city to the other is easily done on foot, even with children. There are also so many things to see on foot that walking will likely become a pleasure for the kids; there are many places for "break," from outdoor dining spots to park benches. Restrooms, however, are not always so convenient, so plan wisely for the little ones.

Attractions for Families

Here are some ideas for a family outing, things to do that should appeal to all ages.

You could begin your outing from on high—atop the **Prudential Tower,** fifty stories above the city. Not only can you see the hills of New Hampshire, but you can look down on Fenway Park, and maybe even see the Red Sox in action!

Looking south, you can see the open expanse of the **Christian Science Center** with its fountains and reflecting pool. After you've soaked in the city from here, take a walk over to the center and enter the **Mary Baker Eddy Library,** where you can now see the world as you probably never have or ever will again. Here's a giant glass globe depicting the world. See how many countries you recognize, and how many you've never heard of. The map was made in the 1930s and has been updated to show how the world has changed since then. Across the street is **Symphony Hall,** where the famous Boston Symphony and Boston Pops play. Quite often there are tours to see this acoustically perfect hall; also ask about the Youth Concerts held Saturdays in January, March, and November. From the Huntington Avenue side of the Prudential Center, you could take a Duck Tour, which even splashes into the Charles River.

THE PUBLIC GARDEN AND BOSTON COMMON

One place that is on everyone's tour list is the **Public Garden.** It has wonderful flower beds and monuments—George Washington on horseback is here—and it's also a wonderland for children, with **Swan Boats** to ride, live ducks, and playful statues of the ducks from Robert McCloskey's classic children's book *Make Way for Ducklings:* Jack, Knack, Lack, Mack, Nack, Ouack, Pack, Quack, and their parents. The Public Garden is even the setting for the story of a swan who was signed up to play the trumpet for the Swan Boats. *Trumpet of the Swan* by E. B. White tells this story, how the swan was at first turned down for a room at the Ritz-Carlton until he played his trumpet. The swan was immediately given a room with a view of the Public Garden. You may want to stop first at the corner of Beacon and Charles Streets and gather picnic fixings at DeLuca's Market, a favorite of Beacon Hill residents.

Adjacent to the Public Garden is **Boston Common** with playgrounds and the Frog Pond for wading in. You might also board the T at Boylston or Park Street stations (this is the oldest part of the oldest subway line in the country). Stop at the Information Center on the Tremont Street side of the Common for a map of the **Black Heritage Trail** that begins nearby or join a guided walk. Pick up a free copy of *Kids Love Boston* for more ideas and fun games. The area is handy to the State House (before touring, ask for a copy of *Under the Golden Dome,* just for kids), too.

From Boston Common it's easy to pick up the **Freedom Trail.** (See the big white steeple nearby? That's Park Street Church, and right in front of the church, you'll see a red line embedded in the sidewalk—the line marking the Freedom Trail.) Follow it and you'll visit some of the most historic sites in the nation. Next to the church is **Granary Burying Ground,** where Paul Revere, three signers of the Declaration of Independence, Ben Franklin's parents, and Elizabeth Vergoose, better known as Mother Goose, lie. In less than a half mile, you'll pass where Ben Franklin went to school, where the Boston Tea Party began (Mom and Dad might want to detour from here down Washington Street to **Downtown Crossing** and the famed, and original, Filene's Basement for some great bargains in clothing), then the **Old State House** and the cobblestones outside marking the site of the Boston Massacre, and on to **Faneuil Hall.**

On the Beacon Street side of the garden, you could stop by the **Bull & Finch Pub,** the setting for the TV show *Cheers,* for a great hamburger, or stop upstairs at the Hampshire House for more elegant dining. From the Public Garden it's also just a short walk to **Copley Square.** The **Hard Rock Cafe** is just off it, or continue into lavish Copley Place, with its stores, theaters, and dining. It leads over a glass-enclosed walkway to the Prudential Center shops with more dining, and to the fiftieth-floor observatory there.

FANEUIL HALL MARKETPLACE

Faneuil Hall Marketplace offers another fun family experience. Faneuil Hall is one of the most historic sites in the nation—a gathering place for calls for freedom from colonial days to the present. Spot the grasshopper weather vane on top of the building. This is also one of the liveliest areas of the city, with lots of interesting shops, street performers, and places to dine. (You'll find lots of kids' favorite foods, too.) The marketplace dates from 1830, and the buildings are all original. In the center **Quincy Market** building is a food feast you won't believe. You can create your own meal, perhaps taking it over to the **waterfront** for a picnic there or onto a ferry boat for a ride to the Charlestown Navy Yard and see the **USS** *Constitution.* For a classic Boston meal, step into **Durgin Park** for hearty food at long tables. It's been a Boston favorite since the mid-1800s. A short walk away, try the **Union Oyster House,** the oldest restaurant in the United States and still at the same location. And do let the kids know that this whole area was part of Boston Harbor 200 years ago.

THE NORTH END

From Faneuil Hall it's just a short walk to the **North End.** And, once again, do walk. You are still along the Freedom Trail. Along the way, on market days—Thursday through Saturday—the streets here will be filled with stands selling fresh vegetables, meats, and other food products. The area along Blackstone Street can be quite littered from this scene. Across the street is the Rose Kennedy Park, a quiet oasis that covers the traffic tunnel through the city. The president's mother was born nearby in the North End. The North

End, Boston's oldest section, is now famed for its Italian flavor—lots of great Italian restaurants and places for pizza. In colonial days, however, it was the home of Paul Revere and the Old North Church from which Revere watched for lanterns to tell him of the British heading to Lexington and Concord—"one if by land, two if by sea." Paul Revere's house is the oldest wooden structure in the city and he raised sixteen children in it—not, fortunately, all at the same time.

THE WATERFRONT

Head over to the waterfront and one of the most popular attractions in the city—the **New England Aquarium,** where you can now also catch a 3-D movie on a huge screen. Just outside the aquarium's doors, you can also board a boat for a **harbor tour** or to join a **whale watch** (easily done in a half day). You'll find lots of food here, too, from quick snacks to fine waterfront dining at the **Chart House.** On the walk from Faneuil Hall, you'll also pass a park where the kids can unwind.

About a half mile from the aquarium (and you can walk on a path all along the waterfront) is the **Children's Museum.** The Children's will delight all ages, with lots of interactive activities, even a climbing sculpture. You can learn about life in Japan, visit Grandmother's Attic, try on some old clothes, or grab a snack at McDonald's. There's a Friday-night performance series ranging from magic to storytelling. Call the museum for information, and ask about its camp-in, an overnight stay in the museum. Outside there's a giant milk bottle—yes, milk once came in glass bottles—and this "bottle" serves up food in summer, just as it formerly did far outside the city.

And almost at the door of this museum is the **Boston Tea Party Ship,** where you can learn about one of the most famous events in Boston history, when colonists dressed as Indians tossed expensive British tea into the harbor. Best of all, you, too, can toss some "tea" into the harbor.

You'll find lots of good food nearby, including the **Barking Crab,** which offers great seafood outdoors or under a heated tent during colder times.

OTHER PLACES TO GO

The **Boston Museum of Science** can easily fill a day (there are even great places to dine inside), with its terrific interactive exhibits, planetarium shows, and the Omni theater, where movies fill a six-story screen with unbelievable sights accompanied by 27,000 watts of sound power.

Franklin Park Zoo is yet another daylong destination. (Unfortunately, it is a bit far out of the downtown area.) Here you can take in one of the largest African tropical forests in the country—it's home to more than 150 animals, including gorillas and monkeys. There's also a petting zoo.

Head over to **Charlestown Navy Yard** (on the Freedom Trail, or hop a ferry from downtown to get there), where you can visit the oldest commissioned warship in the world, the **USS *Constitution,*** learn about the battle of Bunker Hill at the lively and explosive (great sounds) **Bunker Hill Pavilion** nearby, then continue on the Freedom Trail to the top of Bunker Hill, climbing the 236 steps of the monument there for a view of Boston. You'll find lots of good food along the way, from snackies to **Olives** and the **Warren Tavern,** where Paul Revere once hung out.

A visit to the **Museum of Fine Arts** is family fun, too. One of the world's top museums offers Family Place, an exploration of the museum, Saturdays and Sundays October to June. In July and August it meets on Wednesday evenings as part of Family Night Out. At the Information Center you'll find an Activity Book to keep the young ones busy. The museum also boasts one of the finest Egyptian collections in the country, and here families can "unravel" the mysteries of the mummies. Add to the fun of a visit by taking a Green Line trolley (Arborside line) to the front entrance of the museum.

From the downtown waterfront you can take a boat ride through the harbor, out to **Castle Island** or way out to **Boston Light** and explore a Civil War-era fort, sail off for a day's outing to **Provincetown** on Cape Cod, take a **lunch or dinner cruise,** or enjoy a **whale-watch cruise.**

If you just want an ocean swim, take the T Blue Line to **Revere Beach.**

And for sports thrills, take a tour of **Fenway Park,** where the Red Sox play, or the **FleetCenter** for a tour of where the Celtics and Bruins play, or visit the Sports Museum located there.

A Grand Combo

For kids' things, Boston's waterfront can't be beat. All within a short walk—some next door to one another—are the New England Aquarium, the Children's Museum, and the Boston Tea Party Ship and Museum. Take in the waterfront sights, visit the aquarium and see the dolphins play, choose a museum or two, have a snack at the big milk bottle in front of the Children's Museum or the McDonald's at the complex, throw some tea into the harbor for fun and history, wander over to the waterfront Barking Crab for great seafood, check to see whether the Federal Reserve Bank has a tour going in which you might pick up some shredded money, go for a harbor cruise, explore an island or two, climb the oldest lighthouse in the United States, or book a room at the Marriott Long Wharf—it has an indoor pool and is next to the aquarium and the boat trips. You're not far from Faneuil Hall Marketplace, and there's even a waterfront playground at which to relax.

Nearby Trips

No visit to Boston is complete without at least one side trip out of the city to see places that figured prominently in the country's founding and folklore, or just to relax. The Pilgrims, Puritans, witches, presidents' homes, Redcoats, the Industrial Revolution, classic New England villages, ocean beaches and swimming, sand dunes, Peter Rabbit, whaling, the Western Hemisphere's largest casino, and more can all be experienced within an hour to an hour and a half of the city.

For all these adventures, a car is by far the best way to tour. It is quicker, the roads are good and certainly less crowded once outside the Boston city limits, and you'll be able to create your own itinerary based on personal interests. Tour companies also offer day trips to most of these areas, usually combining a few into one trip. Public transportation is also available to most places.

Each of these areas has excellent accommodations for visitors who wish to make it more than a day trip.

Head North

North is the route for witches, Puritans, sea captains, fried clams, and art colonies. The North Shore of Boston is not only the land of the Puritans, who came later than the Pilgrims but were the real founding fathers of Boston, but also where "witches" resided, the China Trade began, and art colonies flourished.

SALEM AND MARBLEHEAD

Salem, about 16 miles north of Boston, is best known for the witch trials of colonial days. Here one can visit the **Salem Witch Museum** and the **Witch Dungeon Museum;** explore the **Salem Maritime National Historic Site,** which focuses on the maritime era; visit the **House of Seven Gables**, made famous by Nathaniel Hawthorne's novel; and stop at the **Salem 1630: Pioneer Village,** the Puritans' first settlement. Also visit the **Peabody Essex Museum,** an internationally known museum with the world's most comprehensive collection of Asian export art, Native American art and culture, and New England decorative art, along with gardens and twenty-four historic properties, some more than 300 years old. The Peabody is one of the finest museums anywhere.

Nearby Marblehead, a North Shore yachting center, is one of the more picturesque coastal villages with many colonial merchant homes open for viewing. In Abbot Hall at the Town Hall is the famed painting *The Spirit of '76* by Archibald M. Willard of a fife player, drummer, and drummer boy.

Salem is reachable by commuter rail from Boston.

CAPE ANN

If you have time, continue along the North Shore to visit the "other Cape," **Cape Ann,** a rocky coastline famed for its fishing, artist colonies, and antiquing. There are beautiful beaches (the water, though, is ice cold), opportunities for whale watching, and historic farms and grand estates—**Castle Hill/Crane Memorial Reservation** in Ipswich is a 1,400-acre ocean-side natural paradise with a great house. Fried-clam lovers will want to stop at **Woodman's** in Essex, where the fried clam was born.

In early October the **Topsfield Fair,** the country's oldest agricultural fair, is held. Children will love **Le Grand David and His Spectacular Magic Companies,** a longtime favorite. Performances are given Sunday at the Cabot Street Cinema theater in Beverly.

By car, take Route 1 or 1A north from Boston.

For more information on Salem, Marblehead, and Cape Ann, call the North of Boston Convention and Visitors Bureau at (978) 977-7760.

LOWELL

Due north of Cape Ann is Lowell, home to the nation's only **Industrial National Park,** which focuses on the place where the Industrial Revolution began. The mills here are a reminder of the textile industry that has long since left the region and also of the beginning of American industrial might. Exhibits re-create those days, from work in the mills to the housing provided for the workers. There are water tours on the canals and trolley tours by land.

The **American Textile Museum** nearby has working looms and exhibits of items made on those looms.

Lowell also has a lively **Folk Festival** each July and also remembers its native son, Beat generation author Jack Kerouac, in a sculpture park.

For more information, call the Greater Merrimack Valley Convention and Visitors Bureau at (978) 459-6150.

By car from Boston, take Interstate 93 north to Lowell.

PORTSMOUTH TO PORTLAND

Just about an hour's drive from Boston is **Portsmouth,** New Hampshire, a charming seacoast town that has been described as the "Nantucket of the north." You will not be disappointed. Also here is **Strawbery Banke,** with four centuries of history and culture. Homes from each period can be visited. Portsmouth was the home of John Paul Jones. Nearby are fine beaches and it's just a short hop over to Kittery, Maine, for outlet shopping.

Continuing on one can visit some of Maine's most picturesque seacoast villages—Ogunquit, York, and Kennybunkport. The cosmopolitan flair of **Portland** is not far, and nearby is the famed L.L. Bean store that never closes. From Portland you can catch an overnight ferry to Nova Scotia and the start of new discoveries.

For Portsmouth information, call the Greater Portsmouth Chamber of Commerce, (603) 436-3988. For Maine information, call (888) 624-6345.

By car, take Interstate 95 north. By train, take the Amtrak Downeaster from Boston's North Station.

Head South

Head south for the Pilgrims and "America's Hometown" of Plymouth. (If you have time, drive an additional thirty minutes and visit Sandwich.)

PLYMOUTH

Plymouth, about 30 miles south of Boston, is the place where the Pilgrims stepped ashore in 1620, earning it the nickname "America's Hometown."

A trip to Plymouth begins on the waterfront to view the famed rock upon which the Pilgrims stepped ashore. Steps away is a full-scale replica of the *Mayflower,* which brought the Pilgrims from Europe. To learn more about the Pilgrims, there are nearby museums filled with history and artifacts.

The best way to learn about the Pilgrims is to visit **Plimoth Plantation,** a re-creation of the 1630s village where they lived. Plimoth Plantation is 3 miles south of the rock. For information, call (508) 746-1622.

Not far from the Plymouth waterfront is **Cranberry World,** a free exhibit that will tell you more about the cranberry than you probably want to know. At **Edaville USA,** in nearby Carver, you can ride a real narrow-gauge steam train through cranberry bogs.

A great time to visit the Plymouth area is fall, when the cranberry harvest takes place (Columbus Day weekend is special), and at Thanksgiving time, when reenactments of the first celebration of the holiday are held.

For information, call (800) 872–1620.

By car, take I–93 to Route 3 south from Boston into Plymouth.

SANDWICH

If you have time, Sandwich, just over the bridge on Cape Cod, is not only one of the prettiest villages on the Cape but also its oldest. You can visit the home of Peter Rabbit, the **Thornton W. Burgess Museum;** the **Sandwich Glass Museum,** featuring items made of that famed glass; and one of Cape Cod's finest attractions, **Heritage Plantation,** a beautiful museum complex in a gardenlike setting filled with Americana, classic cars, and a working 1912 carousel. Its Dexter rhododendrons are world famous. Heritage is now open year-round.

For Sandwich information, call the Cape Cod Canal Area Chamber of Commerce at (508) 759–6000.

Sandwich is about a half-hour drive beyond Plymouth. Take Route 3 to Route 6A, just over the Sagamore Bridge.

PROVINCETOWN

Provincetown, at the tip of Cape Cod, is easily visited from the heart of Boston via (in season) boat excursions. Daily (in season) boat service is also available from Plymouth.

Provincetown is one of the most colorful and scenic Cape Cod towns. Located at the tip of the Cape, the Pilgrims stopped here first before arriving at Plymouth. Do visit the **Pilgrim Monument and Museum.** The monument rises 352 feet above sea level, and the museum contains memorabilia of both Admiral Donald B. MacMillan, the famous Arctic explorer, and Eugene O'Neill, the immortal American playwright, who spent many summers here. Provincetown is a fishing village with many fishermen of Portuguese ancestry. The town, in summer, also has one of the largest gay communities in the East. Beaches and large expanses of sand dunes are nearby.

In Boston, boats leave from Long Wharf. For day-trippers, ample time is allowed ashore before the return voyage.

For information, call the Provincetown Chamber of Commerce, (508) 487–3424.

QUINCY

Just a subway ride away from the heart of Boston is the city of Quincy, home to two presidents: John Adams, perhaps *the* Founding Father of our country, and his son, John Quincy Adams.

Within walking distance of the subway stop is the **Adams Mansion,** home of the first father and son to hold the office of president. John Adams was the second president of the United States, and his son, John Quincy Adams, was the sixth. The mansion, a National Historic Park, is just as it was in the presidents' time. Almost across from the T station is the **First Parish,** where the two presidents and their wives lie in rest. Abigail Adams, John Adams's wife, also made quite a name for herself in the colonial period.

Not far from the city center are the birthplaces of the two presidents, the USS *Salem,* a shipbuilding museum (Quincy was quite famous in shipbuilding history, especially during the Second World War era), quarries from which granite used to build Bunker Hill and other monuments were carved, and the entrance to the 5,000-acre **Blue Hills Reservation,** with lots of natural recreation. Blue Hills is particularly beautiful during foliage season—no need to travel to New Hampshire or Maine when you can visit this colorful paradise just 9 miles from the heart of Boston.

For information, call the Quincy Tourism and Visitors Bureau at 657-0527.

By car, take I-93 from Boston to the Quincy exit. By subway, take the Red Line to Quincy Center (be sure to get on a Quincy train, as Red Line cars also travel to Ashmont in Boston's Dorchester area).

Southwest of Boston

NEW BEDFORD AND FALL RIVER

New Bedford was once a major whaling center. Visit the **New Bedford Whaling Museum,** the largest museum in the world devoted to this topic. It includes a three-quarters scale model of a whaling vessel. The first chapters of Melville's novel *Moby Dick* are set in New Bedford.

Stop also in nearby Fall River to visit **Battleship Cove,** where you can climb aboard the mighty USS *Massachusetts,* one of the most famous World War II battleships, also a PT boat, similar to the one that President John F. Kennedy served aboard, and other military craft. Nearby also is the **Marine Museum,** with *Titanic* artifacts, including a scale model of the vessel. Also in Fall River is the **Lizzie Borden Museum,** site of an infamous ax murder by a daughter of her parents in 1892. You can even stay overnight where the murders took place. Sampling the excellent Westport Rivers wine or Buzzards Bay lager is a treat at **Russell Family Farms** in Westport.

Both New Bedford and Fall River are also known for outlet shopping. For more information, call the Bristol County Convention and Visitors Bureau at (800) 228-6263.

From Boston, take I-93 south, to Route 128, then Route 24 to the cities.

NEWPORT

Newport, Rhode Island, is just over an hour from Boston. Here you can visit the great mansions of the Guilded Age, opulent "summer cottages" of the Vanderbilts, Astors, and others of the nineteenth century's wealthiest families. Newport, known as "America's first resort," is also a beautiful colonial seaport with picturesque homes and buildings. Do visit the Newport mansions, which are open all year. Call (401) 847-1000.

For information, call the Newport County Convention and Visitors Bureau at (800) 976-5122.

Of course, Newport is also home to the famous **JVC Newport Jazz Festival** in early August. For specific dates and other information, call (401) 331-2211.

By car, take I-93 south from Boston to Route 128 to Route 24 south, then Route 138 into Newport.

MYSTIC

If you've ever wondered what life was like in a nineteenth-century seafaring village, this is the place to come. In **Mystic Seaport** in Connecticut, less than two hours from Boston, you can step aboard the last wooden whale ship in the world or cruise the river on a 1908 steamboat. The seaport is home to more than 500 ships and boats.

Nearby is **Mystic Aquarium,** filled with the wonders of the sea. Visitors can even get into the water with beluga whales or get up close to penguins. **The Institute for Exploration** offers a fascinating look at the work of Dr. Robert Ballard and his discoveries including that of the *Titanic*.

Nearby are the **Foxwoods** (the largest in the Western Hemisphere) and **Mohegan Sun** casinos. The **Mashantucket Pequot Museum** at Foxwoods is the world's largest Native American museum and with its state-of-the-art exhibits will keep you fascinated for hours.

Nearby are excellent beaches, a submarine and art museums, and the **Coast Guard Academy.**

For information, call Mystic Places at (800) MY-COAST (692-6278).

From Boston, take I-95 south.

West of Boston

LEXINGTON AND CONCORD

Head west for Lexington and Concord to where the "shot heard 'round the world" was fired—the first shot of the American Revolution. Visit the **Minute Man National Historical Park,** which includes the famed *Minute Man* statue, and North Bridge, where the well-known shot was fired. While there, visit the homes of some literary and philosophical giants of the United States: Louisa May Alcott, Nathaniel Hawthorne (The Wayside, May through October), and Ralph Waldo Emerson (April through October). Also visit the **Concord Museum** for exhibits that will guide you through the areas. You could also walk around **Walden Pond,** made famous by Henry David Thoreau.

For information, call the Concord Chamber of Commerce, (978) 369-3120, and the Lexington Visitors Center, (781) 862-1450.

From Boston, take Route 2 west to Lexington Center, then Route 2A to Concord.

OLD STURBRIDGE VILLAGE

The quintessential New England village, **Old Sturbridge Village** is about an hour's drive west of Boston via the Massachusetts Turnpike. This 1830s village is a collection of genuine homes, shops, and businesses from throughout the region now set up in a classic village scene. Within the village, you can see villagers going about the daily tasks of the period from weaving to sheep shearing, watch blacksmiths work, and see apple cider being made.

The area is also good for antiquing. **Brimfield,** New England's premier flea market and antiques fair destination, holds forth at various times throughout summer and fall nearby.

For Sturbridge area information, call (800) 628-8379.

By car, take the Massachusetts Turnpike from Boston to the Interstate 84 exit. Old Sturbridge Village is the first exit on I-84.

CHAPTER TWENTY THREE

Seasonal Events

There is always something to do in Boston. With the city's riches of universities, museums, and libraries, programs and courses proliferate throughout the year. And the vast areas of parklands in and around Boston offer countless outdoor recreational opportunities, from hiking, biking, and swimming to picnicking and bird watching. Here are some of the many events to be enjoyed. Unless otherwise noted, call the Greater Boston Convention and Visitors Bureau for dates and information: (617) 536-4100.

JANUARY

Food, Wine & Arts Celebration begins, ushering in twelve weeks of more than one hundred events at area hotels, including: Boston Harbor Hotel's Boston Wine Festival, one of the best in the country; the Four Seasons' annual Salute to the Arts Festival; Charles Hotel's annual Jazz Festival; and Langham's fabulous Chocolate Buffet.

Japanese New Year Festival at the Children's Museum, which contains a house that was moved stick by stick from Japan. Tea ceremonies, food, and music.

Martin Luther King Jr. Birthday Celebration. Dr. King studied at Boston University, and many of his personal papers can be seen there.

World of Wheels, Bayside Exposition Center. High-performance and special-interest automobiles.

FEBRUARY

Anthony Spinazzola Gala, World Trade Center. Benefit honors *Boston Globe's* first restaurant critic with a gourmet's feast featuring the works of Boston's finest chefs.

Black History Month. Boston offers a Black Heritage Trail, and many special events are held this month.

Boston Cooks. An expo with the latest trends and innovations in the kitchen, celebrity chefs cooking up their signature dishes, cookbook signings, and a culinary school. Many restaurants feature special meals with celebrity chefs.

Boston Wine Festival, World Trade Center.

Chinese New Year, complete with dragons and firecrackers. Festivities are usually held on Beach and Tyler Streets in Boston's Chinatown.

Presidents' Birthday, third Monday in February. Open house at auto dealers. It all began on Commonwealth Avenue and has spread to the suburbs and other parts of the country. It's a good time just to kick some tires and see what's new in the auto world.

School vacation week, eliciting special programs at museums throughout the area. Check newspaper calendar sections or call the museum information lines.

Thaddeus Kosciuszko Day. Honors the American Revolution's Polish-American hero at the Kosciuszko statue in the Public Garden. Usually the first Sunday in February.

Valentine's Day. Boston's hotels make it special. Did you know more Valentine's Day cards are sold in Boston than anywhere else in the country?

MARCH

Crispus Attucks/Boston Massacre Ceremony. Recalls the March 5, 1770, incident in which Attucks, a former slave, and four others were killed, just outside the Old State House, by British soldiers.

Fromm Concerts, a free presentation of contemporary music by living composers. Held at Sanders Theater in Cambridge. Concerts are also offered in November.

March 17 is not only St. Patrick's Day but also Evacuation Day in Boston, celebrating the day the British left town back in 1776. It's time for the wearing of the green, with St. Patrick's Day celebrations held in Boston and the annual parade going through the streets of South Boston. Just above the South Boston parade site is Dorchester Heights, scene of the cannons that sent the British fleeing in 1776.

The New England Spring Garden and Flower Show, a sure sign of spring. Held at the Bayside Exposition Center in Dorchester, this marvelous display of gardens draws visitors from throughout New England to the oldest continuous flower show in the country. It's also one of the largest shows in the country.

APRIL

Let Freedom Ring, special events along the Freedom Trail.

Patriots' Day, the third Monday in April and a public holiday in Massachusetts. The festivities begin in Lexington, with an early morning reenactment of the Lexington battle on the Green: the ride of Paul Revere and William Dawes through "every Middlesex village and farm" is re-created from Boston, and lanterns are hung in the steeple of the Old North Church in the North End. There are parades in Boston. Also on Patriots' Day is the Boston Marathon, which begins in Hopkinton and runs for 26 miles to Copley Square. The race begins at noon, with the winner typically crossing the finish line between 2:00 and 2:30 P.M. The marathon, which draws thousands of runners—and wheelchair racers—from around the country, turned one hundred in 1996.

Red Sox season begins, Fenway Park. With the curse of the Babe lifted, will this be another championship season?

Swan Boats return to the Public Garden.

MAY

Art Newbury Street. A colorful street any time of the year becomes even more festive with gallery open houses and street musicians performing. All on a Sunday afternoon.

Beacon Hill Hidden Garden Tour. One day a year—the third Thursday in May—it's your chance to discover the hidden beauty of the Hill on a self-guided tour sponsored by the Beacon Hill Garden Club.

Big Apple Circus. From its one ring comes a memorable show.

The Boston Pops returns to Symphony Hall. Get some friends together, book a table, and join in this more than fifty-year-old tradition.

Flowering magnolias add to the beauty of Commonwealth Avenue.

Harvard Square May Fair, usually the first Sunday in May.

Lilac Sunday, Arnold Arboretum. More than 300 varieties are found here.

Memorial Day, the fourth weekend in May.

The Revels, Sanders Theater in Cambridge. In song and dance, the changing of the seasons is celebrated in a Cambridge tradition.

JUNE

The Ancient and Honorable Artillery Company Parade. The nation's oldest military organization parades the first Monday in June from Faneuil Hall to the State House and then on to Boston Common for ceremonies. The parade features a drumhead election, in which ballots are cast on an ancient drum.

The Boston Globe *Jazz Festival.* Takes place throughout the city and features top names in the world of jazz.

Bunker Hill Day, June 17. A parade and other events usually take place the Sunday before Bunker Hill Day.

Cambridge River Festival, held along Memorial Drive in Cambridge. An outdoor community celebration of the arts with musical performances, food, folk art, and more.

Dragon Boat Festival. For one Sunday in June, the Charles River is filled with boats decorated with dragon heads, while along the shore by the Hatch Shell is a Chinese arts festival. Games, dances, and crafts add to the fun.

Irish Festival, at the Irish Cultural Center, Canton. The biggest Irish festival in New England.

Street fairs throughout the city. Marlborough Street between Berkeley and Clarendon Streets is the scene of the Back Bay Street Fair, usually held on the first Saturday in June. Bay Village, a historic area just off Park Square and near the Theater District, holds its fair the first Saturday in June. Little St. Anthony's Festival is the first of the colorful North End celebrations. The St. Botolph Street Fair (just behind the Prudential Center) usually comes on the third Saturday of the month and honors the saint from whom Boston gains its name.

Good Times to Visit

The new year begins in Boston with First Night, on December 31. It's an afternoon and evening filled with spectacular events for the whole family, including a huge parade, lots of indoor concerts and performances, and ending with a spectacular fireworks and laser show. Most happenings are at minimal cost; some are free. Boston was the site of the original First Night, a citywide New Year's celebration that's been copied—but never equaled—throughout the country.

January through March there are grand food, wine, flower, and jazz festivals, many offering special treats for the kids.

April brings Boston's own holiday of Patriots' Day weekend with reenactments of Paul Revere's ride and other colonial activities. The Boston Marathon, now more than a century old, takes place the weekend closest to April 19 as well. Also in April, Boston hosts a terrific kite festival.

May celebrates Museum Goers Month.

June is the time for the Scooper Bowl—it's an all-you-can-eat ice cream festival on City Hall Plaza. It features top ice cream makers and lots of flavors, and it all benefits the famed Jimmy Fund for children's cancer research.

Summer brings free outdoor concerts at the Hatch Shell by the Boston Pops and other music groups. Even free Friday night movies take place at the shell. And, of course, it's the time for lots of outdoor activities, including whale-watching cruises, which leave right from downtown wharves.

August marks the return of Restaurant Week, a highlight of which is a three-course meal at one of the city's top restaurants at a bargain fixed price. Prices are based on the year: In 2005 the price will be $20.05.

Fall offers Youth Concerts at Boston Symphony Hall, foliage viewing, and Head of the Charles Regatta.

Winter brings holiday cheer with colorful displays and grand performances of what many people say is the country's best *Nutcracker,* magically performed by the Boston Ballet. You can ice-skate on Boston Common or even take off for some great skiing within an hour or two, at most, of the city.

Need more ideas for a family outing? Check the *Boston Globe*'s Thursday "Calendar" section for children's activities. Call (888) SEE-BOSTON (733-2678) for current information on seasonal events.

July

Bastille Day, July 14, Boston celebrates everything French throughout the city, and especially at the French Library on Marlborough Street.

Fourth of July festivities: Harborfest is one of the best ways to celebrate the Fourth of July. It takes place along the waterfront; some island tours and activities occur as well. There are a chowderfest, tours of ships, brunches, fireworks, and more. July 4 also brings out the USS *Constitution* for its annual turn-around cruise in Boston Harbor; it is turned so that its sides weather evenly. You can see and hear Old Ironsides fire its twenty-one cannons from Castle Island. The annual concert by the Boston Pops on the Esplanade brings out thousands for the music and fireworks that follow. Another tradition is the 9:30 A.M. reading of the Declaration of Independence from the balcony of the Old State House, where the document was first read to the Boston populace in 1776.

North End festivals, which seem to take over the streets of the North End every weekend in summer. The festivals honor various saints and include parades, lots of food, games, and entertainment. Some of the customs date back hundreds of years. One thing is sure: You won't go hungry in this neighborhood.

Other Festivals. Catch the Boston Seaport, Puerto Rican, or Cape Verdean festivals, or take in the West Indian–American Jamboree.

Pops Esplanade concerts. What could be better than spreading a blanket along the Charles by the Hatch Shell and listening to the Boston Pops? The outdoor concerts are free; bring along a picnic.

U.S. Pro Tennis Championships at Longwood. The oldest tournament in the country usually takes place the second week in July at the Longwood Cricket Club in Brookline.

August

August Moon Festival. The largest Chinese festival of the year, held throughout Chinatown, usually in mid-August or September.

North End festivals continue throughout the month.

September

Art Newbury Street, closing the street to traffic from Arlington Street to Massachusetts Avenue. A grand time to go gallery hopping.

Boston Film Festival takes place at various theaters in the city.

Labor Day, a good time to end summer with a bang. Kidsfair, held on Boston Common during Labor Day weekend, has lots of free things for kids to do, entertainment, arts and crafts, and food.

OCTOBER

Columbus Day, celebrated the second weekend of the month. On Columbus Day there is a parade from East Boston to the North End.

Ellis Memorial Antiques Show. A prestigious antiques event, drawing dealers from around the country.

Foliage season. Traditionally foliage is at its peak in southern New England, including the Greater Boston area, from the first of October to mid-October. Columbus Day weekend is always a prime time to take in the colorful show. Boston's Arnold Arboretum, with the largest variety of trees, shrubs, and plants in North America, is an easy-to-reach place in which to enjoy the foliage. Just 9 miles south of Boston, the Blue Hill Reservation is a good spot for scenic drives through its 5,000 acres as well as colorful vistas from atop Great Blue Hill (you can hike up the 635-foot hill). Or drive to the overlook at Chickatobet Hill, just off the Southeast Expressway in Milton. Another colorful drive is to the Concord/Lexington area and the Minute Man National Park there. Along the way are colorful farm stands. A quick guide to the colors: red—black cherry, pin oak, sumac, white oak; scarlet—red maple, scarlet oak; crimson—blackberry and blueberry bushes; yellow—American elm, beech, birch, Norway maple, poplar, silver maple, striped maple, willow, mountain ash; mixture-ash (yellow–dark purple), black oak (red, orange, brown), sugar maple (yellow-orange, scarlet). The foliage hotline in Massachusetts is (800) 632–8038, or in Boston call 727–3201.

Harvard Square Oktoberfest, Cambridge. The flavor of Germany takes over Harvard Square.

Head of the Charles Regatta. Crews from all over the world join in this event, the largest one-day happening of its kind anywhere. Competition draws more than 3,000 for the 3-mile event from Boston University Bridge to near the WBZ studios on Soldiers Field Road in the Brighton area of the city.

Ringling Brothers and Barnum & Bailey Circus. It's still the Greatest Show on Earth, and it comes to town every October, playing the FleetCenter for two weeks. Check out the circus parade that begins just after the circus train unloads; the elephants and the show have to cross town from where the train stops.

South End annual house tour. Sponsored by the South End Historical Society.

NOVEMBER

Annual International Auto Show, Bayside Exposition Center. Here's your chance to check out all the latest models.

The Boston Globe *Book Festival.* Events are held throughout the city, with talks by authors and special programs for children.

Boston Snow Sports Expo, Bayside Exposition Center. Heralds the start of ski season. Many ski slopes within an easy drive of Boston have already begun making snow, if they don't have it on the slopes already.

Services at the Old South Meeting House, Washington Street. The meetinghouse has its congregation, now in Copley Square, return for a service the Sunday before Thanksgiving. And you are welcome to attend.

Thanksgiving Day. See where it all began in Plymouth. Plimoth Plantation, a re-creation of the Pilgrim village, and other attractions all open, as do area restaurants; and at Plimoth Plantation, Victorian-era themed dinners are held (reservations a must). Old Sturbridge Village features Thanksgiving Day dinners and village tours to show how New Englanders marked Thanksgiving in the 1830s.

DECEMBER

Boston Pops New Year's Eve celebration, Symphony Hall.

First Night, December 31, North America's largest citywide celebration to mark the start of the new year. A wonderful event for families and children. Festivities begin New Year's Eve around 1:00 P.M. and continue past midnight. They include a parade in which everyone can participate, concerts, foods, a laser show at City Hall, and a spectacular fireworks display. More than one hundred events take place, and the purchase of a single First Night button for under $20 provides entry to everything. It's the celebration that cities around the country are copying but never duplicating. Most hotels offer weekend packages that include the button.

Holiday celebrations: The Paul Revere House, in the North End, offers eighteenth-century decorations; a handbell choir performs at Faneuil Hall Marketplace; on Boston Common and at Faneuil Hall, you can see the Christmas lights; you can also see the 50-foot tree at the Prudential Center—an annual gift from the people of Nova Scotia; at Symphony Hall the Handel & Haydn Society's *Messiah* is presented by America's oldest performing organization; the Revels, held at Sanders Theater in Cambridge and featuring music, dance, and skits on the ethnic traditions and rituals of the season, is always popular among all ages; and the *Nutcracker,* at Boston's Wang Center for the Performing Arts, is a tradition presented by the Boston Ballet. Louisburg Square, on Beacon Hill, is known for its Christmas Eve concert by bell ringers and for the candles glowing in the windows of the homes surrounding the park. Also, there are annual performances of Black Nativity by Boston's National Center of Afro-American Artists and of Dylan Thomas's *A Child's Christmas in Wales.* Boston Pops holds special performances.

Tea Party Reenactment at the Boston Tea Party Ship and Museum, December 16. The reenactment has participants tossing the tea overboard. You can see it from Congress Street Bridge for free.

CHAPTER TWENTY-FOUR

You Haven't Seen Boston Until . . .

Okay now, the question is, Have you really seen Boston? Here's a handy checklist of some of the top attractions, grouped by area.

Paul Revere's house, in the North End, is the oldest in the city. Visiting it, you'll discover that Revere did a lot more than take a midnight ride shouting, "The British are coming, the British are coming!" He was an accomplished silversmith, a bell ringer, a bell maker, a goldsmith, an artist, and a manufacturer, having established the first copper-rolling mill in the country, which produced the copper used to cover the State House dome and the hull of "Old Ironsides."

Old North Church, near Revere's house, is the oldest Anglican church in America in continuous service. It is where the famed "One if by land and two if by sea" lanterns were hung, a church of simple beauty and historic sights.

Prudential Tower offers a literal overview of the city. Soar to the Prudential Skywalk—up fifty stories in thirty-two seconds—to soak in a 360-degree view of Boston. Looking down you'll see how green Boston is. Look in at Fenway Park. Looking out you'll see New Hampshire mountains, even the beaches of Cape Cod on a good day. There are lots of interactive displays on Boston history.

Trinity Church is considered by some to be the most beautiful church in the United States, facing another architectural masterpiece—Boston Public Library in Copley Square.

Beacon Hill evokes one of the first images people have of Boston, that of the stately town houses lining the Hill's gaslit streets, all crowned by Charles Bulfinch's renowned, golden-domed State House.

Cheers—the Bull & Finch—is the model for the bar seen on the TV show *Cheers* and has quickly become one of the most popular stops in the city. The Information Booth at Boston Common says that one out of four questions it receives is about Cheers.

Boston Common and the *Public Garden* are two distinctive and neighborly open spaces in the heart of the city; they are places of history and beauty.

Swan Boats, providing a fifteen-minute ride in the Public Garden, have been a tradition for more than 125 years and are unique to Boston.

Boston Harbor, once the most polluted in the nation, has been cleaned up and is again a beautiful sight to see, particularly when one is taking in Boston's skyline from the water. A nice way to do that is to take an inexpensive harbor cruise at lunchtime, picking up a movable feast from Faneuil Hall Marketplace and bringing it along or buying a snack onboard.

Faneuil Hall Marketplace represents a genuine 170-plus-year-old marketplace that has been given new uses and been filled with shops and restaurants. The model for similar restorations around the country, it's lively, historic, and fun.

Filene's Basement is where thousands of thrifty Bostonians shop. Although branches are now spread around the East Coast, the original Filene's Basement, with its automatic markdowns and people trying on clothes in the aisles (there now are some dressing rooms), is a sight to see.

Museum of Fine Arts offers unequaled collections, outstanding galleries of American and European paintings, furnishings, and copious examples of Egyptian and Asian art treasures.

Isabella Stewart Gardner Museum, almost behind the Museum of Fine Arts, is one of those places unique to Boston. Built to resemble an Italian palace, filled with art, and containing a refreshing indoor garden, "the house that Mrs. Jack built" is more than a museum—it's a monument to a legendary woman.

Fenway Park is the oldest and most beautiful of ballparks. Every year, hope springs eternal that the Boston Red Sox will prevail . . . and they did!

Boston Pops may be imitated, but they are never matched. Their blend of classical and popular music is a feast for the ears. Getting a table at Symphony Hall for a Pops concert is nice; nicer still is enjoying the Pops in summer, for free, on the grass at the Hatch Shell.

Freedom Trail, mile for mile, offers an unparalleled amount of American history compressed into just a short distance.

USS Constitution lets you climb aboard and explore the nation's oldest active Navy vessel.

Harvard Square, only a few miles from downtown Boston, offers the nation's oldest and largest private university, Harvard University, which faces a small town square and creates a colorful town scene.

We might also ask, have you seen the glass flowers at Harvard? Tossed some tea into the harbor at the Tea Party Ship? Shopped on Newbury Street? Dined at Durgin Park? Or taken in a summertime North End festival or Harborfest on the Fourth of July? Since Boston is the home of the bean and the cod, have you sampled both, as well as the lobster? It's all waiting for you. Enjoy!

Index

About the Author

Jerry Morris describes himself as a "not-so-proper Bostonian," even though, properly speaking, he was born and primarily educated in the city. He now lives along the state line of Massachusetts and Rhode Island (in the area where Boston's first resident, William Blackstone, fled to avoid the Puritans who were to remake the Shawmut Peninsula into Boston) with his wife, Mary Beth. He is the former travel editor of the *Boston Globe*.